RED INK

· · · · · · · · · · · ·

The Budget,
Deficit, and
Debt of
the U.S.
Government

RED INK

· · · · · · · · · · · · · · · · · · · ·

The Budget, Deficit, and Debt of the U.S. Government

Gary R. Evans

Harvey Mudd College
Claremont, California

http://www.apnet.com/evans

Academic Press
San Diego London Boston
New York Sydney Tokyo Toronto

Copyright © 1997 by ACADEMIC PRESS

Academic Press
a division of Harcourt Brace & Company
525 B Street, Suite 1900, San Diego, California 92101-4495, USA
http://www.apnet.com

Academic Press Limited
24-28 Oval Road, London NW1 7DX, UK
http://www.hbuk.co.uk/ap/

Library of Congress Cataloging-in-Publication Data

Evans, Gary R., date.
    Red ink : the budget, deficit, and debt of the U.S. government /
by Gary Evans.
            p.   cm.
    Includes bibliographical references and index.
    ISBN 0-12-244079-X (alk. paper). -- ISBN 0-12-244080-3 (pbk. :
alk. paper)
    1. Budget--United States.   2. Budget deficits--United States.
3. Debts, Public--United States.   4. Entitlement spending--United
States.   I. Title.
HJ2051.E93   1997
336.3'4'0973--dc21   97-9581
                                                              CIP

PRINTED IN THE UNITED STATES OF AMERICA
97   98   99   00   01   02   QW   9   8   7   6   5   4   3   2   1

Contents

· · · · · · · · · · · ·

Preface

· · · · · · · · · · ·

Very few present-day subjects generate as much public controversy as the budget, the deficit, and the debt of the U.S. government. Although many economists argue that the current concern over the deficit is unwarranted, the majority of politicians, analysts, and the voting public seem to be in agreement on one matter: the deficit is too large. The real controversy revolves around the question of what should be done about it.

The impact of the deficit debate on the national political scene can hardly be overstated. Deficit politics dominated the 1992 presidential election (eclipsing, for example, any role played by the U.S. victory in the Persian Gulf War, forgotten by the public at the time of the election as though it had been fought a generation before, rather than 18 months earlier), and they opened the possibility for the brief appearance of a serious third-party candidate, Ross Perot. Armed with charts and graphs (literally, to be shown on TV, like a college professor might explain the subject) and with a singular enthusiasm for attacking the deficit as the by-product of "politics as usual," Perot proved himself to be a worrisome contender to the established parties until his campaign gradually succumbed to amateurism. Perot quickly faded from the scene but his presence impacted the election in two ways: by splitting off some of the conservative vote, which may have contributed substantially to Bill Clinton's victory, and by forcing the deficit controversy (along with the related issue of stasis—politics as usual—which was to reemerge in congressional elections two years later) to the forefront of U.S. national politics, where it remains today.

The issue returned in altered form in the congressional elections of 1994, when the Republican party tilted the balance of power strongly to the right. At the convening of the 104th Congress in January 1995, Republicans controlled both houses of Congress for the first time since 1955.[1] Democrat Bill Clinton, though, occupied the White House, inviting and generating a strong partisan clash.

In the 1994 election the deficit and deficit reduction did not provide the real focal point of the myriad local campaigns. The public mood seemed generally more conservative, and issues ranging from immigration policy to gun control and crime-prevention measures captured the headlines. The comprehensive health reform program championed through the 103rd Congress by the new president and promoted earnestly by the first lady, Hillary Clinton, perished an ignominious death, receiving only tepid support from Democrats, divided and squabbling among themselves, and was opposed fiercely by Republicans, who were beginning to anticipate their party's ascendancy. After the election the other campaign issues subsided somewhat and the initiative to "downsize" government, especially through budget cuts, began to emerge as the dominant issue to affect the life of the 104th Congress.

A brief campaign document called the *Republican Contract with America*[2] was promoted by some, including the new Speaker of the House, Georgia Republican Newt Gingrich, as the mandate that had caused the shift in power. As is typically the case with platforms and other campaign documents, some of the language of the *Contract* was vague, and some of the text seemed tailored to appeal to the hopelessly sentimental (one provision of the *Contract,* titled *The American Dream Restoration Act,* proposed to restore the American dream with a $500 per child tax credit and the creation of "American Dream Savings Accounts"), but the document also signaled an attack on prevailing budgetary priori-

---

[1]The Senate was composed of 53 Republicans and 47 Democrats. Of the 435 Representatives in the House, 230 were Republicans, 204 were Democrats, and 1 was an Independent. The split in power continued after the 1996 elections. The Republican majority was increased in the Senate and decreased in the House but was still a majority, and Democrat Bill Clinton was reelected to his second term.

[2]The texts of *The Republican Contract with America* and the *Balanced Budget Amendment*, discussed here, are included in appendices.

ties by promising to promote one constitutional amendment to balance the budget and another to require a three-fifths majority vote to pass tax increases. It also included a strong assault on welfare and a vague promise to bolster national defense capabilities and proposed a list of tax cuts, including cuts in capital gains taxes. Finally, the *Contract* promised deficit reduction (aside from the Balanced Budget Amendment) by concluding with a pledge to "enact additional budget savings . . . to ensure that the Federal budget deficit will be less than it would have been without the enactment of these bills." Hardly any of this was new (welfare was trimmed early in the Reagan years, for example, and proposals for a balanced budget amendment and capital gains tax cuts had been around for years), but the likelihood that much of the implied legislation would at least get to the White House for signature or veto was greater than ever.

The *Contract with America* probably had little to do with the Republican victory. Opinion polls taken after the election showed that most Americans were unaware of the *Contract,* and even larger numbers were unaware of its provisions. Instead, a large number of voters seemed to see their federal government as static, expensive, predatory, and financially irresponsible. The Republicans, militant and abrasive after years of frustrating minority opposition, promised radical reform to a public that seemed weary of traditional politics, and anxious, perhaps even angry in some cases, at the financial burden of government. American voters signaled their general discontent as they so often have in the past—by rolling over the government.

Regardless of the cause of the shift in power, when the new Congress convened, the budget and the deficit were again clearly on the front burner. The first partisan shootout was over the Balanced Budget Amendment, which passed in the House but failed by one vote in the Senate after an acrimonious debate, and then failed again in 1996.[3] The tax cut promised by the *Contract with America* was earnestly promoted, but the debate quickly shifted to its estimated financial impact as public opinion polls continued to reveal that the public valued deficit reduction over tax cuts. The vague Republican promise to "get the government off the people's backs" gelled into a very concrete effort to accomplish this by trying to use the budgetary scalpel on a wide range of federal programs. As the 104th Congress steamed on, day after day the news out of Washington concerned itself mostly with the budget.

---

[3]At the time this was written, it was scheduled to come up for a vote yet again in 1997.

The Republicans, especially in the House of Representatives, proved that they were sincere in their efforts at reform. At first (in the "first 100 days") they mostly proposed cutbacks in programs that posed little political danger, typically in welfare (little political danger because the poor are not a recognized constituency—they do not vote consistently nor in large numbers), but the Republican leadership became bolder after the first recess, pushing hard to reduce agricultural subsidies, promoting huge cuts in programs like NASA, and at one stage even proposing the complete elimination of the Departments of Commerce, Education, and Energy.

Health reform continued to matter, but at the core of the debate was the question of how it was to be paid for, especially after it became apparent that changes to the huge Medicare program might strongly impact the largest and most reliable voting constituency in the United States— the elderly. At various junctures of the debate, Republicans proposed fee increases and cutbacks in both Medicare and Medicaid, while Democrats, for once enjoying the luxury of minority opposition, continued to insist on all-inclusive health care reform, attacking the Republican plans as radical and dangerous.

This was not "politics as usual" in Washington. It was, though, potentially dangerous politics for the Republicans, because anything that threatens to cut benefits to a large constituency can reverse the political tide almost overnight. Americans do not like taxes (who does?) nor intrusive government, but they have grown rather fond of the hundreds of billions of dollars in payouts received every year. No one likes the scowling Uncle Sam with his hand out, nor the darkly suspicious Uncle Sam poking his nose into our business, but the cheerfully generous Uncle Sam with the fat wallet and the open checkbook is a welcome relative indeed, or so it seems.

The battle over the budget did not come to a clear resolution. The Republicans could not agree among themselves in every case about the extent of the reform (the House was much more militant than the Senate) and the President quickly discovered that there was no political cost to vetoing legislation he did not like—indeed, his political stature as reflected in one opinion poll after another rose throughout the most acrimonious months of the confrontation.

The Republicans were quick to present a budget that promised no deficit in the year 2002. In one of their many tactical blunders they challenged the President, then on the defensive, to come up with a plan of his own. Discovering that it is rather easy to come up with a balanced budget on paper, he did so, deflating one of the Republican challenges and removing deficit reduction as an election issue. By the time of the spring 1996 primaries, both parties had an official balanced budget plan on the books. The issue waned during the summer and fall campaign.

In the 1996 presidential election campaign, Republican presidential candidate Bob Dole revived the issue by proposing a 15% cut in income taxes (while balancing the budget, of course), a plan that was strikingly similar to that used successfully by Ronald Reagan 16 years earlier. Dole's campaign proposal never caught on with the wiser and increasingly skeptical American electorate, and Bill Clinton was reelected to a second term with a comfortable margin.

The controversy was not closed off, though, by the election of 1996. The deficit-reduction plans—both the Republicans' and the president's—were mostly paper projections, with the substantial cuts backloaded toward the end of the century.

Most of the large programs that drive the budget, including Social Security and the large and expensive medical programs, Medicare and Medicaid, had been placed off limits prior to the 1996 elections because of the political risk of offending the constituencies who benefit from these programs. But these large programs cannot be kept off of the docket indefinitely. Deficit reduction cannot go much farther without them. The real task is just ahead.

What This Book Is About

In the investigation of any aspect of human enterprise, we seldom get very far before we encounter either a budget in some form or a crisis explained by the lack of a budget or by disregard of budgetary discipline. The ultimate constraint on our consumption of goods and services is imposed by a budget that is capped by income and access to credit. Think of how differently we would all live without such constraints (although it wouldn't be in this world–budgets exist because *both* financial and real resources are limited). The business that ignores the financial rules of cost control and cash flow is a doomed business. Although governments have more latitude for fiscal excess, ultimately, financial strength is a necessary prior condition for political and military strength, a lesson discovered by the Soviet Union in the late 1980s. Over time, no regime can endure without good books. And the numbers are indifferent to the politics. No political stance nor ethical imperative, whether liberal or conservative, can override the need to keep the books in order. Resources and programs cannot be paid for with lofty declarations, with the best of intentions, nor with moral righteousness. Just cash. Maybe cash borrowed rather than cash taxed, but only up to a point.

The financial dimension of U.S. politics would be considerably less dramatic if our federal government balanced its books, or if it came close to doing so. But, despite recent progress, it does not yet and really has not for the last two decades or so. The budget deficit—its origin, cause, impact, and resiliency—is a story in itself. Here we concern ourselves less with the arcane politics of the budget, although there is considerable discussion of that subject, and more with the budget itself—in effect, we "open the books" to see what the budgetary documents reveal. Expense sheets and tax schedules are not the stuff of Dickens and Voltaire, but the numbers do tell a story, and while it may be a story that only an accountant could love, it is a revealing and truthful story. We will do more than look at numbers in this book, but looking at numbers is something we are going to do. As the title implies, this book is about the budget.

Despite the solemn tone of the paragraphs above, this book is not alarmist. It is fashionable these days to write apocalyptic books (or the opposite), but our federal government is not going to hell in a hand basket, or the financial equivalent. Despite its five-trillion-dollar gross debt (yes, it is that large) our government is not "bankrupt," nor anywhere near it. Our deficit has been large—too large—but as governments go, it is one of the smallest in the world given the size of the U.S. economy. Although our elected representatives have seemed, at least until recent years, to lack a penchant for fiscal discipline, they nonetheless exercise better discipline than is seen overseas (or to the north or south). Maybe it is small consolation that if all ships are sinking, ours will be among the last afloat, but our own self-criticism should be kept in perspective.

The modern budgetary problem is one of degree, not of absolutes. Given the size of this economy and our historical record, our deficit is too large and our federal debt is growing too fast, and this condition has endured for some time. The problem has *not* been utterly ignored, as we will see later in this book, and the situation looks better than it did a few years back, when the picture was rather grim. But *victory,* which is to say, moderate and sensible budgetary discipline of the kind that was characteristic of this economy decades ago, has proven elusive.

Debt and deficits are hardly a modern problem. The intrepid Queen Elizabeth, whose Tudor regime sank the Spanish Armada and explored the Americas while nurturing a cultural flowering that gave us, among other things, the art of Shakespeare, left a choking legacy of debt to be sorted out by the unfortunate and doomed Stuarts. The heavy use (and abuse) of debt comes and goes in waves or cycles that tend to be self-correcting—either the problem is eventually sorted out or there is a collapse and the financially incompetent are replaced. Unfortunately, we have recently been on the dark side of that cycle.

Fortunately, we seem to be aware of that.

The Plan for This Book

This book is an extension of a series of courses that I have taught since 1983 in which I have focused on the federal budget in general and the deficit in particular. Each year I would look a little more closely at the subject and add more material to my lectures. Finally, given the generous time made available by a sabbatical, I was able to pull the material together and add some more, and this text is the result. Students hearing my lectures in the classroom were being exposed to the material for the first time (in any depth) so my intent was to develop a very detailed introductory survey of our federal government's financial affairs. It should be understandable to any college student or educated reader, regardless of background. The content is *descriptive* rather than *theoretical*—this is not a book on economic theory, although in Chapter 9 I describe some economic theory and use it to discuss the impact of the deficit upon the economy. I use a lot of tables, graphs, and descriptive material to present what I hope is a coherent picture of the budget and an overview of how things are done.

In the approach taken I have tried to be largely nonpartisan and ideologically neutral, not an easy task on a subject as controversial as this, but much of the tone is critical and at times it is hard to take a position without seeming to take sides.

In planning the text I decided that a good overview should include the following information:

1. A clear definition or description of the subject and identification of the problem, to the extent that it is seen as a problem.

2. A description of the historical dimensions of the subject, to place it in a proper historical context (and to a lesser extent, an international comparison to place it in a global context).

3. A careful review of the actual line-item budget in as much detail as possible, knowing that the political "drama" of the budget—the reason that budgetary programs are supported by certain constituencies, are

championed by elected representatives from both parties, and have their own history (like farm subsidies or Medicare, for example)—is easier to understand when the numbers can be seen. How much *is* spent on foreign aid? Is defense spending growing or shrinking? We'll answer those questions by looking at the numbers.

4. A detailed discussion of entitlements and trust funds, with particular emphasis on Social Security, Medicare, Medicaid, and other high-cost programs driven over time by demographics. These are the programs (entitlements) that are in the headlines, for good reason.

5. An examination of taxes—who pays the bills, how has the tax burden changed over the years, and is it possible to achieve deficit reduction without raising taxes?

6. A survey of budgetary procedures describing the roles and practices of the Congress, the President, the Office of Management and Budget, and the Congressional Budget Office and how their activity is constrained and guided (or not) by the current budgetary enforcement laws.

7. A general discussion of the external impact of the budget and the deficit on the economy or on the financial sector. I leave detailed theoretical analysis to the economic texts on fiscal policy, but I provide an overview of some of the major theoretical issues.

8. Prospects for improving the budgetary picture, including, to the extent possible, an overview of the current political climate (an elusive task, because that climate is everchanging).

Some economists argue that deficits of the size seen recently are not harmful and possibly are even beneficial because of their stimulating effect on the economy. Others will insist on the need for a balanced budget. I argue more loosely for "fiscal moderation"—using fairly conservative historical standards as guidelines. There seems to be a rough consensus that $150 or $200 billion deficits, although smaller than the largest deficits we've seen, are still too large, and I agree with that. Accordingly, given the state of the budget at the time this book was written, an underlying goal of deficit reduction at least, if not something more stringent, such as a balanced budget, is implicit in my approach.

The 97% Definitions

The President's budgetary proposal to Congress, submitted each February, is more than 2000 pages long on 8¼-by-11-inch paper. A document published by the Congressional Budget Office that discusses various ways to reduce the deficit has more than 350 pages. The text of legislation affecting a large program like Social Security would fill a bookcase. This little book, intending to provide an introductory overview, is very much shorter.

My purpose in writing this is not to elicit sympathy, but to explain the following writing and editing judgments:

1. I have discovered that detailed tables and visual graphs allow one to pack a lot of summary information into a small textual space that can be reviewed quickly by the reader. Therefore, many such aids will be found in this book.

2. As far as possible, I have probed very deeply into some of the more interesting agency budgets (such as the budget for the Department of Agriculture and other large entitlement programs, for example) because that is where the real budgetary lessons are to be found; I could not do this for all agencies and programs or the book would have been at least double its present length. I therefore tried to make good use of appendixes—offering more detail on such issues as program budgets for the reader who is sufficiently interested in probing the material. Interesting textual materials too detailed to include in the main text, such as the 1995 *Balanced Budget Amendment* and the *Republican Contract with America,* are also found in appendixes.

3. In some areas, I use what I call *97% definitions.*

That needs a little explanation. Technical material—and there is plenty of that in the federal budget—is often difficult to write about because of nuances, subtleties, and small exceptions. How many data tables, for example, end with the inclusive category called "other," equaling perhaps 2% of the total? And yet the explanation for "other," when attempted, is twice as long as the explanation for everything else. Often it is easy to offer the *essence* of a definition or a regulation, or the meaning of some entry in a budget—so long as one ignores or glosses over an exception, a tiny complication, or a qualification that must be made if precision is demanded. Precision, though, is sometimes tedious. Consider the federal expenditure category called an "outlay," for example. *Generally speaking,* outlays are cash disbursements—spending—by our government, unless, of course, you happen to be talking about interfund transfers between federal agencies, fund transfers to undistributed offsetting receipts for federal pensions, or noncash actuarial estimates of the present value of future loan losses for federal credit programs, or . . . well, you get the picture. To reduce the tedium, here and there I use the *97% definitions,* which capture the essence of the point at hand, knowingly allowing some small imprecision because some qualification is not being made. Where this is done I try to get back to the issue later in the text, or when appropriate I try to refer to a more advanced document (usually by referring to a government document or a specialized book), or in the case of a definition, I offer a more complete and qualified definition in the glossary at the back of the book. Look at the definition for the word "outlay" in the glossary, for example. Nevertheless, I apologize in advance for misinforming through simplification.

Red Ink Web Site

Although the general controversies about the budget and deficit reduction sometimes seem timeless, background information and data change frequently. Major programs like Medicare or farm subsidies can be substantially reformed in a single summer, as happened with welfare reform in 1996, for example. Each fiscal year, new budgets are introduced and another year of historical data becomes available. For these reasons it is difficult in a book to keep all of the information presented current.

To provide examples of federal spending (mostly in Chapters 1, 4, and 5), this book uses historical data from fiscal year 1996 for some summary data and data from fiscal year 1995 for detailed analysis of budgetary functions and individual programs. These examples will become less relevant (or less timely) as time passes.

Likewise, some of the individual programs discussed in this book will be altered by new legislation. For example, when this book was being prepared for publication, the Congress was again preparing to submit another vote on an amendment to the U.S. Constitution to balance the budget and the first round of proposals for Medicaid reform were being introduced.

To update a book every few months just to keep it current is not very practical, to say the least. Because of the popularity and availability of the world wide web on the internet, however, it is now possible to provide updates on data and new political developments affecting the budget as an extension of the book. I have agreed to do this for *Red Ink* and have received enthusiastic support from the publisher. The intent is to provide updated data tables as the data become available and to offer descriptions and commentary on changes to major programs or legislation that affects the budget.

The reader and teachers (where this book is used in classes) are invited to find and peruse the supplementary material on the world wide web at the web site for the publisher,

http://www.apnet.com/evans

or the web site for the author,

http://www2.hmc.edu/RedInk[4]

Acknowledgments

I thank Sonia, Leslie, and Jennifer Evans, all of whom contributed in some way to this project, including a lot of proofreading. Without the strong support from my good colleagues in the Department of Humanities and Social Sciences and from the general academic community at Harvey Mudd College, especially by providing me with a sabbatical, this book would have been impossible to complete. I also owe a debt to my students at Harvey Mudd, especially Chris Alef, and to the graduate students at the Peter F. Drucker Graduate Management Center for their patience and receptiveness—there is very little in this book that was not first tried out on them—and to some of the readers of early drafts of this text, including Chris Niggle, Anne Casaletti, Art Svenson, Mayo Toruño, and a number of unnamed reviewers. I am especially grateful to Scott Bentley, Jackie Garrett, and the editorial staff of Academic Press, whose professionalism and courtesy have improved this project considerably while making the experience more enjoyable for the author. And, of course, in academia one always learns from good conversation with professionals in one's own field, and by that account, I will always be indebted to economists Lisa Sullivan, Christopher Niggle, and Thomas Burrows.

---

[4]The commitment to have updates available is a commitment made by the author, not the publisher. The author bears full responsibility for this task and is solely responsible for the accuracy and reliability of any information. Any copyrights or restrictions are included with posted information.

The Deficit and the Debt

n the morning of Monday, October 2, 1995, the House Commerce Committee met to begin "markup hearings" (leading to revision) of an important and controversial piece of legislation moving through the committee structure of the House of Representatives. The bill intended for markup, HR 2425, the Medicare Preservation Act of 1995, represented a Republican-sponsored effort to substantially change the huge, popular, and expensive Medicare program that provides health care for the elderly in the United States. The bill was one of many wending its way through both houses of Congress reflecting the aggressive spirit of change in Washington induced by the Republican victory 11 months earlier.

The House was formally in recess on this Monday, but the committee was meeting anyway because of the gravity of its mission. Legislation was becoming bogged down in both houses because of the scope of the

Republican agenda and, as would be expected, because of resistance by the Democrats, and one legislative deadline after another had been missed throughout this contentious year. Because little else was happening on Capitol Hill, the C-SPAN television network broadcast the hearings to viewers curious about the inner workings of their federal government.

On that morning, viewers got an eyeful. Congressional committee hearings are normally about as exciting as watching the grass grow and tend to move at about the same pace. Although frequently marked by passionate speeches, often intended more "for the record" than for the ears of attending colleagues, the meetings, presided over by the committee chairs, follow strict and elaborate rules of conduct where civility, decorum, and courtesy are expected and are normally observed. Although the references to "my good friend, the distinguished gentleman from Tennessee" (or other similar platitudes) are often uttered through clenched teeth, at least the pretense of polite exchange and solemn dignity is normally honored.

The C-SPAN viewers got their first hint that perhaps dignity might suffer that morning when the committee chair, veteran eighth-term Republican Thomas Bliley, took his seat, appearing somewhat embarrassed and ill at ease. Above him was a large electronic scoreboard with bright lights blazing the message, *Medicare: Countdown to Bankruptcy.* Underneath was the number of seconds left, *197,394,265* (etc.). This was counting down.

Hardly had the opening gavel struck when the incensed Democrats, strongly protesting, sent their own staff members out for impromptu visual aids of their own. As the two sides exchanged verbal volleys, staff members returned properly armed with hand-drawn signs, and the meeting degenerated into a heated, wild circus. At one point while the hapless Bliley (who, given his distinguished record and long career, would have preferred to avoid the histrionics) attempted to restore order, an excited Democrat staff member tried to cover the blinking doomsday clock with an enormous sign that read *Committee to a Tax Cut for the Rich,* while an equally enthused Republican staff member tried to shove the sign away. A Republican accused a Democrat of demagoguery, which is not allowed under House rules. An enraged protest was registered by the former Democrat chair of the committee. Bliley ordered the comment stricken from the record. Then a Democrat called a Republican a liar, also not allowed, resulting in a protest from the other side of the aisle.

Once again the comment was stricken from the record. Finally the Democrats, protesting that the Republicans were allowing too little time for hearings, stormed out of the room, signs and all, to hold hearings of their own, leaving the Republicans with their blinking countdown clock.

It was interesting theater, but lousy politics.

The first session of the 104th Congress (1995) was well on its way to becoming one of the most contentious legislative years in this century. Although everything from the Mexican loan bailout to Bosnia to regulatory reform found its way onto the congressional agenda that year, one issue continued to dominate the political firestorming throughout the session—the budget of the United States government and the related issues of the budget deficit and the federal debt. Program by program, agency by agency, the entire federal apparatus was beginning to come under scrutiny. Medicare, for example, the subject of the chaotic hearings discussed above, was costing too much and growing too fast, at least in the minds of many.

The raging political controversies of the modern era, which are not to be resolved any time soon, concern the sheer size of government, the proper role of government, the division of government among federal, state, and local levels, the regulatory role of government, the ideological orientation of government (even if implicit), the role of government in providing a safety net and income, and the role of government in our private lives. But the primary topic that seems to dominate the political discussion of the federal government in the present era is the fact that the budget runs red ink, year after year. Whether legitimate or contrived, the controversy over the budget deficit—the red ink—has continued to frame the debate over and over.

Key Definitions and Relationships

Any productive discussion of the budget and the deficit requires a careful introduction of some important terms, a somewhat tedious but necessary task. Once past that hurdle, however, we will be equipped to explore much more interesting and fruitful terrain. (We begin and end with definitions—there is a **glossary** at the back of the book that summarizes all of the terms used within.)

In this chapter we begin by defining the deficit (that is, by defining what the word means), then we review the connection between the deficit and the debt. To do this we need to see how the deficit is financed each year.

Table 1.1

Definitions

Outlays Monetary disbursements by the U.S. government, or by agencies within the government, including funds transferred between agencies (see the **glossary** for a more detailed definition).

Outlays (net) Net outlays of the U.S. government to parties outside of government, such as private citizens and corporations, which excludes interagency transfers of funds. Net outlays are always in the form of cash (check) disbursements. When used in the context of the overall budget, the term **outlays** normally refers to **net outlays** and is equivalent to **net expenditures.**

Expenditures Equivalent to net outlays and probably a more appropriate term, but virtually all government documents refer to spending as "outlays" rather than "expenditures," so that term is used throughout this book for the sake of consistency.

Revenues Net receipts of the U.S. government from parties outside of government, typically via taxes. Receipts are always in the form of cash (or equivalent).

Budget Deficit = Outlays – Revenues When outlays are greater than revenues.

Budget Surplus = Revenues – Outlays When revenues are greater than outlays.

Balanced Budget When revenues equal outlays, given some specified tolerance, such as within $100 million.

The Budget Deficit

When we refer to the budget deficit, the budget in question is, of course, of the United States government. Like any fiscal entity, the United States government must finance its vast expenditures from some source and it must keep some degree of budgetary control over its fiscal operations. This is no small task. The federal government will spend about $1.6 trillion in fiscal year 1998 and it will manage a gross debt worth more than $5 trillion. The actual budgetary document released each year, discussed later in this book, is typically close to 2000 pages when appendices and supplements are included, with very little wasted space.

As is summarized in Table 1.1, the **budget deficit,** by definition, is equal to **net government outlays (expenditures)** minus **total government revenues** from all sources. In the event that government revenues *exceed* outlays, the resulting **budget surplus** is defined as government revenues minus government outlays. The **balanced budget** refers to the situation in which revenues roughly equal outlays. Various proposals to require a "balanced budget" would force the government, in some way or another, to match all outlays with revenues.

Table 1.2

Outlays, Revenues, and Deficits
U.S. Government, Fiscal Years 1993–1996
($ billions)

Outlays	1993	1994	1995	1996
Defense	291.1	281.6	272.1	265.4
Social Security	304.6	319.6	335.8	349.6
Medical/health	230.0	251.8	275.3	293.1
Income security	207.3	214.0	220.4	225.3
Interest on the debt	198.8	203.0	232.2	241.1
Other	176.4	190.9	183.3	185.6
Total Outlays	1,408.2	1,460.9	1,519.1	1,560.1
Less: Revenues	1,153.5	1,257.7	1,355.2	1,452.8
Equals: Deficit	254.7	203.2	163.9	107.3

Note: Detailed account explanations are provided in Table 4.2a in Chapter 4.

Source: Budget of the United States Government, Fiscal Years 1996 and 1997, Historical Tables, for FY 92–95. U.S. Treasury estimates at http://www.ustreas.gov/treasury for FY 1996.

Table 1.2 shows major outlay categories, total outlays, revenues, and the deficit for fiscal years 1992 through 1996.[1] As can be seen, in fiscal year 1996 the government spent $1560.1 billion (in other words, about a trillion-and-a-half dollars). Some of the major spending categories are shown: about $265 billion was spent for defense, a little less than $350 billion were outlays for social security programs, and so forth.[2] Revenues for the same year, most of it from tax sources, total $1452.8 billion. Clearly outlays by the government exceeded revenues. The *difference* between the two, $107.3 billion, is by definition the budget deficit for that year. As can be seen in Table 1.2, large deficits also occurred in 1992 through 1995, though in each successive year the deficit has dropped.

A deficit is typical in a budgetary year, at least in the modern era. The U.S. government has run budget deficits of some size since 1969, the year

[1]The U.S. government's fiscal year begins on October 1st. For example, fiscal year 1997 began on October 1, 1996. The aggregate data shown here for fiscal year 1996 had just become available as this chapter was being prepared for publication. For updates on the data discussed in this book, see the section in the Preface entitled *Red Ink Web Site*.

[2]These accounts and what they mean are explained in Chapter 4, where the entire disaggregated line-item budget is examined in detail.

Table 1.3

U.S. Public Debt: Total Interest-Bearing Debt of the U.S. Government as of December 1995 ($ billions)

Instrument	Maturity	Interest category	Amount
Marketable Debt			**3,307.2**
U.S. Treasury Bills	13, 26, 52 week	Discount	760.7
U.S. Treasury Notes	1–10 years	Coupon	2,010.3
U.S. Treasury Bonds	10+ years	Coupon	521.2
Non-marketable debt			**1,657.2**
U.S. government accounts			1,299.6
Foreign governments			40.8
U.S. Savings Bonds			181.9
Other			134.9
Total Debt			**4,964.4**

Source: Treasury Bulletin, March 1996.

of the last budget surplus. In that year, revenues were $186.8 billion, outlays were $183.6 billion, producing a modest **surplus** of $3.2 billion. Since 1950 there have only been five surpluses (the history of deficits and surpluses will be reviewed in the next chapter).

The Federal Debt

The **federal debt,** sometimes called the national debt or the public debt, is in fact the total outstanding debt of the United States government, or to be more particular, of the United States Treasury, the fiscal agency of the U.S. government. So what, then, is the connection between the deficit, as defined earlier, and the federal debt? The answer appears when we ask the question, "How is the budget deficit *financed*?" Like any consumer or business, if the U.S. government spends more than it collects in receipts in any given year, which is what the deficit measures, it must *borrow* the difference. In short, the U.S. Treasury borrows most of the amount necessary to fund the deficit through the sale of U.S. Treasury securities, in particular, U.S. Treasury Bills, Notes, and Bonds. These are sold to a wide variety of buyers in the competitive finance markets.

Table 1.3 shows the total indebtedness of the U.S. Treasury as of December 1995. This is the federal debt, and on that date it stood at nearly $5 trillion. To be precise, when the government runs a deficit, which, remember, is an imbalance between outlays and receipts, it must fund the deficit by selling U.S. Treasury securities, usually of the kind classified as **marketable debt** in Table 1.3. For example, if the government runs a deficit of $250 billion, it will normally finance that by selling $250 billion in new U.S. Treasury Bills, Notes, or Bonds. Therefore, the amount of debt *outstanding* will rise by at least that amount—$250 billion.

In summary—if in any given year the U.S. government runs a deficit, *the federal debt will grow by at least the amount of the deficit.* If over a period of 4 years there are $250 billion deficits in each year, the federal debt will grow permanently by $1 trillion over that period. (We will discuss how this is permanent rather than temporary later.)

Marketable Debt

We saw in Table 1.3 that the amount of marketable debt outstanding in December 1995, which consisted of U.S. Treasury Bills, Notes, and Bonds, stood at more than $3.25 trillion ($3307.2 billion). These financial assets are familiar to most people who trade in the finance markets. They are "marketable" because when they are first issued (sold) by the U.S. Treasury they are sold to any party qualified to bid on them, including private citizens, financial institutions such as banks, mutual funds, corporations, and foreign investors. The securities can also be resold, and they typically are, in a huge secondary market, where they are traded like stocks and corporate bonds. For example, a U.S. Treasury Note with a 5-year maturity might first be sold to a private investor who might resell it six months later to a bank or a mutual fund. Prices of the securities, which fluctuate as market conditions change, are quoted every business day in major financial newspapers, such as *The Wall Street Journal.*

By definition, the securities that make up the marketable debt of the U.S. government differ by their maturity structure. A U.S. Treasury Bill matures in 1 year or less (from its date of issue),[3] whereas a U.S. Treasury

---

[3] A yield-bearing financial asset having a maturity or one year or less is typically called a "bill." Such assets are also called money market assets and money market mutual funds are made up almost entirely of bills. As financial assets, they are characterized by relatively low yields but high safety or low risk (this is especially true of treasury bills).

Table 1.4

Estimated Ownership of U.S. Treasury Marketable Securities (and Savings Bonds), December 1995 ($ billions)

	Amount	Percentage
Commercial banks	285.0	8.7
Individuals (U.S.)	347.7	10.6
Insurance companies	252.0	7.7
Money market funds	71.3	2.2
Corporations	288.8	8.8
State & local governments	420.0	12.8
Foreign citizens & governments	861.8	26.2
Other[a]	768.3	23.3
Total:	3,292.9	100%

[a]Other includes ownership by savings & loan associations, credit unions, nonprofit institutions, corporate pension trust funds, securities dealers and brokers, and certain government accounts.

Source: Treasury Bulletin, March 1996.

Note will mature in 1 to 10 years, and a U.S. Treasury Bond has a maturity date of more than 10 years, typically 30.[4] At maturity, the financial asset is redeemed, or "paid off" by the Treasury. A much more detailed discussion of these financial assets and the markets in which they are traded is found in Appendix A.

As we discussed, virtually anyone can buy these securities, including foreign citizens and governments. Table 1.4 shows the breakdown of ownership of marketable debt (bills, notes, and bonds) for December 1995. As can be seen, the debt is spread around, with more than 25% owned by foreign citizens and governments.

Nonmarketable Debt

The second category within the federal debt is referred to as **nonmarketable debt** (refer again to Table 1.3). These securities are not sold to the public nor to outside agencies, and are never sold on the secondary markets. Some of this debt is owned by foreign central banks and is used in

[4]These bonds should not be confused with the popular and inexpensive U.S. Savings Bonds, which can be purchased for as little as $50. These are classified under nonmarketable debt in Table 1.3, and the amount outstanding at that time was $181.9 million.

their exchange rate stabilization policies. Some is owned by the Federal Reserve System. By far the most important category, representing more than $1 trillion in debt, is the entry for U.S. government accounts. These, generally, are the **trust funds** that one hears so much about.

The two Social Security Trust Funds, which are discussed at length in Chapter 7, are a good example. In any given year, the Social Security System receives more in taxes and other receipts than is paid out. The combined Social Security Trust Funds (for the retirement and disability programs), for example, collected revenues of $396.3 billion in fiscal year 1995, but paid out only $335.9 billion, generating a surplus of $60.4 billion within the Social Security component of the budget.

Because the Social Security program generates this cash surplus, the Treasury "borrows" these surplus receipts to fund spending elsewhere in the budget, treating the surplus funds as though they came from general revenue sources. To compensate for this "borrowing," the Treasury issues nonmarketable U.S. Treasury debt to the Social Security Trust Fund for the amount of the surplus (the $60.4 billion in our example), which thereafter shows up on the books as part of nonmarketable debt under U.S. government accounts. By running such surpluses, the Social Security Trust Funds had accumulated a balance of $483.1 billion by October 1995. All of it was in the form of nonmarketable U.S. Treasury debt, so it constituted about one-third of the $1.66 trillion in nonmarketable debt listed under U.S. government accounts in Table 1.3.

In summary:

Social Security Receipts – Social Security Outlays
($396.3 b)   –   ($335.9 b)

= **Nonmarketable Treasury debt
issued to Social Security Trust Funds**
=   ($60.4 b)

Because the use of trust funds and their impact on the budget is complicated, further discussion will be deferred until Chapters 6 and 7, where the Social Security System and other entitlements programs are discussed in detail. Trust funds were introduced here to explain why the U.S. government, in effect, owes debt to itself. Generally, the U.S. Treasury borrows from special programs that generate surpluses, such as the Social Security Trust Funds.

In summary, most nonmarketable debt represents the internal debt owed by one U.S. government agency to another. Unlike marketable debt, very little of the nonmarketable debt is owed to parties outside of the U.S. government (the $182 billion in U.S. Savings Bonds—about 11% of the total—is the one conspicuous exception).

The Precise Connection between the Deficit and the Debt

Let us now summarize a few points:

1. Deficits are financed by selling marketable debt, contributing to the overall federal debt.
2. For any fiscal year in which there is a deficit, the federal debt will grow by *at least* the amount of the deficit.
3. Some specialized accounts, such as Social Security, generate surpluses and are compensated for this by the issue of nonmarketable debt for U.S. Government Accounts, contributing to the overall federal debt.
4. Therefore, the *increase in federal debt* will be greater than the deficit in any given fiscal year.

To be more precise (with data from fiscal year 1995)[5]:

Change in federal debt =		
($277.3 b)	=	
Budget deficit + Change in trust funds +/– Other		
($163.9 b) + ($99.3 b) + ($14.1 b)		

In Table 1.5, the relationship between the deficit, the change in debt, and the debt is shown for select years. It is clear that the debt has grown (as measured by the change in debt) each year by more than the deficit. This further implies, as a rough generalization, that the total federal debt is equal to the sum of all previous deficits (since 1789!), minus the

[5]The small amount labeled "other" includes such technical adjustments as changes in Treasury cash operating balances, profits made from coinage, and the cashflow impact of certain credit accounts. See Table 13.2 of *The Budget of the United States Government, FY 1996, Analytic Perspectives* for a more complete description.

Table 1.5

The Deficit, the Debt and the Change in Debt
(Select Years, $ billions)

Year	Revenues	Outlays	Deficit	Change in debt	Gross debt
1970	192.8	195.6	2.8	15.1	380.9
1975	279.0	332.3	53.2	58.0	541.9
1980	517.1	590.9	73.8	79.6	909.0
1985	734.1	946.4	212.3	252.9	1,817.5
1986	769.1	990.3	221.2	303.1	2,120.6
1987	854.1	1,003.9	149.8	225.5	2,346.1
1988	909.0	1,064.1	155.2	255.2	2,601.3
1989	990.7	1,143.2	152.5	266.7	2,868.0
1990	1,031.3	1,252.7	221.4	338.6	3,206.6
1991	1,054.3	1,323.8	269.5	391.9	3,598.5
1992	1,090.5	1,380.9	290.4	403.6	4,002.1
1993	1,153.5	1,408.2	254.7	349.3	4,351.4
1994	1,257.7	1,460.9	203.2	292.3	4,643.7
1995	1,355.2	1,519.1	163.9	277.3	4,921.0

Source: Budget of the United States Government, Fiscal Years 1996 and 1997, various tables.

sum of all previous surpluses, plus the value of existing government trust funds:

$$\text{Debt} = \Sigma(\text{Deficits}) - \Sigma(\text{Surpluses}) + \text{Trust Funds}$$

Clearly, when deficits are large, the debt grows.

Why the Debt Will Not Be Reduced (Much)

Reducing the budget *deficit* (the annual difference between outlays and revenues) or even eliminating the budget deficit by balancing the budget clearly has been given a high political priority in recent years, even becoming the focal point of a furious political controversy in 1995 and in 1996, the presidential election year. But what about reducing or even eliminating the *debt*—is that possible?

Given what we have learned so far, it should be clear that eliminating the deficit (by balancing the budget) would stop the marketable debt component of the federal debt—the portion that is used largely to finance budget deficits—from *growing any larger.* On the other hand, a balanced budget would not shrink the debt. A government debt, once in place, normally stays. Modern governments do not "pay off" their debts. They do not substantially reduce the principal value of debt. The debt as a percentage of national output (as measured, for example, by gross domestic product) might decline over time in the face of legitimate budgetary restraint, but the principal value of the debt is not likely to decline much at all.

To reduce the debt (*not* the *deficit,* but the *debt*) requires the government to run a surplus—to have receipts exceed outlays. Generally, the debt would be reduced by the amount of the surplus. To *eliminate* the debt in the case of the United States, the government would have to generate surpluses over the many years, totaling more than $5 trillion. Crudely stating the case, if the government were to run surpluses averaging $100 billion per year, a $250 billion swing from the present state of affairs, it would take about a half century to eliminate the debt. It is inconceivable that such budgetary austerity could be imposed through 4, 5, 10, or any number of presidential elections.

The impact on the economy would likely be intolerable. The regional economic trauma of the aerospace cutbacks in the late 1980s and early 1990s were substantial and long lasting in states such as California, where, as will be shown in a later chapter, the savings were marginal. Reducing the deficit is a daunting enough task by itself.[6]

Finally, there is no real economic reason for eliminating the debt. All modern economies, including our own, have carried some level of debt throughout their history. In the case of the U.S. economy, World War II was largely debt financed, as will be seen in the next chapter, and the legacy of that debt was carried up to the modern era through some of our most prosperous decades—including the "Golden Sixties" without any penalty. The task of modern government fiscal management is to keep the debt growing moderately, if at all, given the size and growth of the economy.

Rolling Over the Debt

Remembering that the deficit is financed by selling U.S. Treasury securities, and these securities constitute the debt, a question naturally arises about the fact that many of these securities are short-term, some with

---

[6]This argument will be much easier to support once the actual budgetary numbers have been seen: these will be introduced in Chapters 2 and 3.

Table 1.6

Average Maturity of U.S. Treasury Debt

Year	Years	Months
1970	3	8
1975	2	8
1980	3	9
1985	4	11
1990	6	1
1995	5	4

Source: Economic Report of the President, 1995, and U.S. Treasury Bulletin, March 1996.

maturities of only 13 weeks. If the debt is never to be reduced, what happens when these securities expire?

The answer should be clear—maturing treasury securities are merely rolled over into new ones. In other words, when a batch of 13-week bills is redeemed, more are sold to replace them, and this procedure of refinance will continue, theoretically, forever. This may strike the reader as odd, because it's a convention that has no true equivalent in the private sector,[7] but this is how governments, including governments of stable and powerful economies, operate. At one time in England the government issued bonds called **perpetuities** or **consols**. These were bonds that, by law, never matured. They simply paid interest to the owner for perpetuity! The U.S. government debt is essentially a perpetuity debt, except that it is financed by rolling over relatively short-term debt instruments endlessly.

Maturing securities are not necessarily replaced with identical securities. The U.S. Treasury frequently changes the composition of its debt, reducing or increasing the average duration, for example, to take advantage of interest rate swings or changing market tastes. For example, in the summer of 1994, after 6 months of a weak stock market and an even weaker bond market, the public found long-term bonds unattractive and began to strongly favor the Treasury's 2-year notes because of their relatively high yield at the time. The Treasury would be imprudent not to take advantage of such changing tastes.

Refer to Table 1.6 for an example of how the Treasury has altered the average maturity of treasury debt over the years. As can be seen, the

[7]Although many large corporations carry some level of debt indefinitely.

average duration has fluctuated considerably, with the maturity tending to lengthen through the 1980s and into the 1990s. In 1993 the decision was made, tentatively, to try to reduce the average duration of the debt to take advantage of the low interest rates on short-term securities.

In summary, using a mix of maturities gives the Treasury more control over management of the debt but is no indication, tacit or otherwise, of any intention to reduce the debt, and it is not a means to do so.

Can the Deficit Be Financed by "Printing Money?"

One sometimes hears that our government finances its deficit by "printing money." Historically, there have been cases in other countries and during our own early history (especially during the Revolutionary War) of governments simply printing whatever money was needed in the form of currency notes, such as our $100 bills.Typically this has had disastrous results in the form of hyperinflation and currency devaluation. Excess currency leads to excess demand for goods that is far beyond the production capacity of the economy, and this imbalance results in severe price inflation. Probably the best example of this is the catastrophic German inflation of the early 1920s immediately after World War I. The unstable Weimar Republic, formed at the end of the war in late 1918, tried to finance both the national budget and the huge debt accumulated during the war by printing marks (Reichsbanknotes), marks, and more marks, producing an inflation that was almost beyond calculation. Consider this graphic example: the author owns (a) a 2 mark note dated August 12, 1914, which would have been worth about 50 cents given the exchange rate at the time, and (b) a 50 million-mark note dated September 1, 1923. Given that by September 1923 the official exchange rate of the mark to the dollar was at about 100 million to one, this 1923 note was also worth about 50 cents. More importantly, by November, only two months later, the exchange rate was more than 4 billion to one, reducing this same note's value to 1¼ cent. This extreme example—not the only one found in history—warns against the expedient of printing money directly to finance budget deficits.

As we have already discussed, U.S. government deficits are financed by selling U.S. Treasury securities, not by printing money. But is the latter a possible option?

Fortunately, the answer is no. Our monetary system and the money-supply process is regulated and effectively controlled by the **Federal Reserve System,** the nation's central banking authority. Technically the Federal Reserve System is not an agency of the U.S. government and certainly not an agency of the U.S. Treasury, although it acts as banker to the U.S. Treasury and it helps the treasury sell its securities.

The Federal Reserve System is "owned" by the nation's private banks that are members of the system (composed of virtually all depository institutions, including banks, in the country), but it, and similar institutions overseas such as the Bank of Japan and the Bank of England, must be thought of as quasi-governmental agencies responsible for executing monetary policy and other regulatory functions. The Federal Reserve System, though, is autonomous and independent of the U.S. Treasury—it does not even receive its funding authority from the U.S. government—and it is not responsible for directly funding Treasury debt, nor would it do so if requested.[8]

In addition, the U.S. Treasury cannot simply print paper notes as in the Weimar Republic. Look closely at a dollar bill and you will see that it is a liability, not of the U.S. government, but of a Federal Reserve District Bank, such as the Federal Reserve Bank of New York or one of the other 11 district banks of the Federal Reserve System. Other than coins, and it would be impossible to mint enough of those, the U.S. Treasury no longer issues paper money. And the U.S. Treasury cannot write a check without funds in its account for the same reason that you cannot—the check will not be honored unless funds are available.

In summary, given at least the *current* rules of federal finance, which are not likely to be changed soon, if the government runs a cash deficit, it has to borrow the shortfall like anyone else. Printing money is not an option.

It *is* possible, however, in the U.S. economy to *indirectly monetize* the debt—meaning that years of excessive government deficits can *indirectly* lead to unacceptably high levels of money and credit formation in the economy. The explanation of this phenomenon, though, requires an understanding of material that is to come in later chapters, so we will return to this topic in Chapter 9.

What Is the Best Measure of Government Debt?

For years a large electronic scoreboard has clicked away over Times Square in New York, keeping tabs on the national debt, allowing anyone in the area to see at a glance a very current estimate of how much money

---

[8]The Federal Reserve System *does* assist in some of the technical aspects of Treasury funding operations, smoothing the impact of the timing of the release of the debt upon the finance markets, for example, and, as stated above, it acts as banker for U.S. Treasury accounts.

Table 1.7

U.S. Government Net (External) Debt as of December 1995 ($ billions)

Category	Amount
Marketable debt	3,307.2
Nonmarketable debt	1,657.2
Total (Gross) Debt	**4,964.4**
less:	
U.S. government accounts	−1,299.6
Net (External) Debt	**3,664.8**
Memo ($ millions):	
Debt subject to statutory limit	4,899,975
Statutory limit (Dec 1995)	4,900,000
Statutory limit (Apr 1996)	5,500,000

is owed to someone by our federal government. Sometime in early 1996 the tally went over $5 trillion. Is this number a reasonable estimate of the "debt of the United States government?"

Not really. The $5 trillion tally, which is reflected as the value of Total debt in Table 1.3, is a good measure of the gross debt of the federal government, but that figure includes $1.3 trillion in internal interagency debt, such as the money technically owed by the U.S. Treasury to the two Social Security Trust Funds.[9]

Table 1.7 shows the net debt, sometimes called the external debt, is a measure of the indebtedness of the U.S. Government to *outside parties*. The material in this table is drawn from the summary of U.S. public debt in Table 1.3. As can be seen, the net debt is equal to the sum of marketable and nonmarketable debt, *less* the category labeled U.S. government accounts, which indicates that the net debt to parties outside of government was $3.664 trillion in December 1995, still a formidable figure. In most contexts this *net debt* is the value that best represents the true indebtedness of the U.S. government.

---

[9]Again, these trust funds will be discussed much more extensively in Chapter 7, where the complicated financial arrangements between the U.S. Treasury and its own trust funds are explained in much greater detail.

What Is the Statutory Debt Limit and What Does It Limit?

One of the more curious spectacles of the 1995–1996 budgetary battles involved the statutory limit on the public debt. Since 1941 this strange law, originating in legislation passed in 1917, has been the most conspicuous example of failed efforts to curb the growth of the national debt. The law is simple—it requires the Congress and the President to set an upper limit on the size of the **public debt subject to statutory limitation**, which is equal to the *gross* debt minus some small exclusions (less than 2% of the total).[10] In effect, the debt limit applies to the gross rather than the net debt.

The potential of the debt limit as a means to control the growth of the debt and thereby the size of budget deficits is obvious. Once the limit is reached, it is illegal for the U.S. Treasury to borrow any new funds. This means that the U.S. Treasury is not authorized to sell U.S. Treasury Bills, Notes, or Bonds for new funding, and if this were done, the Secretary of the Treasury, who technically authorizes such sales, would be violating the law. Therefore, the budget deficit must be eliminated to prevent additional borrowing.

But theory and political reality in Washington sometimes do not match. Characteristically, when the ceiling is hit, the limit is quietly raised (usually quietly; sometimes there will be a righteous speech or two). This step has been taken more than 60 times since 1941—rendering the limit almost meaningless.

In the heated partisan budget wars of 1995, though, the debt ceiling became a very sticky issue. The statutory debt limit had stood at $4.9 trillion since 1993. It was raised in that year of good fellowship and compromise to an unusually high level, given the size of the debt at the time, so that it would not become an issue every few months. The timing was unfortunate. By coincidence, the gross debt subject to statutory limit approached and threatened to exceed the limit in early November 1995. This coincided with the beginning of a bitter fight over the budget between Democratic President Bill Clinton and the Republican Congress just before the government was to be shut down as a casualty of the strife. The debt limit, or the urgent need to raise it, quickly became a hot issue. As part of their effort to try to pressure Clinton to agree to their version of a plan to balance the budget by the year 2002, Congressional Republicans refused to raise the debt limit, a dangerous tactic that provoked the possibility of a technical default on U.S. Treasury debt. This

---

[10]For the actual values refer to Table 1.7.

action forced Treasury Secretary Robert Rubin to "bend the books," taking steps of dubious legality to prevent default, mostly in the form of "borrowing" from the federal employee retirement fund. Republicans became so frustrated at Rubin's success that in early January 1996 House Rules Committee Chair Gerald Solomon threatened to have the treasury secretary impeached. Finally, in late March 1996, after months of fiscal brinksmanship, the debt limit was again raised to exactly $5.5 trillion. That means that the same problem will likely be back to haunt us again around the year 1999.

Will Balancing the Budget Stop the Debt from Growing?

Because some of the debt generated by modern budgetary operations is internal, a balanced budget (no deficit) would have the effect of freezing the *net* debt (the roughly $3.6 trillion value in Table 1.7), because almost all of that is related to the deficit. Nonetheless the U.S. government accounts component of nonmarketable debt would continue to grow as long as some government trust funds, such as the Social Security Trust Funds, continued to generate surpluses (which, remember, are "borrowed" for general treasury obligations), a situation that is projected to continue for decades. Therefore the *gross* debt—the amount tallied by the electronic board over Times Square, would continue to rise, to the tune of about $80 billion per year, *even with* a balanced budget. This would make necessary continuing increases in the statutory debt limit, possibly provoking more partisan controversy, because the debt limit applies to the gross debt, not to the net debt.

Are Deficits and Federal Debt Bad?

It is important to understand that we are going to acknowledge the legitimacy of this question very early in the book—but without answering it completely.

Clearly the entire Republican Party (at least in the 104th Congress), many Democrats, and perhaps a majority of American voters think we ought to "balance the budget." In late 1995 and early 1996 opinion polls showed that Americans gave a very high political priority to balancing the budget. But the polls also showed that for many of the same voters, a considerable part of the support for budget austerity evaporated when they were confronted with a choice between the abstraction of a zero deficit and cutbacks in programs they understood and in some cases benefited from, such as Medicare. And not all of the equivocation seemed to be linked to pure self-interest. In some polls, large numbers of middle-class Americans were reluctant to support sizeable cutbacks in programs designed to help the poor—such as nutritional programs targeted at poor children.

But it is also the case, at least in the modern era, that no large and prosperous industrialized nation has ever required of itself a balanced budget year after year. This is certainly true for the United States. Throughout this century, budget deficits are far more common than are surpluses. And no European government requires a balanced budget— not even close—most run deficits that are much larger than ours when adjusted for the size of the economy. If we in the United States achieve and maintain a balanced budget by the year 2002, it will be a novel experiment, never really tried in the modern era.

On the other hand, there is no doubt that governments must exercise fiscal responsibility and have not always succeeded in doing so. Supporting politically popular and expensive programs with debt rather than with taxes is an attractive expedient for politicians who lack the moral integrity, intelligence, or a sense of obligation to responsibly protect the public purse. Deficits and debts can be too large, and they probably have become too large over the last 20 years.

But we will reserve judgment for a few chapters—or at least until we become more familiar with the subject, make some historical comparisons, and set some loose standards. Then we will come back to the question.

What's Next?

We now have a very precise definition of the deficit and the debt and we understand the connection between the two. But many questions remain unanswered:

1. How common are budget deficits?
2. What is considered a *large* deficit?
3. Given that the deficit is the difference between spending and revenues, (mostly from taxes), what is the money being spent on and what are the sources of taxes and other revenues?
4. Who benefits from government spending?
5. What are the realistic options for changing spending or taxing in the name of deficit reduction?
6. What is the legal framework under which the Congress and the President are required to work—or is there one?

7. What are trust funds, entitlements, appropriations, and all of the other budgetary terms that are so often in the news these days?

Once we have answered these and many more questions, we can return to the fundamental question asked in the previous section.

The approach taken in the next two chapters will be largely historical. To get a sense of where we stand today compared with the past, in the next chapter we will look at the patterns of spending, taxes, deficits and debt in the United States through most of this century. In Chapter 3 we will take a more detailed look at the 1980s and early 1990s, the era of large deficits.

The Difference between Outlays and U.S. Government Purchases from the National Income and Expenditure Accounts

Economics students familiar with the National Income and Expenditure Accounts (which measures gross domestic product, national income, consumption expenditures, and so on) will quickly notice that the value of **U.S. government purchases** as a component of gross domestic product is far smaller than what this chapter describes as U.S. government outlays (expenditures) for any given year. This is because the definitions are entirely different (and the difference is important when studying macroeconomics or when using the data for research). Because this is a technical matter of little interest to the general reader, a discussion of the difference is found in Appendix B. Students studying macroeconomics should read that brief appendix.

The Historical Origins of the Debt

. . . .

. . . .

Budget deficits are not new. In fact, they are typical. During the 96 years between 1901 and 1996 the U.S. government had surpluses in only 28 of those years. Deficits were run in the other 68 years. As we'll see below, though, deficits, or at least peacetime deficits, are more common in the modern era, since about 1960. Only two surpluses have occurred, the first in 1960 and the second, and last, in 1969.

In this chapter we will explore the history of the U.S. government deficits and surpluses through this century up until the last two decades. When discussing the deficits and surpluses prior to 1960, two generalizations will arise:

1. deficits are common during wartime, and
2. deficits, even if short-lived, appear in recession years.

In the next chapter we will also discover that the modern deficits—those seen since 1980—can be classified as *systemic deficits*, enduring

through peacetime and economic prosperity with little historical precedent.[1] The only other period where deficits endured for so long in peacetime was during the Great Depression.

Wartime Deficits

Figure 2.1 shows deficits and surpluses for the years between 1915 and
1955. The dividing line between deficits and surpluses is, of course, zero,
and all entries below that magnitude represent surpluses.[2]
   Upon inspection of this graph, one thing becomes very clear. As stated
above, and as is made evident by the two spikes in the graph, major wars
are deficit-financed. Although the deficits of the early 1940s are small
compared to modern deficits (in 1993, remember, the deficit was $255 bil-
lion, compared to the peak 1943 deficit of $55 billion), the economy was
much smaller then, and the deficits of both world wars were huge, given
the scale of the economy. In 1943, for example, the deficit was about 16%
of gross domestic product (GDP—the level of annual national output),
whereas through the 1980s and early 1990s, when the deficit was per-
ceived to be a growing problem, it never exceeded 6% of GDP in any year.
By comparison, if the deficit in 1995 was as proportionately large as the
1943 deficit compared to the scale of the economy, it would have been
nearly $1 trillion rather than the still unacceptable $163 billion.
   Before we discuss the wartime deficits, another interesting feature can
be seen in Figure 2.1. The government ran surpluses throughout the 1920s
and deficits during the 1930s. This is hard to see on the scale of Figure 2.1,
so data for the interwar period will be shown later in this chapter.
   When we remember that the deficit is equal to outlays minus revenues,
the best way to explore the origins of deficits and surpluses over any period is to see how these two financial categories play against each other.
If a deficit looms in the historical data, we might care to know if the
cause was a sudden surge in outlays or a loss of revenues. Therefore, we

---

[1] This term—*systemic deficits*—is the author's own. A systemic deficit is a large
deficit that endures for years regardless of economic conditions (i.e., through recession and high growth) due to some systemic and lasting fundamental budgetary problem. See a more detailed discussion in the glossary. The purist might want to compare
this definition to the definition of *structural deficits*, which is an estimate of what a
deficit would have been had the economy been operating at full employment.

[2] Data used in all graphs in this chapter, unless otherwise indicated, are from the
same source: various tables in *Budget of the United States Government, Fiscal Year
1995, Historical Tables*.

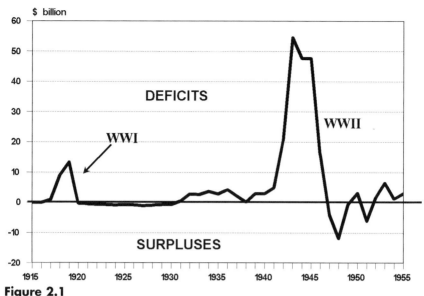

Figure 2.1
U.S. Government Budget Deficits, 1915–1955

will break down the period between 1915 and 1955 by looking at data for revenues and outlays.

World War I

Figure 2.2 shows U.S. government receipts and outlays for the years from 1915 to 1922. Remember that the difference between outlays and receipts is equal to the deficit.

The United States was a late entrant into World War I. Archduke Franz Ferdinand was assassinated in Sarajevo on June 28, 1914, and shortly thereafter Germany and Austria-Hungary were engaged in combat with Great Britain, France, and Russia. The United States tried to follow a policy of neutrality in the early years of the war, but after repeated German attacks upon U.S. shipping, the United States finally entered the war in April 1917. The U.S. economy, which was still largely agricultural, flourished during the war, partly because of munitions exports (which explains why Germany was sinking U.S. ships) but mostly due to agricultural exports to a continent ravaged by war.

Inspection of Figure 2.2 clearly shows that the wartime deficit arose because of the surge in outlays, which were obviously war-related. Receipts

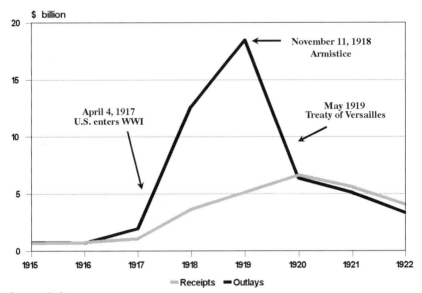

Figure 2.2
U.S. Government Receipts and Outlays, World War I

did rise some. This was due in part to the prosperity associated with the war but also because of a series of taxes imposed during the Wilson administration. These taxes consisted of new tariffs, a graduated income tax that had an upper tax bracket of 75% for the wealthiest citizens,[3] a 65% excess profits tax, and a 25% inheritance tax. Most of these taxes were gradually rolled back after the end of the war. Income taxes were cut in 1921, 1924, and 1926. Revenues rose sharply, but clearly not by enough to finance the war. World War I was debt-financed.

As soon as the Treaty of Versailles was signed in May 1919, federal outlays fell back from more than $18 billion in that year to little more than $5 billion in 1920. In the years that followed, they would eventually fall well below $4 billion, less than 25% of the peak.

World War II

The same pattern was repeated, on a grander scale, two decades later during World War II. Figure 2.3 shows U.S. government receipts and outlays between 1939 and 1960, and includes the war years.

[3]The federal income tax was authorized by the Seventeenth Amendment to the U.S. Constitution and it was first imposed in 1913.

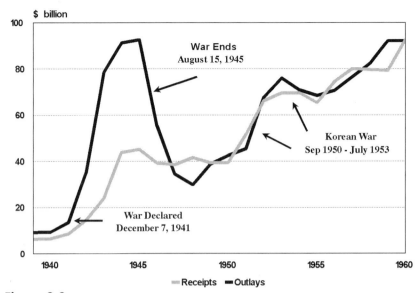

Figure 2.3
U.S. Government Receipts and Outlays, World War II and after

When the United States entered the war after the bombing of Pearl Harbor on December 7, 1941, the government was already running a small deficit and it had been running small deficits for the previous decade (the reason for this will be discussed below). Once again, outlays, largely war-related, shot up to multiples of what they had been prior to the war. In 1940 federal outlays were only $9.5 billion. By 1945 they would soar to $93 billion, nearly a 10-fold increase in only five years. Once again, tax receipts rose substantially (from $6.5 billion in 1940 to $45 billion in 1945), generally for the same reasons as during World War I. World War II fiscally kicked the U.S. economy out of a depression that had burdened it for more than a decade, and the general prosperity, even though war-related, increased tax revenues. Most of the revenue increase, though, was due to higher taxes.

Very heavy excise taxes on amusements and luxuries were imposed,[4] as were steeply graduated income and corporate profits taxes. Personal income taxes had an upper bracket of 94%. Corporate profits had an

[4]And the definition of a luxury was vastly more inclusive than would be accepted today—tires and sugar were luxuries. In addition to the rationing programs used during the war, excise taxes were justified more to discourage civilian consumption of critical war materiels than as a means of raising revenues.

upper bracket of 40% and there was a 95% tax on what was defined to be "excess corporate profits." A unique salary limit was imposed that forbade after-tax salaries of more than $25,000 per year. Most important, though, the income tax, which had been largely applicable only to the wealthy, was expanded to include the employed middle class and payroll withholdings were instituted for the first time.

As was the case in World War I, revenues shot up but were not nearly enough to finance the war. The second war was, like the first, generally debt financed. To see the extent to which it was, please review Figure 2.4. This graph shows the deficit as the percentage of outlays during World War II (or, in other words, what percentage of outlays were borrowed during the war). As can be seen, in 1943 only 30% of federal outlays were financed with tax receipts and other revenue sources; the remaining 70% was borrowed. Data for World War I (not shown here) are similar. In 1919 the deficit was equal to 72% of outlays.

Even with the large peacetime deficits of recent years, only in 1985 was the deficit more than 25% of outlays. The wartime deficits really were exceptional.

As might be guessed when reviewing this data, the *federal debt,* which, we remember, is equal to the sum of previous deficits plus the growth of

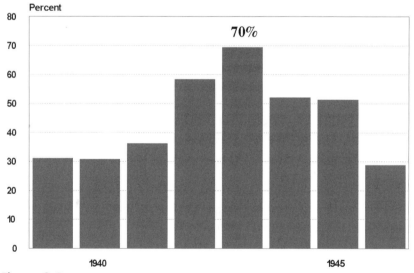

Figure 2.4
Deficit as a Percent of Outlays, World War II

Table 2.1

Federal Debt, End of Year 1940–1945 ($ billions)

Year	Debt
1940	50.7
1941	57.5
1942	79.2
1943	142.6
1944	204.1
1945	260.1

Source: Budget of the U.S. Government, Fiscal Year 1995, Historical Tables.

government trust funds,[5] was compounded substantially by both wars. The extent to which the debt grew is made evident in Table 2.1, which shows the magnitude of federal debt outstanding at the end of each year between 1940 and 1945.

In 1940, the total federal debt stood at only $50.7 billion, most of that amount was caused by the deficits from two decades earlier in World War I. After 1942, each year's *deficit* was around the size of the 1940 *debt,* so that by the end of the war, the debt had increased fivefold, from $51 billion to $260 billion.[6]

Public support for the new indebtedness was substantially bolstered by a very effective campaign to encourage civilians to buy the small-denomination U.S. Savings Bonds (sometimes called war bonds) so popular in that era. Advertisements and slogans were omnipresent throughout the war—even movies and cartoons exhorted the public to save and to buy bonds. (A similar campaign had been used in World War I to promote the sale of Liberty Bonds.) The campaign was instrumental in keeping consumer spending relatively low, saving resources for military use,

[5]The Social Security System, beginning fiscal operations only in 1936, was already running a trust-fund surplus of nearly $1 billion by 1942, an impressive amount, given that federal outlays were about $35 billion that same year. By 1942 the Social Security Trust Fund had already accumulated more than $3 billion. This will be discussed in Chapter 7.

[6]To get some idea of the scope of this increase, in which the debt roughly doubled every other year, it would take 30 years for the debt to double again—in 1975 the debt grew to $542 billion.

and providing a means for consumer spending to help stimulate the economy after the war. As a means of financing the deficit the popular bonds, although contributing somewhat, were less instrumental. Most of the debt was financed by large-denomination U.S. Treasury securities, a considerable part of which was purchased by U.S. banks.

The Era between the Wars: 1920 to 1940

The two decades between the great wars were economic antipodes. While the 1920s, sometimes called the Roaring Twenties, were prosperous years of almost unconstrained economic enthusiasm, the dark and dismal 30s, the decade of the terrible Great Depression, were truly the opposite. U.S. government fiscal affairs in those two strange decades are well represented in Figure 2.5. Two peculiar features become immediately apparent: through the prosperous 1920s the government consistently achieved budget surpluses, but through the grim 1930s there was a deficit in every year, carrying the legacy of deficits into World War II.

Before discussing these two decades, it should be stated that the prosperity of the 1920s was mixed and possibly premature. The two decades are very closely linked. While the 1920s gave the first glimpse of many modern technologies and the corporations that were to make them available to the market, the agricultural sector, still the largest sector in the economy, did not partake in the prosperity. Prices for farm products fell after the first war, and the farm industry, somewhat myopic and overenthusiastic during the war years when exports flourished, had become heavily indebted. More importantly, the euphoria of the decade gave rise to excessive speculation in real estate and stocks, and the crash of the stock market in October 1929 truly burst the bubble. True prosperity would not be seen again until the early 1940s.

As seen in Figure 2.5, both revenues and outlays fell sharply after World War I. They stabilized in 1922 and they remained remarkably constant thereafter, with receipts exceeding outlays by a substantial margin in relative terms. However, in absolute terms government economic activity was subdued. During this decade the three presidents who were to leave their legacy—Warren G. Harding, Calvin Coolidge, and Herbert Hoover—were conservative and they generally promoted small government and low taxes, at least by modern standards. Income taxes were cut from their high wartime levels three times between 1921 and 1926. The 1920s probably represent the last decade where old-fashioned conser-

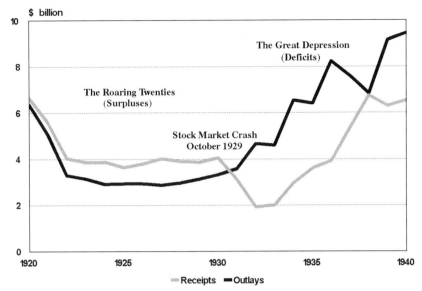

Figure 2.5
U.S. Government Receipts and Outlays, 1920–1940

vatism prevailed, embracing both low taxes and minimal government, at least in a fiscal sense.

Budget deficits appeared in the 1930s and were to last through the decade into World War II. The deficits were small in absolute terms, especially compared to the scale that was to be encountered during the war, but they were very large in relative terms. For example, the deficit as a percent of total outlays exceeded 50% in 1936, a level that had never been approached in the modern era.

The obvious effect of the depression upon tax receipts allows a generalization that continues into the modern era: *when national income falls in a recession or a depression, tax receipts fall as well.* This is because the tax base falls, and is especially true of an economy that relies very heavily upon income taxes for tax receipts in general.

The clear break in trend in tax receipts during the depression is apparent in Figure 2.5. The worst years of the depression were those between 1930 and 1933. After 1933 the economy began a slow recovery (although national income had not recovered to its 1929 level even as late as 1939). With the recovery, tax receipts began to increase. There was a recession within the depression in 1938, and receipts slipped back the following year. Finally, as was seen earlier, receipts shot up during the war.

During the administration of Franklin D. Roosevelt, the only U.S. president elected to more than two terms (four), outlays rose in one of the earliest applications of activist fiscal policy, as a part of the effort to defeat the depression. Roosevelt's recovery program, instituted very aggressively, was called the New Deal, and among its achievements it included the creation of the Public Works Administration, which was to spend $3.3 billion on roads and structures, the passage of the Agricultural Adjustment Act in May 1933, which was to lead to the long tradition of price supports, production restrictions and subsidies that continue in altered form to the present day (authorized mostly through subsequent legislation passed in 1938), the creation of the Federal Emergency Relief Administration, which would dispense $500 million to relief organizations, the Civilian Conservation Corps (CCC), which would spend $500 million employing men between ages 18 and 25 in conservation projects, and the huge Works Progress Administration (WPA), which spent more than $10 billion before it was dismantled during the war.

Most of the New Deal programs were eliminated by the end of World War II, although many of the agricultural programs continue to the present day. Perhaps the most lasting legacy of the New Deal came with the creation of the Social Security System, authorized by the Social Security Act of 1935. As we will see in later chapters, the impact this system on contemporary fiscal affairs can hardly be overstated.

The Golden Decades: 1950 to 1970

After World War II, U.S. government financial operations settled into a period lasting two decades that might be described as "fiscal tranquility." As the economy expanded in its post-war prosperity, government outlays and receipts, as seen in Figure 2.6, expanded as well, and at nearly the same pace. Although there were only five surpluses in the 21 years between 1950 and 1970 (in 1951, 1956, 1957, 1960, and 1969) the deficits tended to be very small, even in recession years. Aside from the two recession-related deficits in 1959 and 1968, where the deficits were about 14% of outlays, deficits as a percentage of outlays were never more than 6% (as opposed to levels as high as 25% in the present era). Even the Korean War, fought on a much-reduced scale when compared to World War II, did not have a large fiscal impact. Outlay increased somewhat during the war (September 1950 to July 1953) but rising receipts kept the

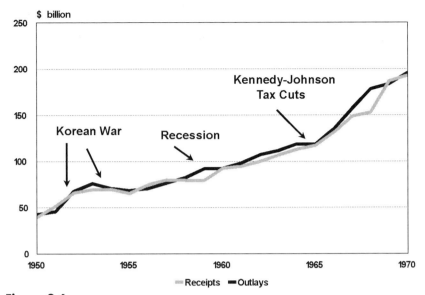

Figure 2.6
U.S. Government Receipts and Outlays, 1950–1970

deficit manageable. The war in Vietnam would have a similar fiscal impact; no clearly discernable deficit arose from that war.

The two recessions of this era, beginning in 1957 and in 1970, were relatively mild and short-lived. In 1957, the impact upon tax receipts caused a small surge in the deficit lasting only one year. The 1970 recession was so mild that it had no significant impact upon receipts at all.

Toward the end of the era a fiscal experiment with tax cuts was initiated by President John F. Kennedy. In June 1962, the Kennedy administration proposed a substantial cut in personal income and business taxes as a stimulus to the economy. The economy was relatively strong, but the stock market had experienced a sharp decline (the Dow Jones Industrial Average had fallen from around the 720 level in March of that year to around 520 in early June). In his public appeals for tax reduction in the following months, Kennedy justified intentional deficits. His *Economic Report to Congress* presented on January 21, 1963, included this passage: "Let me make clear why, in today's economy, fiscal prudence and responsibility call for tax reduction even if it temporarily enlarges the federal deficit—why reducing taxes is the best way open to us to increase revenues."[7]

[7]This passage is quoted in Michael G. Rukstad's book, *Macroeconomic Decision Making in the World Economy, Text and Cases.* See the Bibliography, Section 7.

Congress debated the tax-cut proposal for more than a year. Kennedy was assassinated in the interim, but the legislation was promoted by the new President, Lyndon Johnson, and it was signed into law on February 26, 1964.

Beginning in 1965, marginal tax rates on personal income taxes were reduced from 91% to 70% at the upper ranges and from 20% to 14% at the lower end. A minimum standard deduction was allowed for low-income families. The maximum corporate tax rate was reduced from 52% to 48%. Despite this substantial reduction in tax rates, there was clearly no immediate impact upon tax receipts, although receipts did stagnate for 1 year in 1968, producing an unusually large deficit (for the era) of $25 billion.

In summary, in reviewing the era between World War I and 1970, we see that deficits were more typical than surpluses, but surpluses were fairly common. The largest deficits by far were associated with wartime spending—of the $381 billion federal debt that existed at the end of 1970, more than two-thirds of it was accumulated during the 7 years of the two world wars. Finally, the mild recessions of the era produced brief deficits that were caused by lower tax revenues.

What's Next?

In contrast to what we have seen to this point, the modern deficits that emerged in the 1980s were not caused by war spending nor by recessions. They were systemic deficits that have little historical precedent. In the next chapter we will begin exploring the reasons for the emergence of enduring peacetime deficits.

3

The Deficit and the Debt in the Present Era

· ·

· ·

The deficits of the past 15 years, in contrast to those earlier in the century, have not been associated with wars nor recessions. They can be described as *systemic deficits,* enduring as a feature of the contemporary economic structure and the political system that is responsible for generating them.

In this chapter we explore in more detail the emergence of systemic deficits and the growth of the federal debt over the last 25 years, with emphasis on the period that begins in the early 1980s. As before, we we will look at patterns of outlays and revenues to see what they yield, and will explore some of the legislative and economic developments of the early 1980s that appear to have contributed to the emergence of the deficit as a *chronic* problem rather than one that is temporarily associated with recessions. At the end of the chapter we put the issue in perspective, adjusting the figures and the data to the growth of the economy and to other normalizing influences. There we will find some comfort in evaluating the

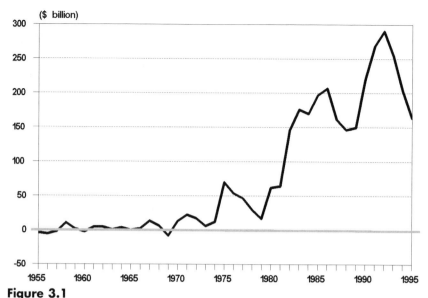

Figure 3.1
U.S. Government Budget Deficits, 1955–1995

systemic deficit: we will see that such deficits are now commonplace around the world, even among the most prosperous and stable countries, and that the budgetary situation in the United States is actually better than it is in most countries.

Deficits in the Present Era

In Figure 3.1 we see the history of budget deficits from 1955 until 1995. As can be seen, deficits since the early 1980s consistently move into a range above $150 billion, and years when the deficit exceeded $200 billion were not uncommon. The deficit in 1992 reached nearly $300 billion. The first prominent spike can be seen in 1975, but that deficit was related to the recession. The economy was already beginning to experience some inflationary pressures in the early 1970s, and the OPEC oil embargo of 1973 (there was another in 1979), in which petroleum prices shot up to multiples of what they had been, contributed to a sharp recession that began in 1974 and continued into 1975. After the recession the deficit subsided, and by 1979, while Jimmy Carter was still President, outlays exceeded revenues by only $40 billion.

We will begin to evaluate the origins of modern deficits by looking at the history of receipts and outlays, which is shown in Figure 3.2. As can

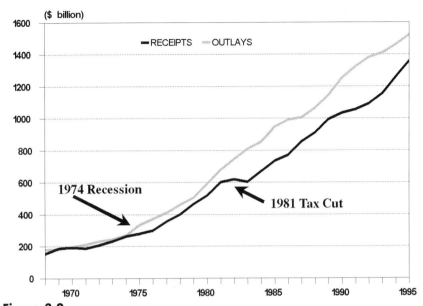

Figure 3.2
Federal Receipts and Outlays, 1968–1995

be seen, receipts and outlays spread apart beginning in 1981 and in 1982, and they never converge again. This spread is due to a sharp drop in receipts rather than to any fluctuation in outlays.

Table 3.1 shows that outlays experienced robust growth through the late 1970s and into the 1980s; this was certainly enough to keep pace with the overall growth of the economy. The Reagan administration slowed the growth rate substantially from what it had been during the Carter era (from an inflation-adjusted real growth rate of about 44% to 33% in Reagan's first term in office, then to about 18% during his second term). It cannot be said a lid was kept upon federal outlays, nor did they increase to unnaturally high levels, given the growth and size of the economy at the time. Receipts, though, clearly break trend in 1981 and 1982, and although their growth rate resumes thereafter, the breach between receipts and outlays became permanent. Part of the sharp reduction in receipts can be attributed to the very deep double-dip[1] recession that began early in 1980 and ended in the summer of 1982. The tax base stagnated in those years, at least in inflation-adjusted real terms.

[1]There was a short-lived and modest recovery in 1981, followed by another sharp contraction from late 1981 through the summer of 1982—hence the term "double-dip."

Table 3.1

U.S. Government Outlays
Four-Year Growth Rates for Three Presidents

President	Budget years	Nominal growth rate	Inflation-adjusted growth rate
Carter	1978–81	65.7%	43.8%
Reagan I	1982–85	39.5%	33.3%
Reagan II	1986–89	20.8%	18.0%
Bush	1990–93	23.2%	19.9%

Source: Original data for calculation of inflation adjustment from Economic Report of the President, February 1994.

But the recession cannot explain the entire downturn in receipts, nor can it explain why there was no convergence of receipts and outlays once the recovery was underway in 1983, as we would have expected had the deficit been linked only to the recession. With the recovery there should have been a substantial reduction in the deficit, but there was not. The deficit soared to record levels. Revenues never again returned to the level of outlays. The explanation for this has to be found in some of the legislation that was passed in that era.

The Economic Recovery Tax Act

Ronald Reagan was elected President with the promise of significant tax cuts. At the time Republicans controlled the Senate and Democrats held only a slim margin of control in the House of Representatives. In what might be described as a nonpartisan political frenzy to support radical tax cuts, Reagan's promise was fulfilled with astonishing speed, and it resulted in the sweeping *Economic Recovery Tax Act (ERTA)* passed in August 1981, only 8 months after he assumed office. Here are the primary features of that legislation:

1. Cuts that ultimately equaled 22% to 24% (depending upon how the tax cut is calculated) of tax brackets for personal income taxes were phased in over the next 2 years. To understand the significance of this tax cut, refer to Table 3.2, which shows by example the impact of the Economic Recovery Tax Act upon the taxes owed by a married couple filing jointly with a taxable income of $35,000. This couple would have paid

Table 3.2

Federal Taxes Owed for Married Filing Jointly with Taxable Income of $35,000

Tax year	Tax owed	Percent yearly reduction
1981	$7,996	
1982	$7,265	9.1%
1983	$6,572	9.5%
1984	$6,225	5.3%
Net Percentage Reduction:		22.1%

Source: IRS 1040 tax tables for 1981–1984.

$7,996 in taxes in 1981, but they paid only $6,225 on the same income in 1984, which is a net reduction of more than 22%.[2]

2. Beginning in 1985, income tax brackets and exemptions were indexed for inflation. The Carter administration made a serious mistake by failing to see the political damage caused by inflated marginal tax brackets. Brackets were not adjusted for inflation, and the torrid price increases of the late 1970s were pushing taxpayers into higher marginal tax brackets even though, in real inflation-adjusted terms, their incomes were falling. This unhealthy combination certainly contributed to Carter's defeat in his bid for a second term 1980. The fact that taxes were too high (or the "burden of government too great") was a major campaign theme of Ronald Reagan.

3. The top marginal tax bracket was reduced from 70 to 50%.

4. An extremely generous set of depreciation schedules (called the *Accelerated Cost Recovery System*) was initiated for businesses. The legislation allowed very brief depreciation periods[3] and it accelerated depreciation methods. It allowed passive losses in real estate.[4] Finally, all wage

[2]When filing personal income taxes, after all adjustments to income are made, one looks up the tax by finding the bracket in which adjusted income falls, then recording the tax for that bracket. To say that taxes were cut by 23% means that, on average, the tax associated with any given bracket fell by 23%. Reagan had initially asked for 30%!

[3]For example, autos and trucks could be depreciated in only 3 years. Owner-occupied commercial real estate could be depreciated in 10 years, as opposed to 25 years or more under earlier legislation.

[4]Losses for tax purposes could be declared on profitable real estate because of accelerated depreciation "expenses," which, of course, involved no cash payments to anyone. This is no longer allowed.

earners were allowed to deduct $2000 per year for contributions to Individual Retirement Accounts (IRA) from their taxable incomes.

Although the indexing of tax brackets (provision 2 above) made good economic sense, the rest of the tax reform package was too severe, at least in terms of its impact upon the deficit. Because of these reforms, revenues fell in 1983, contributing to the break in trend in revenues and introducing a systemic deficit that would endure through the 1980s.

In the heady enthusiasm of the early years of Reagan's first term there were few critics of radical tax reduction. Most supporters believed or at least they argued, that deficits would not be a problem, and, indeed, they might be reduced. Reagan gave many early speeches promising a balanced budget. A document released from the executive office in February 1981 entitled *"America's New Beginning: A Program for Economic Recovery,"* the first substantial document proposing the 30% tax-bracket reduction advocated by the administration, showed a budget balanced by 1984 and a surplus of $30 billion by 1986.[5]

Supply-Side Economics[6]

The primary theoretical support for severe tax cuts was provided by a corpus of economic theory very much in vogue at the time called **supply-side economics.** Early supporters of the Reagan plan certainly believed in the fundamental message of supply-side economics.

What was the appeal of supply-side economics? To understand we have to remember that in an economy relying mostly on income-based taxes (corporate and private), tax revenues, generally speaking, will be equal to the product of tax rates times the tax base (or income):

$$\text{Tax revenues} = \text{Tax rate} \times \text{Tax base (income)}$$

Supply-side economists argued that in a market economy where productivity is based upon private incentives, excessively high taxes discour-

---

[5]In fact, the deficit was $185 billion in 1984 and $221 billion in 1986.

[6]Not all economists agree, of course, with the author's explanation of the impact of the 1981 legislation. To review representative articles, both in favor and against, see the Bibliography, Section 9, and especially the material by Alan Auerbach, Lawrence Chimerine, Daniel Feenberg and James Porterba, Lawrence Lindsey, Paul Samuelson, and Joel Slemrod.

age innovation, risk, and investment (in effect, why bother working hard if the rewards are to be taxed away?). This gradually retards economic growth and it diminishes the growth rate of income and the tax base. In other words, high taxes engender a stagnant economy.[7] Therefore, the argument continues, if tax rates are cut, even if substantially, the economy will prosper and income and the tax base will grow. If the base rises proportionately more than the rates are cut (if, for example, the effective tax rate is cut 10% and *as a result* taxable income rises 12%), tax receipts will *rise because of* the tax cut. Assuming that government outlays are growing normally over the same period, the deficit should fall. There was considerable faith in 1980 and in 1981 that this would happen.

When considered out of context and stated generally, supply-side economics had some fundamental truths. In a private market economy it is certainly possible for the tax rate to be so high that it is a disincentive for growth. And the tax cuts of the early 1980s almost certainly had a stimulating effect upon the economy, which experienced non-inflationary robust growth for 7 years, although this can be attributed partly to extremely easy credit conditions and to the very substantial use of debt by consumers and businesses over the same period. But it is entirely another matter whether the economic growth that resulted from tax cuts would be substantial enough to offset the reduction in rates to such a degree that the deficit is trimmed. It soon became apparent that in the case of the U.S. economy in the early 1980s, when given the economic structure and tax levels of the time, economic growth would not be high enough to reduce the deficit. Quite to the contrary; the deficits began to grow. This is made very apparent when we review Table 3.3, which shows receipts, outlays, their growth rates, and deficits between 1979 and 1996. Fiscal year 1983 (October 1982 to September 1983) is conspicuous because that was the year when receipts experienced the sharpest break in trend, following the recession of 1982 and reflecting the final cuts in the Economic Recovery Tax Act of 1981.

Although growth rates of receipts and outlays were volatile throughout the period, outlays generally outpaced receipts (each year on average,

---

[7]The ailing economy of Great Britain, where marginal tax rates were absurdly high—and much higher than in the United States, was an oft-cited example in those years. Prime Minister Margaret Thatcher had been swept into office the year before Reagan's election with a similar political platform. Like Reagan she cut *income* taxes, trimming the top marginal bracket from 83 to 60%, for example, but unlike Reagan, she offset these cuts by substantially increasing the Value-Added Tax (or **VAT**—essentially a national sales tax) from 8 to 15% for non-food commodities. The British VAT is now 17.5%.

Table 3.3

U.S. Government Outlays, Receipts and Deficits (FY 1979–1996, $ billions)

Year	Outlays	% Growth outlays	Receipts	% Growth receipts	Deficit
1979	504.0		463.3		40.7
1980	590.9	17.2	517.1	11.6	73.8
1981	678.2	14.8	599.3	15.9	79.0
1982	745.7	10.0	617.8	3.1	128.0
1983	808.4	8.4	600.6	−2.8	207.8
1984	851.8	5.4	666.5	11.0	185.4
1985	946.4	11.1	734.1	10.1	212.3
1986	990.3	4.6	769.1	4.8	221.2
1987	1,003.9	1.4	854.1	11.1	149.8
1988	1,064.1	6.0	909.0	6.4	155.2
1989	1,143.2	7.4	990.7	9.0	152.5
1990	1,252.7	9.6	1,031.3	4.1	221.4
1991	1,323.4	5.6	1,054.3	2.2	269.2
1992	1,380.8	4.3	1,090.5	3.4	290.4
1993	1,408.7	2.0	1,153.5	5.8	255.1
1994	1,460.9	3.7	1,257.7	9.0	203.2
1995	1,519.1	4.0	1,355.2	7.8	163.9
1996	1,560.1	2.7	1,452.4	7.2	107.3

Source: Budget of the United States Government, Historical Tables, Fiscal Year 1996.

outlays grew 7.72% and receipts grew 6.85%), and by the end of the decade the government was consistently running deficits of $250 billion.

In the years that immediately followed the Economic Recovery Tax Act, more sober recognition of the emerging deficit defused some of the enthusiasm for tax cuts, and some reductions were reversed or eliminated as other taxes were gradually raised.

A second major piece of tax legislation, the Tax Reform Act, was passed in 1986. This law reduced the number of marginal tax brackets from 14 to 4 and it substantially reduced the top marginal individual income tax bracket from 50 to 28%, while the maximum corporate tax rate was cut from 46 to 34%. To offset this the maximum tax rate on capital gains was increased from 20 to 28% and extremely generous accelerated depreciation schedules, allowable passive losses and $2000 IRA deductions were eliminated by this law. Additionally, during the entire decade Social Security taxes crept relentlessly upward. These changes in the tax structure, especially when compared to the lasting impact of those features of the Economic Recovery Tax Act that were retained, did very little to provide budgetary relief.[8]

It should be remembered that supply-side economics and the tax cuts of the early 1980s were not justified as a means of reducing deficits. In the sweep of conservative enthusiasm during that era, they were viewed as a nearly revolutionary and long-overdue stimulus to an ailing economy— or to use language reflective of the excitable rhetoric of the time—they rekindled the fires of private enterprise. This aggressive policy, oriented toward improving business conditions and increasing economic growth, was promoted with the promise that it also would not produce red ink. But it did.[9]

Debt and Interest on the Debt in the Present Era

If we remember from earlier discussions the connection between *deficits* and the *federal debt*, what we have seen so far would lead us to believe that the debt would have grown markedly over the period in question. As is made evident in Figure 3.3, that has clearly been the case. The higher line shows total gross debt outstanding, which includes nonmarketable interagency debt within the U.S. government (such as the Social Security Trust Fund, for example). The lower line, labeled net debt, represents debt by the U.S. government to outside parties—the real net debt of the U.S. government to everyone else.[10]

In looking at the graph, a couple of interesting observations can be made:

1. We remember that most of the debt accumulated before the modern era was generated in World War II (in 1946 it stood at $271 billion). More than 2 decades later at the point when the data presented in Figure 3.3 begins, the debt had grown by only 35% (in 1968 it stood at $369 billion). In the 10 years that followed (until 1978) it would more

---

[8]The impact of the 1986 Tax Reform Act has also been debated a great deal. For a good description of the 1986 law and a suitable starting point for the debate see the article by Barry Bosworth and Gary Burtless, Bibliography, Section 9.

[9]It should be noted here that the new supply-side economics of the mid-1990s has moved away from support for a general reduction in tax rates to advocacy for reductions in the highest marginal tax rates and a flatter tax structure. We return to this subject, with citations, in Chapter 9.

[10]If this is confusing, refer back to Table 1.7 in Chapter 1.

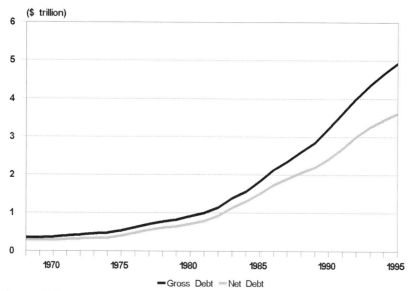

Figure 3.3
Total Federal Debt, 1968–1995

than double, and in the next ten years (from 1979 until 1988) it would more than triple.

2. Total debt did not reach $1 trillion until 1982, having required nearly two centuries (from 1789) to reach this level. The debt increased to $2 trillion by 1986, in only four years. The $3 trillion debt level was surpassed in 1990 and the fourth trillion-dollar increase was reached two years later in 1992. In 1996 the level of debt reached $5 trillion.[11]

One would expect the debt to increase in a growing economy,[12] but these figures are unusually large even when nominal economic growth is taken into account. National income or gross domestic product, even when it is not adjusted for inflation, does not double every 4 years.

The primary *internal* problem associated with rapidly growing debt for any economic entity, whether government, business, or consumer borrowing is *debt service,* or in a few words, finding the means to make payments associated with the debt. The higher the debt relative to the means to pay, usually some form of income, the more serious the debt burden.

[11]Net debt (gross federal debt less the amount held by government accounts); more representative of the government's true debt burden, took a little longer to reach these milestones. The $1-trillion mark was passed one year later than gross debt in 1983, the second trillion in 1988, and the third in 1993.

[12]This will be discussed in the next section.

Debts are normally *amortized* in some form or another, meaning that periodic payments are required on the interest and usually on the principal.

In this regard, the task is a little easier for a federal government than it is for a corporate or a consumer borrower. The payment obligation for corporate or consumer borrowers assumes some principle reduction. For the federal government debt service essentially consists of making only the interest payments on the outstanding debt. As discussed earlier, governments do not reduce the debt principal.

Even so, the task of debt service can be formidable. Figure 3.4 illustrates the amount of interest paid for the securities outstanding that make up the debt. In recent years this has been above $200 billion.

Interest expense is part of the line-item federal budget (as will be seen in the next chapter), so any potential debt service problem would be reflected in interest as a percentage of outlays as shown in Figure 3.5. Here we see that interest expense has risen from about 6% at the beginning of this era to about 14%. Note the flattening of this expense after 1990 (we will discuss this later).

Again, a number of observations can be made:

1. Any such increase of debt service in any budget, government or otherwise, puts a tremendous overall strain on the budget. Every dollar

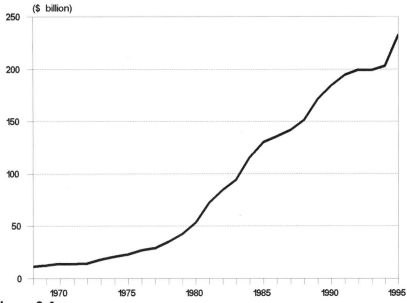

Figure 3.4
Interest on the Debt, 1968–1995

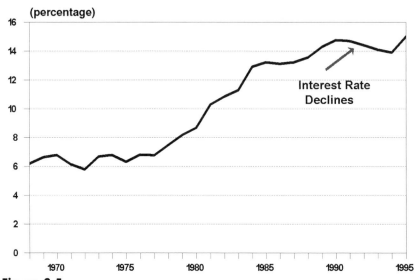

Figure 3.5
Net Interest as a Percentage of Outlays, 1968–1995

spent for debt service is a dollar that cannot be spent for traditional government services.

2. As this percentage grows, ever larger cuts must be made in the discretionary part of the budget (such as defense, education, and so on) merely to maintain the status quo.

3. The 6% figure at the beginning of the era (1968) is fairly large given the budgetary moderation seen through the 1950s and 1960s. That 6% almost entirely reflects the interest-service cost of the debt built up in World War II, more than two decades earlier. This shows how much of the interest burden of debt can "stick" intergenerationally. Whether deficits are the result of efforts to finance wars or are due to political problems, they result in episodic surges of debt. Because there is never any debt reduction even in years of balanced budgets, interest as a percentage of the budget tends to ratchet up stepwise. This reflects an old problem and it becomes a new one.

Interest Rates and the Interest on the Debt

The level of interest payments, in absolute terms and as a percentage of outlays, reflects the size of the debt itself, as was shown earlier in Figure 3.3 and in Table 1.3, and the level of interest rates paid by the government for the myriad U.S. Treasury securities that make up the debt. As a rule of thumb, an increase of 1% (for example, from an average of 7% to 8%) in the average interest paid by the U.S. Treasury for its portfolio of securities will increase this interest expense (and hence the deficit) by approximately $30 billion. A decrease in interest rates of the same amount would have an equivalent effect in the opposite direction.

There is a difference between the effective interest rate paid by the U.S. Treasury and the prevailing, often volatile, market rates of the same securities. Once the Treasury issues a note or a bond, the rate is locked in for the duration of that issue. When market rates rise by, say, 1%, rates paid by the Treasury will slowly follow as old debt is redeemed and new debt is issued. The effective rate paid lags behind market rates, where the extent of the lag is determined by the average maturity of the securities that make up the debt—the longer the average maturity, the longer the lag.

In Figure 3.4 we saw that interest flattened after 1990, remaining just under $200 billion, but not growing even though the debt grew. Figure 3.5 showed that interest as a percentage of outlays declined slightly after 1990. This reflects declining interest rates in those years, which can be seen very closely in Figure 3.6. The more volatile line represents the market rate paid on newly issued 3-month Treasury Bills. Effective interest

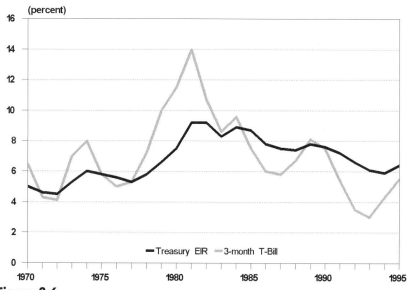

Figure 3.6
Effective Interest Paid on Federal Debt and 3-Month T-Bill Rate

paid, which is essentially a long-weighted moving average of the full range of previous bill, note, and bond rates, is relatively smooth. The effective interest followed market rates up during the inflationary period of the late 1970s, rising above 9% in the early 1980s. Both rates then began to decline with the abatement of inflation through the remainder of the decade. Market rates fell so sharply in the recession that began in 1990 that they were well below the effective rate and they pulled it down in the early 1990s. It's for that reason that interest expense stabilized in the early 1990s, despite continued high deficits and growing debt.

Interest rates have remained low since a small increase in 1994. But a substantial rise in market rates of perhaps 2% would increase the effective rate only slightly, around 0.25%. Even so, that would add approximately $10 billion to the deficit.

To summarize the point raised at the beginning of this section, the primary *internal*[13] problem posed by growing debt is the debt-service burden, here represented as interest expense. As the relative importance of this category grows, more Draconian choices have to be made in the discretionary areas of the budget if deficit reduction is the goal.

Perspectives

In a prosperous economy one would expect debt and deficit figures to grow larger over time. Economic growth and inflation ensure that all measures of economic activity rise over time. For that reason some comparative yardsticks will put the deficit and the debt in better historical perspective.

Figure 3.7 shows the deficit as a percentage of gross domestic product. This ratio normalizes the deficit in relation to the size of the economy. It would be difficult to find a consensus among economists about what a prudent ceiling for this ratio should be. Many conservative economists promote a balanced budget, which would imply that 0% should be the ceiling. The European standard, in contrast, sets a ceiling of 3%. The omnibus 1992 **Maastricht Treaty,**[14] which governs the formation of the **European Union (EU)**—or more precisely, it governs the transformation

[13]By this we mean the internal *accounting* problem of dealing with an unbalanced budget—where governmental budgetary integrity is the issue. There is also the *external* problem of the effects of all budgetary decisions upon the economy, which is discussed in Chapter 9.

[14]All references to the Maastricht Treaty are taken directly from the Treaty, which is available at the EU Europa Web Site, http://europa.eu.int.

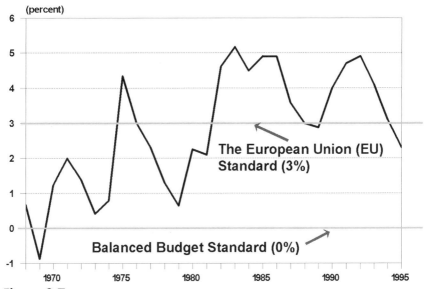

Figure 3.7
The Deficit as a Percentage of GDP, 1968–1995

from the old European Economic Community (EEC) to the more extensive and ambitious European Union (EU), also called the European Community (EC)—includes very specific provisions on deficit targets. Article 104c of Title II of the Treaty mandates that EU member nations generally "shall avoid excessive governmental deficits," and Treaty protocols specifically define acceptable upper limits as "3% for the ratio of planned or actual government deficit to gross domestic product at market prices; [and] 60% for the ratio of government debt to gross domestic product at market prices." In other words, this means that EU member nations are expected to keep their deficits below 3% of GDP and their net debt below 60% of GDP.[15] Failure to comply can result in a substantial penalty;

[15]These limits refer to *general* rather than *federal* government deficits and debts. In the United States, this would be equivalent to combining all levels of government; federal, state, and local, into one budget. The issues that arise in this difference and the means of comparing the European *general* standard to the U.S. *federal* standard are discussed in the next section. The requirement that "planned or actual" budget deficits fall below 3% of GDP implies that in a situation where recession or slow growth causes high unemployment and the actual budget deficit exceeds the 3% limit, an estimate of what the deficit would be under the assumption of full employment— the "planned" deficit—(which, of course, would be lower than the actual deficit) might be regarded as an acceptable substitute for the actual deficit number.

Articles 109j and 109k of the Treaty declare that members that fail to meet this standard might be denied the rights and privileges extended by the European Central Bank (ECB), and they also might be denied the right to adopt the new European single currency (now called the European Currency Unit, or ECU, eventually to be called the Euro), scheduled by the Treaty to go into common use on January 1, 1999. (The EU, never short of acronyms, now designates the proposed organization of EU members who will be allowed to use the single currency after 1998 as the **Economic and Monetary Union,** or **EMU**—so now the failure to meet the deficit and debt limit could result in the denial of the right to become a member of the EMU.) The track record of these EU nations in meeting their standards is discussed below in the next section.

The range of possibilities, therefore, would seem to lie between a conservative U.S. standard of 0%—a balanced budget (though many U.S. economists would find the European standards acceptable)—and the more generous European standard of 3%. A middle-ground position might place the limit between 1 and 2%, where the deficit would be expected to be below 2% in normal years, possibly peaking above 3%, but only temporarily, in recessions. However, ranges above 3% that approach 6% in the upper extremes are certainly too high to endure by any standard. As can be seen in Figure 3.7, where the balanced-budget and 3% European standards are drawn for reference, throughout the 1980s and into the 1990s the budget deficit was higher than even the upper threshold, an unacceptable level. A deficit of 1% of GDP in 1995, for example, would be about $75 billion (as opposed to the actual figure of $163 billion). At this level it would not have received nearly as much attention.

In terms of internal debt-service thresholds, the debt-to-revenues ratio, shown in Figure 3.8, is a more reliable indicator. We show net debt, which excludes debt within the government to its own trust funds. This is roughly equivalent to the debt-to-income ratio of financial entities in the private sector. Debt-to-income ratios are revealing because they reflect the debt divided by the short-run means of servicing the debt (income). Clearly, the higher the ratio, the greater the percentage of income required to service the debt. Although there may be no threshold that is universally seen as prudent, a substantial rise in this number is clearly inauspicious.

Figure 3.8 presents a curious spectacle. It is apparent that the net debt-to-revenues ratio was exceptionally high in 1948 because of the debt accumulated during World War II. Budget moderation gradually reduced the relative burden of debt for 3 decades, pulling the ratio down below 2

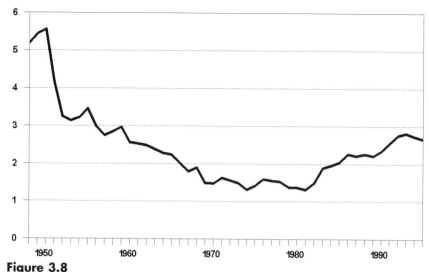

Figure 3.8
Net Debt-to-Revenues Ratio, 1948–1995

in the late 1960s, to a relatively stable level of 1.5 through the 1970s. Then it began a slow climb, approximately doubling in the decade of the 1980s. This time, though, the rise could not be attributed to a war. By any reasonable accounting standard this would not be regarded as a healthy sign.

International Perspectives: How We Compare to Other Countries

When judging our national performance on the budget and the deficit it helps to make some comparisons to our international competitors. As we will see, by that standard the U.S. government is faring relatively well.

People sometimes want to know if the U.S. has the "Argentina problem." Are we now borrowing as heavily as some of the less-developed nations, such as Brazil, Argentina, or Mexico, that sometimes make headlines because of their grave economic problems?

The answer is no; the problem of the U.S. Treasury is not even close to some of the worst seen internationally. For example, 1983 was a bad year for Mexico and it was typical of the worst years experienced throughout the Americas in the 1980s. In that year the Mexican government had a budget deficit that was equal to about 37% of outlays and 11% of

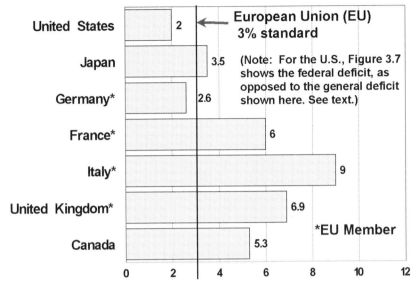

Figure 3.9
General Government Deficits as a Percentage of GDP in 1994
Source: OECD Economic Outlook, December 1995.

GDP.[16] The worst U.S. deficits during the 1980s were at about half this level, never higher than 23% of outlays nor 7% of GDP.

The United States compares favorably to a select group of nations for good data are available, including some of the EU nations that must comply with a 3% deficit limit as discussed earlier.

Figure 3.9, which uses OECD (Organization for Economic Cooperation and Development) data, compares general government deficits as a percentage of GDP in 1994 for the nations shown. Because the structure of government differs from one nation to another, and because various types of funding are drawn from different levels of government (for example, in the United States, defense is funded largely at the federal level while education is funded at the state and local level), the only meaningful international comparisons are for general government. This account consolidates taxing, spending, deficits and government indebtedness from all levels of government. The comparison, therefore, is not strictly at the federal level, because such a comparison would have little meaning.

[16]The deficit that year was about 40.3 billion pesos on outlays of 108 billion pesos, and GDP stood at 373.7 billion pesos. In that same year the money supply also doubled and inflation was above 100%.

As can be seen in Figure 3.9, the U.S. general government deficit of 2% of GDP compared favorably to all countries.[17] Germany, despite serious financial problems associated with the inclusion of what was formerly East Germany, was a little higher than the United States, while Canada and the United Kingdom had relative deficits that were more than double or triple those of the United States. Italy, a member of the European Union, *is* in essence having an "Argentina problem," with deficits at nearly 9% of GDP.[18] As was mentioned earlier, EU members are supposed to exercise sufficient fiscal discipline to keep their general government budget deficits at less than 3% of their GDP (as indicated by the 3% threshold line on Figure 3.9). Clearly some EU members included here are not having much success in meeting this goal. Indeed, preliminary data for 1995 shows that only 3 EU nations, Denmark, the Republic of Ireland, and Luxembourg fell below the 3% ceiling in 1995.[19]

Gross debt as a percentage of GDP, also defined as an EU standard, and the *net* interest as a percentage of GDP (derived from net debt rather than gross debt) are shown in Figure 3.10 and in Figure 3.11.

That the deficit has been a chronic problem in Italy is made very evident by both graphs (that data in Figure 3.11 imply that more than 11% of Italy's national output is used to make interest payments on Italian government debt) and it serves as a warning of the future that might await any country that allows deficits to grow into the double-digit ranges.

---

[17]The source for these data is *The OECD Economic Outlook, December 1995.* These data are volatile from year to year—Japan's figure in 1993, for example, was only 0.3%. Also, in some cases the estimates for these numbers and especially for the data in Figure 3.10 are little more than crude estimates, although the data for the EU nations are probably reliable. The EU also monitors this data to evaluate the "convergence criteria" (the 3% deficit and 60% debt limit) of member nations for joining the Economic and Monetary Union (EMU). Their data are published in *Money and Finance,* a Eurostat quarterly. To evaluate the status of all EU nations, four of which are shown in Fig. 3.9, this document should be consulted. Comparing data from the 1994–5 edition, in some cases the EU figures are slightly different from the OECD numbers used here.

[18]The emergence of the relative values shown here reflects less an improvement in the U.S. position than a deterioration of the European position. Both France and the U.K. were always below 3% between 1985 and 1991, but their positions deteriorated after 1991. Italy and Greece (not shown) have always been near the double-digit range in the modern era.

[19]See "How to Shift the Goal Posts," *The Economist,* April 20, 1996, p. 43. The 15 EU countries are Austria, Belgium, Denmark, Finland, France, Germany, Great Britain, Greece, Ireland, Italy, Luxembourg, the Netherlands, Portugal, Spain, and Sweden.

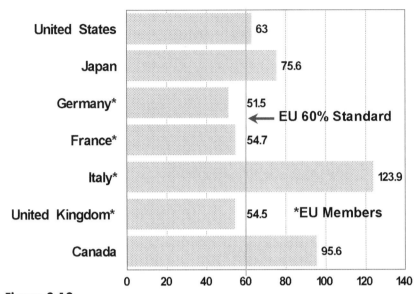

Figure 3.10
General Government Gross Debt as a Percentage of GDP in 1994
Source: OECD Economic Outlook, December 1995.

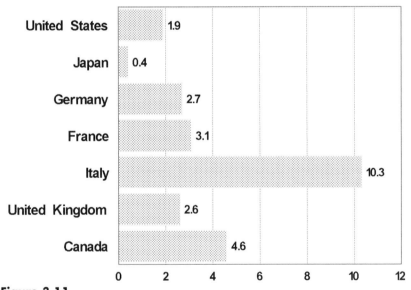

Figure 3.11
Government Net Debt Interest Payments as a Percentage of GDP in 1994
Source: OECD Economic Outlook, December 1995.

It is something of a relief that the United States is nowhere near that threshold. The domestic problem is serious, but not nearly so serious as it might be. Japan, with fairly high gross debt but low interest payments, presents an interesting case. Japan faces the same problem as the one now emerging in the United States—the financing of entitlements. Japan ran a tiny deficit in 1993 (at 0.2% of GDP) and a much larger deficit in 1994 (at 3.5% of GDP, as shown in Figure 3.9). The 1993 deficit was the first since 1986—between 1987 and 1992 the general government of Japan ran small surpluses, to the envy of much of the rest of the world.[20] This was possible for Japan, however, because the country has a relatively new social security system that generates, by itself, a large surplus that offsets the rest of the budget. Because the system is newer, the ratio of contributors to beneficiaries is much higher than within the social security system in the United States.[21]

If we exclude from the accounting Japan's social security system, the rest of the budget generated a deficit at a value equal to 4% of GDP in 1993, and much higher in 1994. More remarkably, Japan's *net* government debt was only 7.6% of GDP, but Japan's *gross* government debt, which includes the generic debt of the Japanese government to its own social security trust fund, stands at a phenomenal 75.6%, as shown in Figure 3.10, which is even higher than the U.S. gross government debt (at 63% of GDP). More important, because of the rapid aging of the Japanese population, social security taxes are projected to rise very sharply over the next 35 years to levels that might be politically intolerable in the United States. This will be discussed in more detail in Chapter 7.

To summarize, the United States looks rather strong compared with the rest of the world, including even Japan. The strength is *relative*, however, and it is due largely to a gradual, uneven deterioration of the European position over the last 5 years and an improvement in the U.S. position

[20]Some smaller European nations and Australia also generated surpluses for many years. Included are Denmark, Finland, Sweden, and Norway. All of these countries had deficits by 1993.

[21]Although the Japanese and U.S. social security systems are similar, there are some differences that make comparisons difficult. Part of the trust fund in Japan is returned to the private economy for investment, much as would be the case with a private pension plan. In the United States the entire trust fund is "invested" in U.S. Treasury nonmarketable securities. This subject will be discussed extensively in Chapter 7. Some of the material here came from an interesting article on the subject by Robert Price, *"Spotlight on Japan—Public Finances," The OECD Observer No. 185,* December 1993/January 1994.

in 1994 and 1995. As such, this does not necessarily mean that the United States does not have a problem—it might instead mean that the problems of Europe, Canada, and possibly Japan are more serious.

What's Next?

Now that we have seen the relative scale of budgetary operations over time and in comparison with other countries, it will be interesting to see where the outlays go and where revenues come from. It is time to look at the actual line-item budget. That is the subject of the next chapter.

The Line-Item Budget

· ·

· ·

W*e cannot get very far* in any discussion of the federal budget unless we take a close look at the line-item budget itself. That is what we are going to do in this chapter. We begin by looking at the budget desegregated by 19 major outlay (expenditure) categories (called "budgetary functions") for the fiscal years 1986 through 1995. In a few words, we'll see how tax money and money borrowed was spent. We will also examine proportions, or how the budgetary dollar is divided (for most people who have never studied the actual line-item budget, there are often surprises here), and we will look at growth rates of the major spending categories. What we see will lead to some important generalizations, especially when we entertain the question of how the budget deficit might be reduced if we are to accomplish that primarily through outlay cuts.

After reviewing outlays, we will then turn our attention to taxes to see the relative importance of the different tax categories and to see who pays and how that has changed over the years. And again we can evaluate, at least superficially, what changes would be necessary to raise tax revenues in any effort to reduce the deficit via taxes.[1]

Finally we will look at the federal budget organized by agency. In Chapter 5 we will continue a more detailed discussion of agency budgets and special spending categories, such as defense, agriculture, energy, and so on.

A few words should be said about what will *not* be included in this chapter. The important distinction between mandatory and discretionary spending (and a budget that distinguishes between the two) will be discussed in Chapter 8 rather than here.[2] The issue of entitlements and how they fit into the budget will be reserved for Chapter 6.

About Budgets

A look at the definition of the word *budget* makes it clear that a budget can be many things, or more precisely, that there are many aspects to budgeting:

> **bud·get** (buj´it), *n.,adj.,v.,* –et·ed, et·ing. —*n.* **1.** an estimate, often itemized, of expected income and expense for a given period in the future. **2.** a plan of operations based on such an estimate. **3.** an itemized allotment of funds, time, etc., for a given period. . . .[3]

A budget, therefore, can be a *planning* document, projecting estimated revenues, expenses, and surpluses or deficits into the future, which typically includes a presentation of *historical* financial accounts along with an interpretive discussion. In another context a budget can be a set of restrictive rules, regulations, or limits, typically on spending.

The document actually called *The Budget of the United States Government,* officially released by the office of the President every February for the following fiscal year[4] conforms to the first definition. Table 4.1

---

[1]In this chapter we address only this issue of reducing the deficit superficially. After more groundwork has been completed, we return to the same question more earnestly in later chapters.

[2]As we will see, these terms are important when discussing legislation affecting the budget, but the concepts are too complicated to introduce here.

[3]This partial definition is taken from *The Random House Dictionary of the English Language,* Second Edition Unabridged, 1987.

[4]In other words, the budget for fiscal year 1997, which began on October 1, 1996, was released in February 1996.

Table 4.1

Budget of the United States Government
List of Documents and Their Purposes

Document	Pages	Contents/purpose
Budget of the United States Government, Fiscal Year 1997 *and* *Budget Supplement*	20 183	From the perspective of the office of the President and his budgetary office, the Office of Management and Budget, offers a general overview of the budget. Sets priorities, makes strong program recommendations for next fiscal year, discusses compliance with budget legislation such as the Budget Enforcement Act and makes general five year projections (to FY 2002) for agencies and major spending categories.
Budget of the United States Government, Appendix, Fiscal Year 1997.	1174	The real heart of the budget. A detailed budget estimate by department or agency summarizing appropriations, outlays, authorizing legislation and descriptions of programs. Does *not* include a five-year forecast, which is done only at major agency level.
Budget of the United States Government, Historical Tables, Fiscal Year 1997.	267	The historical component of the budget, showing patterns of spending, taxing, deficits, debt, etc. over long historical periods.
Budget of the United States Government, Analytic Perspectives, Fiscal Year 1997.	514	Discusses the economic assumptions used to generate projections and technical issues of the deficit, debt, trust funds, federal credit, etc.
Budget Systems and Concepts of the United States Government.	16	A brief description of terms, primary budget laws, and an overview of the budgetary process.

lists the five budgetary documents released in February 1996 and it briefly describes the contents or purpose of each document. This budget is a planning document that always includes a 5-year projection for revenues, major spending categories, and deficits.

The President's budget is also a *political* document and for that reason it does not meet the second component of the definition—it does not set final limits or restrictions on spending. Instead, it is presented to Congress as a planning or advisory document and it clearly represents the political perspective of the President. Rather than being a final document setting limits, the *Budget of the United States Government* actually *begins* formally the long debate over actual spending and taxing decisions. Congress may not like what it sees in the budget (and often it does not), so final decisions and budgetary limits come in the months that follow after long and sometimes invidious political battles. This element of the budgetary process—the political side of the issue, including the timetable for the budget as a *restrictive* document—is discussed fully in Chapter 8.

The remainder of this chapter focuses on the *historical* component of the budget to the present time. We will evaluate the financial status of the federal government for the present and the near past.

Unified and Agency Budgets

The fiscal operation of the U.S. government is an immense enterprise. Our federal government is the largest spending entity in the world, sending out checks totaling more than $1.5 trillion in fiscal year 1996. Clearly, we can expect its budgetary statements to be complex.

There are different ways of presenting the historical component of the federal budget. The most revealing arrangement, at least for purposes here, is a budget presentation called the *unified* budget organized by budgetary *function*. That will be the first budget we see.

The term *unified* means that the consolidated revenues and outlays (expenditures) of all government agencies and trust funds are represented in a single budgetary document. This term is now used partly for historical reasons. Traditionally, two types of spending existed—one called "on-budget" spending and the other called "off-budget" spending. These outdated distinctions are still made in the present-day budget (most social security spending is off-budget while most defense is on-budget), but the distinctions are now meaningless. At times in the past, mostly for rather questionable political reasons, only on-budget spending constituted the budget and references to the deficit were references to only the on-budget deficit. These arcane categories may seem strange today, until one asks the question, What political options are there if new categories of spending emerge at a time when deficit reduction has been promised to the public? Back in the days of on-budget and off-budget spending, one solution would be to classify the new spending as off-budget.[5] Fortunately, everyone now uses the *unified* budget and on-budget and off-budget spending is fading into the past.

The unified budget can be organized either by budgetary *function* or by listing federal *agencies* (such as the budget of the Department of Defense, the Department of Commerce, and so forth), and summing their individual budgets. The budget by *function* segregates all categories of spending into functional categories that identify the major purpose of the spending. We begin our discussion with a budget organized by *function*. Later in the chapter we will look at a federal *agency* budget.

A private corporation will sometimes budget on what is called an *accrual basis* rather than on a *cash basis*. A corporation often divides its budget into two components (at least), a *capital budget* and an *operating* or *cash* budget, but the federal government does not make such distinctions. The federal government operates with a unified cash budget. These accounting distinctions, which are important when discussing some of the subtleties of deficit reduction, are far too technical to discuss here, and a full understanding requires at least some familiarity with basic accounting principles. It is for that reason that a full discussion of *cash* versus *accrual* accounting and the absence of a true capital budget in the federal budget is provided in Appendix C for those who are interested. Because information included in this chapter helps explain the material in that appendix, it should not be read until this chapter is completed.

Finally, it is possible (and necessary in some contexts) to organize the budget according to classifications of *mandatory* and *discretionary* spending. These are complicated legal concepts and will be discussed in Chapter 8, along with a budget that shows these classifications.

The Unified Budget of the U.S. Government: Outlays by Function

In Table 4.2a we see the unified federal budget by function for the fiscal years 1986 through 1996 (the fiscal year begins on October 1, so FY 1997,

---

[5]For example, until FY 1995, the U.S. Postal Service always had a small operating deficit. In 1994 the Postal Service had operating expenses of $51.0 billion, but revenues of only $49.8 billion. The resulting $1.2 billion deficit had to be financed from the general budget. In the past, a portion of the deficit could be hidden (or removed from consideration in debates over the budget *and* in public pronouncements about the results of those debates) by classifying it as off-budget.

Table 4.2a

Unified Budget of the United States Government Net Outlays (Expenditures) by Function, $ billions FY 1987 to 1995

Outlays by Function	Number	1987	1988	1989	1990	1991	1992	1993	1994	1995
Social Security	650	207.4	219.3	232.5	248.6	269.0	287.6	304.6	319.6	335.8
National defense	050	282.0	290.4	303.6	299.3	273.3	298.4	291.1	281.6	272.1
Net interest (2)	900	138.7	151.8	169.3	184.2	194.5	199.4	198.8	203.0	232.2
Income security (1)	600	123.3	129.3	136.0	147.0	170.3	196.9	207.3	214.0	220.4
Medicare	570	75.1	78.9	85.0	98.1	104.5	119.0	130.6	144.7	159.9
Health (4)	550	40.0	44.5	48.4	57.7	71.2	89.5	99.4	107.1	115.4
Education, training, employment, social services	500	29.7	31.9	36.7	38.8	43.4	45.2	50.0	46.3	54.3
Veterans benefits	700	26.8	29.4	30.1	29.1	31.3	34.1	35.7	37.6	37.9
Transportation	400	26.2	27.3	27.6	29.5	31.1	33.3	35.0	38.1	39.4
International affairs	150	11.6	10.5	9.6	13.8	15.9	16.1	17.2	17.1	16.4
Agriculture	350	26.6	17.2	16.9	12.0	15.2	15.2	20.5	15.1	9.8
Natural resources and environment	300	13.4	14.6	16.2	17.1	18.6	20.0	20.2	21.1	22.1
Energy	270	4.1	2.3	2.7	3.3	2.4	4.5	4.3	5.2	4.9
General science, space, technology	250	9.2	10.8	12.8	14.4	16.1	16.4	17.0	16.2	16.7
Community and regional development	450	5.1	5.3	5.4	8.5	6.8	6.8	9.1	10.5	10.6
Commerce and housing credit (1)	370	6.2	18.8	29.2	67.1	75.3	10.1	-22.7	-5.1	-14.4
Justice	750	7.6	9.2	9.5	10.0	12.3	14.4	15.0	15.3	16.2
General government	800	7.6	9.5	9.0	10.7	11.7	13.0	13.0	11.3	13.8
Undistributed offsetting receipts (3)	950	-36.5	-37.0	-37.2	-36.6	-39.4	-39.3	-37.4	-37.8	-44.5
Total Outlays		1,004.0	1,064.1	1,143.2	1,252.7	1,323.4	1,380.9	1,408.7	1,460.9	1,519.1
Total Revenues		854.1	909.0	990.7	1,031.3	1,054.3	1,090.5	1,153.5	1,257.7	1,355.2
Budget Deficit		149.8	155.1	152.5	221.4	269.2	290.4	255.1	203.2	163.9

Notes: (1) See Table 4.2b for disaggregation.
(2) Does not include interest paid to government accounts and trust funds.
(3) Mostly federal employer contributions to pension funds. See Glossary and explanation in Chapters 2 and 7.
(4) Includes Medicaid.
Source: Budget of the United States Government, Historical Tables, various years & various tables.

for example, began on October 1, 1996). As can be seen, outlays are segregated into nineteen budgetary functions. Two of those budgetary functions, *income security,* a large catch-all category, and *commerce and housing credit* are further desegregated in Table 4.2b.

Total outlays, total revenues, and the *budget deficit* can all be seen near the bottom of Table 4.2a. For example, in FY 1995, outlays equaled $1.519 trillion, revenues equaled $1.355 trillion, which produced a deficit of $163.9 billion. Aside from these summary totals, this table emphasizes outlays. The tax sources that sum to *total revenue* will be shown later in Table 4.4a.

Table 4.2c shows proportions for these same outlays. These three tables will be used in combination to make generalizations about the budget.

Reviewing Outlays

When looking at Table 4.2a, remember that the outlays are listed by budgetary function rather than by agency. The function numbers used in the actual budgetary documents are shown in the column entitled *number* (the numbers shown have no meaning aside from this classification). For example, the function number for the National Defense function is 050, so all spending by any agency that has the primary purpose of contributing to national defense is classified under function 050 and is typically further classified in a subfunction (not shown) such as 053, atomic energy defense activities.

In many cases the total for the budgetary function is not close to the budget for the associated agency. An extreme example is found in function 350, agriculture. As can be seen in Table 4.2a, that outlay for 1995 was $9.8 billion. But budget outlays for the Department of Agriculture in 1995 (this will be seen later) was $56.6 billion, more than five times the amount! When looking at the detailed and diverse budget of the Department of Agriculture, one finds rural electrification programs classified as function 271 (energy), rural waste and water disposal grants classified as function 452 (community and regional development), and the food stamp program classified as 605 (food and nutrition assistance under function 600, income security). So only about one-third of the budget of the Department of Agriculture is classified primarily as an agricultural function.

It might useful to depart from this text for a moment to take a careful look at the spending categories shown in Table 4.2a. Look also at the

Table 4.2b

Disaggregation of Two Major Outlay Functions Shown on Table 4.2a Income Security and Commerce and Housing Credit

Income security expenditures	1987	1988	1989	1990	1991	1992	1993	1994	1995
Federal employee retirement (1)	43.7	46.9	49.2	52.0	56.1	57.6	60.0	62.5	65.8
Housing assistance	12.7	13.9	14.7	15.9	17.2	18.9	21.5	23.9	27.5
Unemployment	17.1	15.3	15.6	18.9	27.1	39.5	37.8	28.7	23.6
Food & nutrition assistance	18.9	20.1	21.2	24.0	28.5	32.6	35.1	36.8	37.6
General income security (2)	10.9	27.9	29.7	31.4	37.0	42.9	48.4	56.4	60.8
Special retirement	5.6	5.3	5.7	5.1	4.9	5.5	4.3	5.7	5.1
Other (3)	14.4	-0.1	-0.1	-0.3	-0.5	0.0	0.1	0.0	0.0
Total:	123.3	129.3	136.0	147.0	170.3	197.0	207.2	214.0	220.4

Notes: (1) Includes federal employee disability

(2) Prior to 1987, this category was Supplemental Security Income (SSI) only. Now includes SSI (aid for aged, blind, disabled) family support payments, and earned income tax credit.

Commerce and housing credit	1987	1988	1989	1990	1991	1992	1993	1994	1995
Mortgage credit	-6.7	5.0	5.0	3.8	5.4	4.3	1.6	-0.5	-1.0
U.S. Postal Service (1)	1.6	2.2	0.1	2.1	1.8	1.2	1.6	1.2	-1.8
Deposit insurance (2)	3.1	10.0	22.0	58.0	66.4	2.5	-28.0	-7.6	-17.8
Commerce (3)	1.6	1.5	2.1	3.1	2.1	2.1	2.0	1.7	6.2
Total:	6.2	18.8	29.2	67.1	75.3	10.1	-22.7	-5.1	-14.4

Notes: (1) Subsidy (+ value) to or surplus (– value) from the U.S. Postal Service only. Postal Service budget (revenues about $55 billion in FY95) is independent of federal budget, except for small subsidy or surplus.

(2) Includes savings and loan bailout of the 1980s and reflects deposit insurance rates in the 1990s.

(3) 1995 and after includes FCC Universal Service Fund, funded in part by telecommunications fees assessed on carriers and auctions.

Table 4.2c

Unified Budget of the United States Government Outlays, Revenues, and Deficit as a Percent of Total Outlays FY 1987 to 1995

Outlays by function	1987	1988	1989	1990	1991	1992	1993	1994	1995
Social Security	20.7	20.6	20.3	19.8	20.3	20.8	21.6	21.9	22.1
National defense	28.1	27.3	26.6	23.9	20.7	21.6	20.7	19.3	17.9
Net interest	13.8	14.3	14.8	14.7	14.7	14.4	14.1	13.9	15.3
Income security	12.3	12.2	11.9	11.7	12.9	14.3	14.7	14.6	14.5
Medicare	7.5	7.4	7.4	7.8	7.9	8.6	9.3	9.9	10.5
Health	4.0	4.2	4.2	4.6	5.4	6.5	7.1	7.3	7.6
Education, training, employment, social services	3.0	3.0	3.2	3.1	3.3	3.3	3.5	3.2	3.6
Veterans benefits	2.7	2.8	2.6	2.3	2.4	2.5	2.5	2.6	2.5
Transportation	2.6	2.6	2.4	2.4	2.4	2.4	2.5	2.6	2.6
International affairs	1.2	1.0	0.8	1.1	1.2	1.2	1.2	1.2	1.1
Agriculture	2.6	1.6	1.5	1.0	1.1	1.1	1.5	1.0	0.6
Natural resources and environment	1.3	1.4	1.4	1.4	1.4	1.4	1.4	1.4	1.5
Energy	0.4	0.2	0.2	0.3	0.2	0.3	0.3	0.4	0.3
General science, space, technology	0.9	1.0	1.1	1.1	1.2	1.2	1.2	1.1	1.1
Community and regional development	0.5	0.5	0.5	0.7	0.5	0.5	0.6	0.7	0.7
Commerce and housing credit	0.6	1.8	2.6	5.4	5.7	0.7	-1.6	-0.3	-0.9
Justice	0.8	0.9	0.8	0.8	0.9	1.0	1.1	1.0	1.1
General government	0.8	0.9	0.8	0.9	0.9	0.9	0.9	0.8	0.9
Undistributed offsetting receipts	-3.6	-3.5	-3.3	-2.9	-3.0	-2.8	-2.7	-2.6	-2.9
Total Outlays	100.0	100.0	100.0	100.0	100.0	100.0	100.0	100.0	100.0
Total Revenues	85.1	85.4	86.7	82.3	79.7	79.0	81.9	86.1	89.2
Budget Deficit	14.9	14.6	13.3	17.7	20.3	21.0	18.1	13.9	10.8

Source: Calculated from values in Table 4.2a.

disaggregation, percentages and growth rates in Tables 4.2b, and 4.2c. It might be useful to ask the following questions:[6]

1. Are there any surprises? Are any of the categories much larger or much smaller than expected?

2. Where does the bulk of spending seem to go?

3. Which was the largest spending category in 1986? Which was the largest in 1995?

4. What has happened to the relative importance of national defense over the years shown (consult Table 4.2c)? How extensive have the defense cutbacks been since 1989?

5. The budgetary impact of interest payments on the national debt, largely payments to the holders of marketable U.S. Treasury securities (one-fourth of which are owned by foreigners) was discussed in the previous chapter. This category is recorded in the unified budget as net interest. How large, both absolutely and relatively, is net interest? How much taxpayer money is spent annually for Net Interest?

6. In terms of their relative contribution to total outlays, what is the importance of such categories as transportation, international affairs, agriculture, energy, commerce, justice, and so on. (Again, consult Table 4.2c in addition to Table 4.2a.)

7. At first glance, if one wants to reduce the budget deficit by outlay cuts, what are the primary candidates? Do any of these seem politically difficult to reduce or to alter in a substantial way?

Certain Questions and Answers about the Budget

Some smaller popular or topical items are well hidden in the budget, and people who review the budget for the first time often want to know where they are or how large they are. Some of these categories will be discussed in much more detail in the last section of this chapter, and some major categories, such as social security and medical outlays, are discussed at length in later chapters. Here, though, are some of the more common questions and their answers:

Question: How much of the agricultural function (of $9.8 billion in 1995) is used for farm subsidies?

---

[6]All of the categories introduced in these questions, including defense, Medicare, and Medicaid, are discussed in detail in later chapters. This exposure is meant to be an introduction to these subjects.

Answer: In 1995 about $7 billion of this amount was for price support programs and other subsidies to farmers. This was substantially below the total for 1994 when about $12.4 billion of the total budget of $15.1 billion was spent for price support programs and other subsidies. The savings, though, cannot be attributed to program reform. They are due mostly to very favorable crop prices in 1995, which substantially reduced the need for price support payments. Legislation was passed in 1996 that will change the nature of subsidies in the future, though not necessarily by reducing program outlays from 1995 levels. Farm programs and these subsidies are discussed extensively in the next chapter.

Question: Under which budgetary function can the savings and loan bailout be found and how much did it cost?

Answer: The savings and loan bailout is found under budgetary function 370 commerce and housing credit. Look at how that category ballooned after 1988. We can see the disaggregation of this spending function on Table 4.2b under deposit insurance where the cost of the bailout is easy to see. In 1993, though, this deposit insurance category ran a huge surplus of $28 billion.[7] Legislation in 1989 established three new insurance funds, the Bank Insurance Fund (BIF), the Savings Association Insurance Fund (SAIF), the FSLIC Resolution Fund (FRF), and an agency that was created to dispose of the assets of insolvent thrifts, the Resolution Trust Corporation (RTC) and its revolving fund. In 1993 these four funds began generating large surpluses. These deposit insurance funds in 1995 accumulated a huge collective surplus of $17.8 billion (on net, premiums paid by the insured intermediaries plus RTC proceeds from selling seized assets exceeded outlays by this amount), causing the commerce and housing credit budgetary function to also run a large surplus. Therefore, to some extent, the public is being "paid back" for some of the excesses of the 1980s.

Question: Where in the budget can we find foreign aid? How much is it? Is it a large part of the deficit problem?

Answer: What is normally thought of as foreign aid is found under budgetary function 150, international affairs, and it makes up about $12.9 billion of that $16.4 billion category in 1995. As such, it constitutes less than 1% of total outlays. More than half of foreign aid is for military goods. To be specific, in 1995, $7.6 billion was spent under function 151, international development and humanitarian assistance, and

---

[7]These are outlay categories, so a *negative* entry means that the fund associated with the entry took in a net surplus of cash.

$5.3 billion was spent under function 152, international security assistance, the military component of foreign aid. Of the latter, the Arms Export Control Act required that, in 1995, a minimum of $1.2 billion be granted as aid for Israel ($1.8 billion in 1994), and a minimum of $815 million ($1.3 billion in 1994) be granted as aid for Egypt. Foreign aid likely will remain at around the $12 billion level for the next few years.

Question: Is function 900, net interest, the interest paid by the U.S. Treasury on the federal debt that was discussed in Chapter 3?

Answer: Yes. This is the net interest payment on the debt. As long as deficits are generated and the debt grows, this figure will increase. As a line-item category it cannot be cut, of course (like defense), although it may fall somewhat in a year of sharply declining interest rates. As we saw in Chapter 3, a decline in the effective interest rate paid (see Fig. 3.4 and Fig. 3.5) of 1% absolutely (for example from 6% to 5%) will reduce this category by about $30 billion. A similar increase in rates will raise it by about the same amount. This is the expense that becomes a problem, both in absolute terms and as a percentage of outlays, if control is lost over the deficit. Table 4.2c shows net interest above 15% of outlays in 1995. This was also seen in Figure 3.5. This category is *net* rather than *gross* interest, and it does not include interest paid to U.S. government agencies, such as the social security trust fund (nor should it). A reasonable political objective might be to keep this category from growing more as a percentage of outlays.

Question: Where can we find welfare outlays?

Answer: In the United States, most welfare outlays are financed at the state and local level, although federal spending is substantial. Welfare outlays are scattered around in the federal budget. What is classified as welfare is rather arbitrary (is social security disability a form of welfare, for example, or are subsidized student loans, or the program that provides medical care to the elderly, Medicare, forms of welfare?). Most assistance to the poor is found under budgetary function 600, income security, which is desegregated in Table 4.2b. Clearly, not all of that category can be classified as welfare. Federal employee pensions and other retirement programs are included in this category and they constituted $70.9 billion of the total in 1995. Unemployment, at nearly $24 billion in 1995, $29 billion in 1994, and $38 billion in 1993 (the $14-billion difference between 1993 and 1995 reflects the clear benefit of a stronger economy), is not really welfare and is offset in part (though not entirely) by unemployment taxes, which were $29.0 billion in 1995. Housing subsidies (604), food & nutrition assistance (605), which includes the food stamp program and the old Aid to Families with Dependent Children (AFDC) program, and Supplemental Security Income (609) are traditional welfare programs for the poor and totaled $126 billion, which was about 8% of outlays. We will see a very extensive discussion of need-based entitlements programs, including all of those listed above, in Chapter 6. The health-care component of welfare is too complicated to discuss here and it is discussed separately in Chapters 6 and 7.

Question: What is the large negative category called undistributed offsetting receipts (950) near the bottom of the table?

Answer: Most of this consists of contributions made by the various agencies of the U.S. government to their employees' retirement funds (including military retirement). These contributions are recorded as outlays by the agencies that make them (such as the Department of Defense to the military retirement funds and the Department of Transportation to the civilian government employee retirement funds). As such, they are reflected in the unified budget, but the money never leaves the government nor is it spent (although it will be someday). The sum proceeds are listed as undistributed offsetting receipts, a negative entry, to eliminate double counting.[8]

Question: Where are the "block grants" that Congress always argues about?

Answer: The term block grant is to some extent an ill-defined political term. The federal government makes direct transfers of money to state and local governments in the name of many of these budgetary functions. These grants are earmarked for certain purposes and they typically have many restrictions attached to them. They are scattered throughout the unified budget, and in 1995 they constituted about $225 billion of the $1.52 trillion spent, or about 15% of the total. For example, of the $54.3 billion spent for function 500, education, training, employment, and social services, in 1994, $34.1 billion was in the form of grants to state and local governments. A political proposal for block grants is generally a proposal for grants to state and local governments that is still earmarked for certain programs or spending functions, but with far fewer restrictions than in

[8]This budgetary function includes some other small categories of spending as well. These can be seen in *Budget of the United States Government, Analytic Perspectives, FY 1997*, Table 4.3.

prior programs. The issue involves a matter of degree, and generally the appeal for block grants is an appeal for more autonomy at the state and local level.

Deficit Reduction on the Outlay Side

In reviewing Table 4.2c, which shows the relative percentages of the budgetary functions, the difficulty of achieving deficit reduction through expenditure cuts becomes readily apparent. The budget is fairly lopsided. Consider that the budget deficit is usually between 10 and 25% of outlays. Yet, as is described in Table 4.3, the top six categories listed, defense, Social Security, the medical programs, income security and interest on the debt, comprise an astonishing 88% of outlays in 1995. Even when the welfare provisions are removed from income security, the total is still about 80%, with the residual roughly the same size as the budget deficit in a bad year. The bottom 12 categories (which includes, among other things, education, veterans' benefits, transportation, agriculture, foreign aid and the budget of the Department of State, energy, the Department of Justice and the federal court and prison systems) contribute relatively little to total outlays, so substantial cutbacks in these areas will not contribute much to deficit reduction. This considered, it is plainly very hard to envision significant deficit reduction on the outlay side without most of it coming from the top.

Yet even in the top six categories the options are limited. Net interest on the debt cannot be cut—the goal here would be to keep this category from growing any more. Within the income security category, nearly half of that amount is for pensions ($71 billion)[9] or unemployment ($24 billion). And the others, including defense, Social Security, and at least the Medicare component of medical spending are among the most popular programs in government and, more important, reflect the interests of extremely powerful constituencies.

Of course, no sensible deficit reduction plan will propose eliminating the deficit in a single fiscal year. Even the most ambitious of plans would spread outlay reductions for large programs out over at least 5 years. Given this kind of planning horizon the task becomes a little easier. Some programs can be cut outright, as defense was between FY 1992 ($298 billion) and 1995 ($272 billion). In the case of rapidly expanding programs

---

[9]This includes military retirement programs costing about $28 billion in FY 1995.

Table 4.3

An Obstacle to Deficit Reduction: Disproportionate Spending

Category	% outlays	Residual
Top 6 budgetary functions (FY 1995)	87.9%	12.1%
Top 6 budgetary functions excluding welfare provisions of income security but including retirement programs and unemployment from the same	79.6%	20.4%
Sum total of education, transportation, agriculture, energy, veterans affairs, justice and international affairs, i.e., traditional budgetary functions other than defense	11.8%	
The Deficit:		10.8%

like Medicare, which has grown annually at nearly double-digit ranges, a program "cut" in the name of deficit reduction might instead amount to a substantial reduction in the annual growth rate of the program, perhaps from 10.5 to 5%. Likewise, budgets can be frozen at funding levels from prior years.

We can ask if the latter two examples, cutbacks in growth rates and frozen funding levels, are really budget cuts? The answer is yes. Tax revenues will rise each year in which there is economic growth (assuming no changes in tax rates, of course). The rough rule of thumb is that each 1% of GDP growth will add about $15 billion to tax receipts. In a strong growth year such as FY 1996, receipts can rise by more than $50 billion due to economic prosperity alone. If the growth rates of large programs are frozen or curbed, over a number of years this *may* be enough to achieve substantial deficit reduction.[10]

Nonetheless, even this gradualist approach to deficit reduction is unlikely to work unless most of the reduction is concentrated in the largest spending categories. It will not do much good to freeze educational

---

[10]The balanced-budget plans of both the Republicans of the 104th Congress and President Bill Clinton generally followed this format. Both set their balanced budget target for FY 2002 (the Republicans did this first, then the President followed suit), and both rely heavily on economic growth, proposing only moderate program cuts. We return to a discussion of these plans in later chapters.

spending or to reduce the growth rate of spending by the Department of Justice. Some of the restraint has to be in defense, health care, Social Security, income security—the large programs at the top.

This first glance at the data allows us to draw some conclusions. Because of the concentration of the bulk of federal spending in just a few areas, and given the contractual classification (interest, retirement, and unemployment) of part of the spending, the popularity of other parts (Social Security and Medicare) and the obvious necessity of most of what remains (defense), there are likely to be many constraints to cutbacks in outlays. This problem has grave political overtones.

Taxes

Table 4.4 shows the composition of taxes from fiscal years 1986 through 1995. The relative percentages for 1995 are shown in the far right column and can also be see in Figure 4.1. Personal taxes (including the employer contribution to Social Security) make up about 80 % of the total.

Although the composition of taxes has remained relatively steady over the last decade, Figure 4.2 shows that through the 1970s and early 1980s the relative importance of corporate income taxes fell by nearly one-half, from a little below 20% to the present level of slightly more than 11%, although all of the decline was experienced before 1985. As corporate taxes fell, social insurance taxes rose in relative importance with the increase in tax rates of some of the entitlement programs—especially Social Security and medical taxes. As will be seen later, this reflects the relative growth in the importance of entitlements.

The bottom part of the table shows effective tax rates as a percentage of various measures of national income. For example, total federal taxes collected as a percentage of gross domestic product stayed steady at around 18 to 19% through the decade. Personal income taxes as a percentage of personal income have remained below 10% and social insurance taxes stayed at 8%. Corporate income taxes now constitute a relatively small percentage of total revenues (about 11%), but the effective corporate tax rate as a percentage of corporate profits before taxes typically is above 25%. These or similar ratios in effect would have to be adjusted upward if deficit reduction is to be achieved through an increase in tax rates.

Table 4.4

Unified Budget of the United States Government
Tax and Revenue Sources and Related Data, $ billions
FY 1987 to 1995

Revenue sources	1987	1988	1989	1990	1991	1992	1993	1994	1995	1995 % tot
Personal income taxes	392.6	401.2	445.7	466.9	467.8	476.0	509.7	543.1	590.2	43.6
Social insurance taxes (total)	303.3	334.3	359.4	380.0	396.0	413.7	428.3	461.5	484.5	35.8
OASI (Social Security)	194.5	220.3	240.6	255.0	265.5	273.1	281.7	302.6	284.1	21.0
Disability (Social Security)	18.9	21.2	23.1	26.6	28.4	29.3	30.2	32.4	67.0	4.9
Hospital	56.0	59.9	65.4	68.6	72.8	79.1	81.2	90.1	96.0	7.1
Unemployment	25.6	24.6	22.0	21.6	20.9	23.4	26.6	28.0	28.9	2.1
Other social insurance	8.3	8.3	8.3	8.2	8.4	8.8	8.6	8.4	8.5	0.6
Corporate income taxes	83.9	94.5	103.3	93.5	98.1	100.3	117.5	140.4	157.0	11.6
Excise taxes	32.5	35.2	34.4	35.3	42.4	45.6	48.1	55.2	57.5	4.2
Estate and gift taxes	7.5	7.6	8.7	11.5	11.1	11.1	12.6	15.2	14.8	1.1
Federal Reserve interest (1)	16.8	17.2	19.6	24.3	19.2	22.9	14.9	18.0	23.4	1.7
Customs fees	15.1	16.3	16.3	16.7	15.9	17.4	18.8	20.1	24.3	1.8
Other	2.5	2.7	3.2	3.0	3.7	3.5	3.6	4.3	3.5	0.3
TOTAL	854.20	908.90	990.60	1,031.20	1,054.20	1,090.50	1,153.50	1,257.70	1,355.20	100.00
Gross Domestic Product (2)	4,452.40	4,808.40	5,173.30	5,481.50	5,676.40	5,921.50	6,258.60	6,633.60	7,004.50	
Effective tax rate (as % GDP)	19.19	18.90	19.15	18.81	18.57	18.42	18.43	18.96	19.35	
Personal income	3,877.30	4,172.80	4,489.30	4,791.60	4,968.50	5,264.20	5,479.20	5,750.20		
Personal income ETR (as % PI)	10.13	9.61	9.93	9.74	9.42	9.04	9.30	9.44		
Social insurance ETR (as % PI)	7.82	8.01	8.01	7.93	7.97	7.86	7.82	8.03		
Social Security ETR (as % PI)	5.50	5.79	5.87	5.88	5.92	5.74	5.69	5.83		
Corporate profits before taxes	293.60	354.30	348.10	371.70	374.20	406.40	464.30	528.20		
Corporate profit ETR (as % CPBT)	28.58	26.67	29.68	25.15	26.22	24.68	25.31	26.58		

Notes: (1) The Federal Reserve System owns a large portfolio of U.S. Treasury securities. They return interest beyond their operating costs to the Treasury, reflected here.
(2) This is Fiscal Year GDP (Oct 1–Sep 30). Personal income and corporate profits are ordinary annual (Jan–Dec).
Source: Budget of the United States Government, Historical Tables, and Economic Report of the President, 1994, 1995, 1996, and 1997.

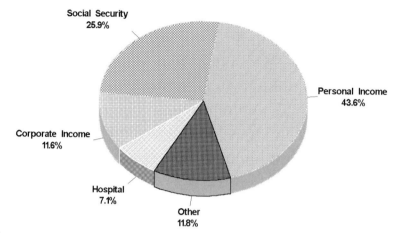

Figure 4.1
Composition of Tax Revenues, FY 1995

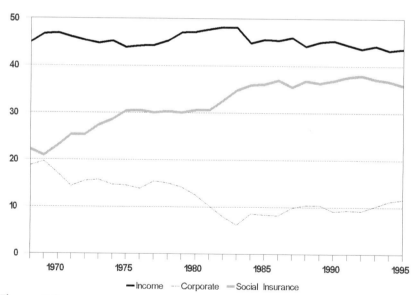

Figure 4.2
Tax Sources, Percent of Revenues

At first glance it might appear that some of the effective tax rates shown are lower than they should be. For example, the actual Social Security tax rate including the employers' contributions through the 1980s was around 14%, at least up to the income cap on Social Security (the social security tax rate in 1986 was 7.15% for *both* the employee and the employer up to income cap of $42,000), yet in no year are Social Security collections as a percentage of personal income above 7%. How is this explained?

It is explained partly by the fact that some earned income, such as interest, is not in the form of wage income and some income earned is above the cap. But for the most part this apparent discrepancy reflects the peculiar math of entitlements-linked taxes. In the Social Security program, for example, a person is either contributing to the program through taxes or is a beneficiary. Both have personal income (and in the case of the beneficiary, Social Security is part of the *source*) but only the former is paying full Social Security taxes. Therefore the social security tax rate as a percentage of *total* personal income will always be lower than the rate paid by any person who actually pays the tax. As entitlements tax rates increase over time *for those actually paying the taxes,* the general increase in *aggregate* effective rates does not rise nearly so much.

Tax Rates and the Flat Tax

Personal income tax rates are graduated in the United States—taxpayers with high taxable incomes pay higher rates than those with lower incomes. As shown in Table 4.5, there are five income tax brackets for taxable personal income, with the lowest rate at 15% and the highest at 39.6%. These rates are assessed against *taxable* income, which is income after all authorized deductions, ranging from dependent deductions to home mortgage interest, have been taken. The tax brackets for the two most common filing categories, *single,* and *married filing jointly* are shown for tax year 1995. These brackets are indexed each year to prevent inflation from pushing taxpayers into higher tax brackets. As a result, they are slightly higher each year.

For example, a single taxpayer with taxable income of $25,000 in 1995 would have owed a tax equal to 15% of the first $23,500 ($3,502), and 28% of the remaining $1,500 ($420), for a total tax bill of $3,922, equal to 15.7% of her taxable income. Because this taxpayer has taxable income greater than $23,500 but less than $56,550, she is said to be in

Table 4.5

Personal Income Tax Rates and Tax Brackets 1995 Tax Year

	Brackets for	
Marginal tax rates	Single	Married filing jointly
15%	$0	$0
28%	23,350	39,000
31%	56,550	94,250
36%	117,950	143,600
39.6%	256,500	256,500

Notes: (1) These rates apply to *taxable* income, after deductions, such as those for dependent children and mortgage interest, have been taken.

(2) Income earners must also pay FICA payroll tax for Social Security and Medicare at 7.65% of earned income, an amount that is matched by the employer.

Source: IRS form 1040, 1995 tax year.

the 28% *marginal tax bracket,* which means that each additional dollar she earns in income is taxed at that rate.

To provide another example, a married couple filing jointly in 1995 with a taxable income of $100,000 would have paid 15% on the first $39,000, 28% on the next $55,250 (i.e., up to $94,250), and 31% on the final $5,750, for a total tax bill of $23,102, or about 23% of total taxable income. They would have been in the 31% marginal tax bracket.

We should remember that the personal income tax is not the only tax paid at the personal level—the FICA payroll deduction tax earmarked for Social Security and Medicare[11] accounts for nearly one-third of all federal revenues. The FICA tax is effectively a flat tax—income earners pay 7.65% of earned (not taxable) income and employers make a matching contribution (another 7.65%), though there is a cap on the Social Security component of the tax ($62,700 in 1996).

---

[11] This tax and its history are discussed extensively in Chapters 6 and 7 where the Social Security and Medicare programs are addressed.

Some politicians and economists propose that the system of graduated brackets be replaced with a flat tax—a single bracket paid by everyone, regardless of the level of income. The flat tax-level would have to depend upon which if any tax deductions (such as mortgage credit and dependent children) would be retained. The flat tax with the greatest chance of success would likely retain the FICA payroll tax as it now stands and it would still allow major deductions, such as mortgage interest credit, because these are so popular.[12]

Tax reform on this scale, though, seems to have little strong support in the present era. Such drastic changes very strongly affect the distribution of income, Some groups gain and others lose income, which draws support from the gainers and enmity from the losers. This is the undesirable consequence of risky political decisions. For example, eliminating graduated income taxes would shift income somewhat (perhaps substantially) toward high-income earners and away from those presently in the lowest tax brackets. Given that there are much larger numbers of the latter than of the former (though the former contribute more to political campaigns) the flat tax stands on rather shaky ground as a viable political option, even though it might substantially simplify tax filing.

The Impact of Tax Rates upon Revenues and the Deficit

An evaluation of the impact of these effective tax rates upon revenues and the deficit produces interesting results. For example, *as a first approximation*, if the effective tax rate as a percentage of GDP is raised from the 1995 level of 19.35 to 20.30% of GDP (this would be about a 5% tax *rate* increase), revenues would have been about $67 billion higher. Given that the deficit is three times this scale, the relatively small gain in revenues in this example serves as an early warning that substantial deficit reduction and certainly balancing the budget would be an onerous task if it were to be accomplished primarily through tax increases, even if they were spread out over a number of years.

Of course, nothing is ever as simple as this crude first approximation. This simple approach assumes that a 5% increase in the generally effective tax rate would leave GDP unaffected, a dubious assumption. With tax matters there is the potential for complicated feedback effects. A

---

[12]Many tax proposals have been considered in recent years—too many to be discussed in detail in this book. A review of flat-tax proposals can be found in the book by Douglas R. Sease and Tom Herman. Please see the Bibliography, Section 9.

sizeable tax rate increase can decrease disposable (after-tax) personal income, the ultimate source of consumption in this economy. The growth rate of GDP (in other words, the tax *base*) could slow down in response, diluting the revenue gains of the tax-rate increase. Therefore the $67 billion revenue gain should be regarded as the *maximum* likely revenue gain, with the expectation that the final revenue gain might be considerably less.[13]

To amplify this point, Table 4.6, which shows the annual growth rates as percentages of the same tax and revenue categories that we considered earlier, clearly illustrates the sensitivity of tax revenues to economic conditions and tax rates. In 1988, for example, social security taxes were increased by 5% in absolute terms (the employer and employee tax rate was raised from 7.15 to 7.51% of income up to a limit of $45,000) and as a result, Social Security revenues jumped by more than 13%. The volatility of corporate income taxes through the years included in the table largely reflects the volatility of corporate profits. Likewise, the impact of the recession of the early 1990s on personal income tax collections is easy to spot. Tax revenues from this source in 1991 were essentially flat (growing at only 0.2%) because of the recession. In summary, the growth rate of revenues is as sensitive to the growth rate of income (the tax base) as it is to tax rates, and any interplay between the two must be taken into account.

Finally, it should not be forgotten that our discussion ignores the political feasibility of sizeable tax increases. The economics of the issue are largely irrelevant if the political climate renders large tax increases impossible.

The Agency Budget

In the remainder of this chapter we will look at the *agency budget* and compare it to the budget arranged by *function* that we have already seen. The comparison will be partial at this stage. To fully understand all of the elements of the *agency budget,* which lists the individual departments and agencies of the federal government, we will need to review the structure and the function of federal *trust funds,* a complicated subject that

---

[13]With tax matters there is always the possibility of complicated feedback effects. These issues will be covered more thoroughly in Chapter 9 when we discuss the economics of deficit reduction.

Table 4.6

Unified Budget of the United States Government Percentage Annual Growth Rates of Tax and Revenue Categories FY 1988 through 1995

Revenue sources	1988	1989	1990	1991	1992	1993	1994	1995	Avrg
Personal income taxes	2.2	11.1	4.8	0.2	1.8	7.1	6.6	8.7	5.3
Social insurance taxes (total)	10.2	7.5	5.7	4.2	4.5	3.5	7.8	5.0	6.1
OASI (Social Security)	13.3	9.2	6.0	4.1	2.9	3.1	7.4	-6.1	5.0
Disability (Social Security)	12.2	9.0	15.2	6.8	3.2	3.1	7.3	106.8	20.4
Hospital	7.0	9.2	4.9	6.1	8.7	2.7	11.0	6.5	7.0
Unemployment	-3.9	-10.6	-1.8	-3.2	12.0	13.7	5.3	3.2	1.8
Other social insurance	-0.0	-0.0	-1.2	2.4	4.8	-2.3	-2.3	1.2	0.3
Corporate income taxes	12.6	9.3	-9.5	4.9	2.2	17.1	19.5	11.8	8.5
Excise taxes	8.3	-2.3	2.6	20.1	7.5	5.5	14.8	4.2	7.6
Estate and gift taxes	1.3	14.5	32.2	-3.5	0.0	13.5	20.6	-2.6	9.5
Federal Reserve interest	2.4	14.0	24.0	-21.0	19.3	-34.9	20.8	30.0	6.8
Customs fees	7.3	0.6	2.5	-4.8	9.4	8.0	6.9	20.9	6.4
Other	8.0	18.5	-6.3	23.3	-5.4	2.9	19.4	-18.6	5.2
Total	6.4	9.0	4.1	2.2	3.4	5.8	9.0	7.8	6.0

Source: Calculated from Table 4.2a.

will be included in Chapter 6. For that reason, the aggregated agency budget will be introduced here, then some of the less complicated programs will be discussed in the next chapter, including defense, energy, agriculture, and transportation, education, and some specialized programs. The more complex components of the budget—especially those involving major entitlements and large trust funds—will be evaluated in Chapter 6. These will include social security, all of the health programs, welfare entitlements and retirement entitlements.

Table 4.7 shows outlays for the unified budget arranged by federal department or agency rather than by budgetary function. A comparison to the Table 4.2a will show that total outlays are the same. Beyond that, however, some categories do not match up very well. For example, as was noted earlier, budgetary function 350, agriculture, had outlays of $9.8 billion in 1995, but the Department of Agriculture within the agency budget spent $56.7 billion in the same year, more than five times that amount! Likewise, the Department of Energy had outlays totaling $17.6 billion in 1995, but only $4.9 billion falls under the budgetary category 270, energy.

These anomalies are easy to explain once the individual agency budgets are examined, which we will do in Chapter 5. Before leaving the aggregate budget, though, a clear generalization once again emerges: most of the spending is concentrated in the four categories at the top of the budget. The Department of Defense, the Treasury (for the most part due to interest payments on the debt), the newly-formed Social Security Administration,[14] and the huge Department of Health and Human Services have individual budgets summing to $1.31 trillion, which equals 86% of the budget. Once again, at first glance it appears that if deficit reduction is to be achieved through outlay cuts, a considerable part of it must come from these top four categories. Departments like Justice, State, and Commerce do not have budgets large enough to matter much in an environment of deficit reduction.

What's Next?

Again, the reader is reminded that the highly technical issues of *cash* versus *accrual* accounting techniques and the fact that the federal government does not distinguish between an *operating budget* and a *capital*

[14]The Social Security Administration was given separate agency status effective March 31, 1995. Before that it was a division of the Department of Health and Human Services.

Table 4.7

Outlays by Department/Agency
FY 1992 to 1995, $ billions

Department or agency	1992	1993	1994	1995	1995%
Social Security Administration	307.19	327.39	345.82	362.12	23.84
Department of the Treasury	292.99	298.80	307.58	348.58	22.95
Department of Health and Human Services	231.56	253.84	278.90	303.08	19.95
Department of Defense	314.90	307.84	299.05	291.23	19.17
Department of Agriculture	56.44	63.14	60.75	56.67	3.73
Office of Personnel Management	35.60	36.80	38.60	41.28	2.72
Department of Transportation	32.49	34.46	37.23	38.78	2.55
Department of Veterans Affairs	33.90	35.49	37.40	37.77	2.49
Department of Labor	47.08	44.65	37.05	32.09	2.11
Department of Education	26.05	30.29	24.70	31.30	2.06
Department of Housing and Urban Development	24.47	25.18	25.85	29.04	1.91
Department of Energy	15.52	16.94	17.84	17.62	1.16
NASA	13.96	14.30	13.70	13.38	0.88
Funds appropriated to the President	11.11	11.53	10.51	11.16	0.73
Department of Justice	9.80	10.17	10.01	10.79	0.71
Department of the Interior	6.55	6.78	6.90	7.41	0.49
Environmental Protection Agency	5.95	5.93	5.86	6.35	0.42
Department of State	5.01	5.38	5.72	5.34	0.35
Department of Commerce	2.57	2.80	2.92	3.40	0.22
Judiciary branch	2.31	2.63	2.68	2.91	0.19
Legislative branch	2.68	2.41	2.56	2.63	0.17
General Services Administration	0.47	0.74	0.33	0.71	0.05
Small Business Administration	0.55	0.79	0.78	0.67	0.04
Executive branch	0.19	0.19	0.23	0.21	0.01
Undistributed offsetting receipts	−117.11	−119.71	−123.47	−137.63	−9.06
Other	18.63	−10.08	11.41	2.21	0.15
Total	1,380.86	1,408.68	1,460.91	1,519.10	100.00

Source: Budget of the United States Government, Historical Tables, various years.

budget are addressed in Appendix C. For the interested reader, this might be the time to read that appendix, although some parts of what promises to be a complicated discussion might be easier to understand after more detailed budgeting practices are reviewed in Chapter 8.

In Chapter 5 we will take a closer look at some of the individual agency budgets, beginning with defense. We will explore the question of why there is such a large discrepancy between certain budgetary functions, like agriculture, and the departments or agencies that are normally associated with those functions. As we look at the individual budgets it will also be easier to understand why cutbacks in some of these agencies are a little more difficult to achieve once we learn what the money is being spent for or which constituency the spending represents.

Individual Agency Budgets

n the last chapter we looked at two aggregate budgets—outlays arranged by budgetary *function* and by *agency* (or department). Although both budgets summed to the same totals, the picture presented within was rather different when we compared one budget to the other. By clear inspection, some departments, like the Department of Agriculture, have spending functions that are not clearly linked to the functions with which the department is associated in the public eye. In the case of agriculture, for example, we will see that most of the spending in the budget of the Department of Agriculture supports various welfare programs, most of them classified somewhere under budgetary function 600, income security.

Agency budgets truly reveal the complexity of the federal budget and they make it easier to understand why there are many obstacles to budget cutting. With virtually any line-item category one can identify constituencies who feel that the spending is necessary and justified, and whose votes are guided by those sentiments, even if they generally embrace a philosophy of fiscal austerity. There are programs that benefit farmers, students, the elderly, the poor, the infirm, corporations and businesses of all sizes and interests, and myriad special interests. By example, some of these will be apparent as we disaggregate some of the larger and more important or interesting agency budgets.

Unfortunately, it is impossible to review completely every agency budget. To do so would require one to reproduce and expand upon the huge *Appendix* to the *Budget of the United States Government,* a document that even in its cryptic presentation is more than 1000 pages long.

Hoping to generalize from an exposure to some of the more important agencies, in this chapter we will explore in greater detail the budgets of the Departments of Defense, Energy, Agriculture, Transportation, and Education. We will also discuss direct grants, some welfare expenditures, and a special category called *Funds Appropriated to the President.* The more complicated discussion of trust funds and the large entitlements programs like Social Security and Medicare is reserved for the next chapter.

Finally, a much more detailed presentation of outlays for fiscal year 1995 and estimates for fiscal year 1996 arranged by budgetary function is presented in Appendix D: Outlays by Function, Subfunction, and Major Program, which lists all programs with outlays exceeding $100 million. Although not organized by agency, most well-known federal programs can be found by scanning though the listings. The reader is invited to consult that appendix after reading this chapter for detailed spending records.

Defense

Defense enjoyed a surge in popularity and budgetary importance during the Reagan era of the 1980s and was, in fact, a program favorite of the conservative President. But when deficit reduction became an earnest goal at the end of his presidency, the axe fell hard on defense. As was shown in Table 4.2a, function 050, national defense, was the largest single category in the unified budget at 28.1% of all outlays in 1987, but had declined to only 11.9% of the budget seven years later, a very substantial cut in relative terms.

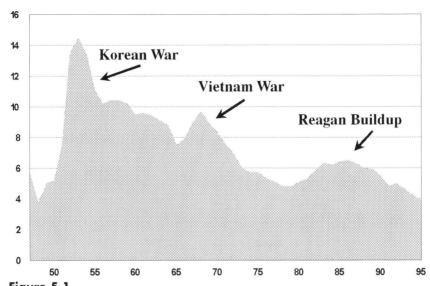

Figure 5.1
Defense Outlays as a Percentage of GDP, 1947 through 1995

Although it was commonly thought that the Reagan Administration had built up defense spending to record peacetime levels, Figure 5.1 shows that the surge in defense spending in the 1980s merely reversed temporarily a long cyclical decline coming off of the peaks of the Korean War and the Vietnam War (spending for World War II is not shown, but as one might guess, was between 18% and 40% of the budget during the war years).

In current budget projections defense is frozen roughly at 1995 levels after an adjustment for inflation, so the projections continue the decline. Outlays in 1995 put defense at only 3.9% of GDP, the lowest level since 1948, and estimates for the year 2000 place the same figure at 3.3%. It has not been that low since 1940. These projections add up to one clear message: even considering the peace dividend, a *further* cutback in defense is not a likely candidate for substantial deficit reduction, and there is occasional agitation from conservatives to raise defense spending.

Table 5.1 shows outlays for both the Department of Defense, which in the budget is divided into two components, military and civil (the latter having nothing to do with what people call "civil defense," an old term that brings up memories of air-raid sirens and local militias), and for the

Table 5.1

Defense Outlays ($ billions)

	1994	1995	1996e	1995% tot
Department of Defense				
Military	268.6	259.6	254.3	
Civil, incl. military retirement	30.4	31.7	32.3	
050 National Defense Function	281.6	272.1	265.6	100.0
Military personnel	73.1	70.8	67.2	26.0
Procurement	61.8	55.0	48.1	20.2
Operation & maintenance	87.9	90.9	91.5	33.4
Research, devmnt, test, eval	34.8	34.6	34.4	12.7
Atomic energy defense	11.9	11.8	10.2	4.3
Memo:				
602 Military retirement net outlay	26.7	27.8	28.5	

Notes: Civil defense is mostly Corps of Engineers, with most spending under function 300 Natural resources and envmnt.

Military retirement is not listed under function 050, but rather 600 income security and is part of the Federal employee retirement category of income security.

Procurement is largely for acquisition and modifications of weapon systems.

Atomic energy defense, although clearly a defense function, is funded in the Department of Energy.

050 National Defense Function in the unified budget. The latter shows, for example, that about 26% of defense spending is allocated to personnel. As can be seen, the figures for the agency and the function do not match, although they are not as skewed as those for agriculture.[1]

Reasons for the mismatch become readily apparent with some explanation. First, the civil component of the budget of the Department of Defense includes the budget of the Department of Army Corps of Engineers with an annual budget around $3.7 billion. The Army Corps of Engineers is responsible for flood control projects and inland waterways, among other things, so their outlays are typically classified under 300, natural resources and environment, rather than defense. Most of the rest

[1]The figures provided for 1996 are estimates and in the case of individual programs they may deviate substantially from the values to be spent in FY 1996. The estimates are OMB estimates and to some extent they therefore reflect the budgetary plans coming from the Office of the President. Getting reliable estimates for 1996 is compounded by the fact that the FY 1996 budget procedure was never completed because of substantial disagreements between the President and the new Republican Congress. This is discussed in the final chapter.

of the civil budget (but not all of it) is where one finds the Military Retirement Fund, which shows payments for military retirees of $27.8 billion in 1995, about 40% of all federal retirement expenditures, and clearly an entitlement which cannot be cut. This payment is classified as an outlay under function 600, income security, but is *also* partly reflected in the defense category 051 Military personnel as an expenditure on military personnel. The Military Retirement Fund is a trust fund, and its complicated accounting is explained and summarized in Chapter 7.

Finally, there is a strange anomaly in the defense budget, found in the spending category called atomic energy defense. As will be seen below, this is clearly a defense expenditure but it is found in the agency budget of the Department of Energy rather than the Department of Defense.

Energy

At $17 billion, the budget of the Department of Energy is large and it therefore provides at initial glance opportunities for cutbacks in an era of deficit reduction. One often hears in public political discussions suggestions of huge energy subsidies and wasteful research. A closer inspection of the disaggregated budget, though, produces a complex picture. Table 5.2 shows the figures for both the budgetary function 270, energy and the budget for the Department of Energy. Note the difference in expenditures—the budget of the Department of Energy is more than four times the scale of expenditures for the energy function!

The departmental budget shows why.[2] First, more than $11 billion of the $17 billion departmental budget, or 67% of the budget, is classified as atomic energy defense activities under budgetary function 053, a defense category. Virtually all of this money is used for nuclear weapons research, development, testing, and for the disposal of nuclear waste. Despite progress toward world disarmament, this sizable component of the budget continues to receive substantial funding (though a considerable part of that is for winding down nuclear weapons activities or for

---

[2]The figures shown within the departmental budget include some outlays, typically small amounts, to other areas of the federal budget (there are interagency transfers throughout the federal budget), and even from one budget category to another within the Department of Energy. For that reason totals of outlays do not sum up to net outlays for the department. Also, some of the outlays shown, especially those under the category Power Marketing Administration, are present-value estimates of future loan obligations rather than actual cash disbursements. For more explanation, see the definition of the word **outlay** in the glossary.

Table 5.2

Energy Outlays ($ millions)

	1995	1996est	1995%	Comments
270 Energy function	4,936	3,217	100.0	
Energy supply	3,584	2,009	72.6	
Energy conservation	671	681	13.6	
Emergency energy preparedness	223	171	4.5	
Energy information, policy, regulation	458	356	9.3	
Department of Energy	17,617	14,678		
Atomic energy defense activities			66.8	Essentially nuclear weapons
Weapons activities	3,656	3,389		development, testing, and
Defense envnmtl restoration	5,621	5,237		transportation. Most outlays are
Other defense AE support	2,486	1,601		under budget function 053.
Energy research				
General science & research	1,340	978		Mostly high-energy physics.
Energy supply research	3,327	3,042		
Fossil energy research & devel	440	426		
Clean coal technology	243	311		
Energy conservation	671	681		
Resource supply & stockpiling				
Uranium supply & enrichment	109	48		
Naval petroleum & oil shale res	203	178		
Strategic petroleum reserve	212	261		
Regulation & other				
Federal Energy Regulatory Comm	−5	5		Costs transferred to fees of
Economic regulation	12	8		regulated businesses by 1996.
Office of Inspector General	28	27		
Energy Information Administration	86	72		
Energy departmental admin	309	253		Reflects transfer of duties &
Uranium decontamination	349	287		funds.
Nuclear Waste Disposal Fund	375	218		
Power Marketing Administrations				These are agencies that sell
Alaska Power Administration	4	9		hydroelectric power, mostly
Southeastern Power Administration	23	20		from dams built by Corps of
Southwestern Power Administration	35	27		Engineers. Outlays here are not
Western Area Power Administration	285	219		cash, but present value estimates
Bonneville Power Administration	−121	−43		of future costs for loan service.
Colorado River Basins Power	11	0		See text.

Notes: Some outlays shown are to other agencies of government or funds within Department of Energy, so do not total to net outlays for department.

Some classifications of major categories are done by author, not all outlays are shown, but all large outlays are shown.

Some outlays, especially those for power administration, are financed by loans.

disposing of the harmful byproducts), whereas tiny and inconsequential programs draw attention.

Once the atomic energy component is removed from the departmental budget the only remaining large-scale spending categories (above $500 million) are found in the area of energy research. The amounts funded there are sizeable, totaling more than $5 billion annually (relatively small amounts of these funds are transferred to other federal accounts). The first category shown, general science and research, though reduced in recent years, mostly funds high-energy and nuclear physics, and included from 1992 through 1995 more than $1 billion squandered on the Texas superconducting supercollider, an enormous hole in the ground through which no proton will ever be accelerated (wind-down costs for the supercollider program were budgeted at $513 million in 1993 and $639 million in 1994). The second category shown, Energy supply research is a generalized category providing funds for research in myriad energy technologies, including nuclear fission, solar energy, magnetic fusion, and energy-related environmental safety.[3]

Energy regulation (see regulation and other in Table 5.2) does not cost much, totaling less than $200 million. To this figure, though, must be added the sizeable (relative) budget of the Nuclear Regulatory Commission (not shown here), which has separate agency status and its own budget, for which outlays were $525 million in 1995.

Finally, the issue of energy subsidies arises occasionally in public discussions of deficit reduction. The Department of Energy sells a large amount of electricity from hydroelectric dams. The agencies under which the electricity is sold are called power marketing administrations, shown at the bottom of Table 5.2. It is debatable whether the energy is subsidized—it depends upon what one calls "cost." Federal law requires that energy rates periodically be adjusted so that the government ultimately "recovers all costs of operation and all capital invested in power, with interest."[4] And, of course, restricting pricing to "cost" is not the same as pricing to make a profit, which is how electricity is priced by the private sector. Substantial authority to borrow has been extended to some of these agencies to upgrade capital equipment and to promote conservation measures, and some portion of the relatively small outlays shown are from borrowing authority.

The complexities of large hydroelectric projects are demonstrated by the venerable Tennessee Valley Authority (TVA), created during the Great Depression and privileged to have its own agency status that is separate from the Department of Energy. With an annual budget above $5 billion, most of it funded through energy sales, the TVA is the sole provider of

---

[3]Research funds for the National Science Foundation, which does include some energy-related research, are not found in the energy budget. The National Science Foundation has agency status and its own budget, which has been about $2 billion annually in recent years.

[4]This passage is quoted throughout the authorization discussions of the various power administrations listed in Table 5.2.

electric power to an area of 80,000 square miles in seven states. Additionally, though, it manages navigational channels, recreational and educational activities, and environmental programs, which in the past have been supported by user's fees but, are are also subsidized in part by federal money. By law, direct costs of power distribution are supposed to be self-supporting through fees charged to energy users, but some of the cost of capital investment (nearly $2 billion in 1995) finds its way into the federal budget. The TVA had net budgetary outlays of $912 million in 1994 and $1.3 billion in 1995. Sentiments in recent years have favored phasing out the small subsidies to such agencies as the TVA, encouraging them to be completely reliant on revenues generated through power sales and user fees.

Generally speaking, energy subsidies are nonexistent or, given the scale of the budget, so tiny as to be of no real consequence if deficit reduction is the goal.

Agriculture

The budget of the Department of Agriculture is controversial because of its overall size and because of the common knowledge that it includes large agricultural subsidies. The subsidies are generally regarded as wasteful by nearly everyone who chooses to talk about them, including some of the farmers who benefit from them. But they endure year after year despite the fact that the constituency that favors them is a small segment of the U.S. population.[5] Congressional floor votes and debates on agricultural issues, including funding, are typically spirited and emotional, and are one of the few areas where the debate does not split along partisan lines. Partisan allies in almost every other endeavor part company when it comes to agricultural issues and the budget of the Department of Agriculture. New alliances and divisions emerge—urban versus rural, farm regions versus industrial regions. Republicans and Democrats who bitterly dispute almost all other matters along strict party lines form strong and emotional bonds (for at least the duration of a debate) when the issue is the peanut price support system or marketing aid for California wines.

Table 5.3 shows the budgetary breakdown for both function 350, agriculture and the Department of Agriculture. Once again, a tremendous discrepancy between the two figures is seen. The reason becomes

[5]Less than 2% of the U.S. population earns its livelihood from farming, although the farming community is politically active on farm issues to such a degree that farm support tends to be nonpartisan.

Table 5.3

Agriculture Outlays ($ millions)

	Funcn	1994	1995	1996est	1995%
350 Agriculture Function		15,121	9,773	7,718	
Department of Agriculture		60,753	58,571	54,064	100.0
Agricultural research & education	352	1,773	1,804	1,826	3.1
Agricultural inspection programs	352	1,086	1,043	999	1.8
Commodity Credit Corporation	351	9,752	5,555	6,000	9.5
Soil, watershed, & other conservation	350	3,508	2,848	3,055	4.9
Forest Service	302	3,343	3,765	3,151	6.4
Food Stamp & other nutritional programs	600	36,679	36,968	38,756	63.1
Rural Housing & Community Development	452	1,605	2,124	1,652	3.6
Public Law 480 Foreign Aid	151	1,376	1,066	963	1.8

Notes: Commodity Credit Corporation is where most farm subsidies and price support programs are found. See text.

Spending for the Food Stamp program was $25.554 billion in 1995, for school lunch programs, $7.499 billion.

Outlays for Rural Housing Assistance reflect, in part, present cash value of future loan subsidies. See text.

Function numbers are functions within which most, though not all, spending is classified for the category shown.

CCC estimate for 1996 is made by author based upon recent legislative changes.

fairly obvious when looking at the disaggregated budget. General low-income welfare nutritional programs, including the food stamp program, which spent more than $25 billion in 1995, constituted more than 60% of the departmental budget. The nutritional programs are nominally agricultural because they involve food, but they are classified under budget function 600 income security. The myriad rural housing assistance programs (under 450, commercial and regional development) are mostly loan subsidies for low-income rural housing.[6] Low-income and welfare expenditures, therefore, make up about 65% of the departmental budget.

The expensive food stamp program, which does not involve any *direct* purchases of agricultural products (food stamps are given to low-income

[6]Outlay data for categories like this (loan subsidies) do not reflect cash outlays alone—they also include an estimate for the present value of future subsidy costs. For a more detailed explanation of this complication, see the definition of the word **outlay** in the glossary at the end of this book.

recipients and can be used by them for the purchase of groceries), generally has the support of the same farming constituency that support farm subsidies. At the opening of the 104th Congress, for example, after the Republican sweep of both houses of Congress in the fall elections, efforts to substantially curb both the food stamp program and the smaller child nutrition program (which provides school lunches for the most part and cost about $7.5 billion in 1995) met strong opposition from farm-belt members from both parties.

Most but not all of the farm subsidy programs are found in the budget of the venerable Commodity Credit Corporation, a government-owned corporation created to ". . . stabilize, support, and protect farm income and prices; help maintain balanced and adequate supplies of agricultural commodities, their products, foods, feeds, and fibers; and help in their orderly distribution."[7]

The job of the Commodity Credit Corporation and the general support of the federal government for farming activities, including subsidies, was substantially revised by a sweeping agricultural law passed in 1996, which is described in detail in the next section. Because the effects of the law have yet to be seen and because the new programs legislated by the law may turn out to be temporary (ending in the year 2002) both the old system (prior to 1996) and the new approach will be described.

The many types of farm support programs are summarized in Table 5.4. Prior to 1996, the most common programs were *price supports,* which were applied to corn, cotton, wheat, rice, peanuts, tobacco(!), barley, oats, rye, grain sorghum, sugar, honey, milk, oilseeds, wool and mohair.[8] For each of these commodities a minimum price was set (by the Congress, effectively), and if market prices fell below that threshold, the Commodity Credit Corporation (CCC) would purchase sufficient quantities of the commodity (or use another of the options shown in Table 5.4) to bring the price back up to the support level. In the case of wheat, for example, in years of bumper crops the CCC would buy surplus wheat, store it in granaries (general storage costs for CCC products would typically exceed $2 billion per year), and would eventually try to market it, often overseas. If all of the wheat could not be sold, it could be destroyed.

Table 5.5 shows the target crop prices for wheat, corn, rice and cotton under the farm legislation in effect in 1994, along with actual market

---

[7]*Appendix, FY 1995,* p. 150.

[8]Not all of the price support programs require heavy subsidies. The price of sugar is supported by strict acreage limitations, which limits supply (as does the embargo of Cuban sugar). For a discussion of this and the political prospects of subsidy reductions, see "Plowing a New Field," *National Journal,* January 28, 1995, p. 212.

Table 5.4

Types of Agricultural Subsidy and Support Programs

Old law

Price support	Using any one of the methods below, such as direct purchases or commodity loans, the commodity price is prevented from dropping below a price floor set by legislation. Market prices are allowed to be *higher* than the price floor.
Direct purchases	Typically for a price support program, certain quantities, usually surplus production given some price floor that is above what would be the market price without intervention, are purchased from producers or processors.
Commodity loans	Loans are made with commodities as collateral and upon maturity the borrower may repay the loan (if prices are high for the commodity in question) or forfeit the commodity collateral without making monetary payment—turning the crop over if prices are low.
Acreage limitations	Restricting the acreage that any producer in the program can use for one crop, sometimes without payment and sometimes with **land diversion payments.**
Land diversion payments	Direct payments to producers to withhold land from production (acreage limitations).
Disaster payments	Direct payments for crop loss from weather disasters.
Marketing programs	A situation in which the government undertakes part or all of the cost of marketing a commodity, especially overseas.

1996 law

Production flexibility contracts	Replaces price support program for grain, cotton, and oilseed crops. Removes all crop restrictions and makes direct subsidy payments to farmers. See text.

Note: 1996 law does not necessarily eliminate programs described under old law. See text.

prices seen on two dates in 1995 and 1996 (the relevance of these market prices will be explained later). These price supports were suspended in the 1996 farm bill (price supports for dairy products, sugar, and peanuts were retained), although they may be restored in the future, probably at different levels.

Table 5.5

Target Crop Prices for Federal Commodity Programs for 1994 and Market Prices for 1995 and 1996

Crop	Price support	Price 11/15/95	Price 5/30/96
Wheat (per bushel)	$ 4.00	$5.17	$6.29
Corn (per bushel)	$ 2.75	$3.13	$4.78
Rice (per hdwgt)	$10.71		
Cotton (per pound)	$ 0.729	$0.840	$0.829

Source for support prices: *Reducing the Deficit: Spending and Revenue Options,* Congressional Budget Office, March 1994, p. 212.
Source for quoted prices: *The Wall Street Journal.* Wheat prices quoted are for hard KC, corn prices are for No. 2 yellow, Cent. Ill.

Changes Made by the 1996 Farm Bill

On April 4, 1996, President Clinton signed HR 2854,[9] a sweeping agricultural act (given the dubious title, "The Freedom to Farm Act," by its sponsors) that made significant changes in price support and quota programs. Generally, the law suspended through the year 2002 the price support authority, quotas, and acreage limitations for grain crops, cotton and oilseed, and replaced them with what were called **production flexibility contracts.** Farmers are eligible for these production flexibility contracts if at anytime between 1991 and 1995 they had acreage planted with any of these crops or they had enrolled in the old acreage reduction programs.

The production flexibility contracts, which are not tied to price supports or any form of market activity, make no restrictions on farmers except for those that apply under conservation and environmental laws, and farmers are no longer obliged, as they might have been under the old law, to restrict output. Grain, upland cotton, and oilseed farmers can participate freely in the market, as though there were no government program at all—except that they get federal payments that are effectively little more than welfare checks based upon their prior participation in the old program.

The funds explicitly authorized by the farm bill for the annual payments for the production flexibility contracts are shown in Table 5.6, along with the crop allocations (for example, corn farmers will get

[9]All references that follow are from the text of this bill, now Public Law 104-127.

Table 5.6

Select Provisions of HR 2854, the 1996 Agriculture Act

Funding made available for production flexibility contracts ($ millions)

FY 1996	$5,570
1997	$5,385
1998	$5,800
1999	$5,603
2000	$5,130
2001	$4,130
2002	$4,008

Crop allocation percentages for production flexibility contracts

Wheat	26.26%
Corn	46.22%
Grain Sorghum	5.11%
Barley	2.16%
Oats	0.15%
Upland Cotton	11.63%
Rice	8.47%

Milk price support for mild with 3.67% butterfat, per hundredweight

1995	$10.10
1996	$10.35
1997	$10.20
1998	$10.05
1999	$ 9.90

Source: Text of HR 2854, now Public Law 104-127. 1995 milk price is from prior law, and is provided for reference.

46.22% of the more than $4 billion set aside for production flexibility contracts in FY 2002). Again, these are not price support payments, but they are direct entitlement payments that replace the old subsidies. In some of these years, especially 1996, they will likely exceed the amount that would have been spent under the old price support program. The funding does taper down (in the name of deficit reduction), but it does not taper down much and it does not taper down to zero. In a few words, it is likely to have the final effect of reducing farm subsidies (although possibly not), but not of eliminating them.

The dairy price support program was relatively unaltered by the bill and it preserved milk price supports until 1999 (the levels are also shown in Table 5.6). The peanut price support was preserved, but it was dropped from $6.85 to $6.10 per ton. A quota system was retained that could allow the Secretary of Agriculture to keep the effective floor above $6.10. The sugar program was relatively unaltered. The new or altered programs will still be administered by the Commodity Credit Corporation.

The farm welfare payments to the grain, cotton, and oilseed growers are justified as necessary to help farmers through the period of "transition," as perhaps they are, but the law does not guarantee a transition. The old price support payments and production quotas are not eliminated, and careful language was chosen in the law to ensure they would not be—they are suspended until the year 2003. More important, as can be seen in Table 5.6, the funding for the final year does not converge to zero as it would in a legitimate transition program.

The fiscal impact of the new farm bill is mixed. It probably does reduce agricultural spending somewhat from what it would have been under the old farm bill (though that is not assured—in years of high crop prices such as 1995 subsidies would likely be lower for the grain crops than the new welfare "transition" payments) but it keeps taxpayer-financed subsidies intact, albeit under a new arrangement that has shifted from a price-support program to an entitlements program.

Commodity Credit Corporation (CCC) Funding

The cost of price support and other programs is high, although not nearly so high as it was in the early 1980s. A summary of CCC funding for select years, including an estimate for 1995 made in 1994, is shown in Table 5.7. What counts as a subsidy depends upon interpretation. Certainly, direct producer payments are subsidies. Commodity loans are subsidies only if the loans are not repaid (which was the case in 1993 for a little more than $1 billion dollars), which would be the case only if crop prices fall below the support level. Commodity purchases, part of which are dedicated to other federal programs or resold by the government, and the cost of storage (of purchased grain, for example) fall into a gray area, although few of these expenses would be funded if agriculture were truly on its own. If CCC net outlays are treated as the effective cost of farm support, then clearly that figure covers a wide range, because the amount exceeded $15 billion in 1993, but was less than $6 billion in 1995.

Table 5.7

Commodity Credit Corporation Gross Outlays, Offsets, and Net Outlays 1993, 1994, 1995 estimates, 1995 ($ millions)

Program	1993	1994	Estimated 1995	Actual 1995
Gross outlays	25,793	19,134	21,821	17,692
including				
Commodity purchases	1,761	1,620		909
Storage, transportation	2,846	2,173		1,194
Direct producer payments for				
Feed grains (corn)	2,597	4,098	1,641	0
Wheat	1,946	1,102	1,446	86
Rice	923	646	635	468
Cotton	1,412	555	390	45
Commodity loans	9,067	6,430		9,231
Less offsetting collections	−10,737	−9,382	−12,009	−12,137
including				
Sales to federal sources	−617	−930		−681
Sales to non-federal sources	−458	−311		−257
Loans repaid	−7,849	−6,234		−9,430
Equals net outlays	15,055	9,752	9,812	5,555

Notes: Estimates for 1995 were made in early 1995 at the same time the 1994 figures were released.

The unanticipated sharp declines in 1996 direct crop payments were due to unusually high commodity prices.

Source: Budget of the United States Government, Appendix, for FY 1995, 1996, 1997.

Other subsidies for programs outside of CCC jurisdiction, such as crop insurance and myriad programs under the rubric "soil conservation," can add another $3 billion or so to the total.

The effort to estimate subsidy costs and the CCC budget is difficult because the subsidies are *entitlements*, just like Social Security, and outlays depend largely upon volatile world commodity prices. A banner year for weather and crops, to the extent that it reduces commodity prices, can wreak havoc for the CCC budget. In contrast, a year of exceptionally high crop prices can have the opposite effect, as happened in 1995. Net outlays by the CCC declined very sharply in 1995 not because of program changes or reforms (the first budget to be affected by the new farm bill will be the 1996 budget), but because commodity prices, and especially wheat and corn prices, rose to record levels, far above price support levels. These prices were shown in Table 5.5; wheat was selling for $6.29 per bushel and corn for $4.78 per bushel in May 1996, far above their respective price support floors (under the old law) of $4.00 and $2.75 per bushel respectively. It is for that reason, when comparing estimated to actual 1995 outlays in Table 5.7, that the CCC estimates for 1995 direct producer payments were so much higher than actual payments for the same year.

Of course, direct producer payments for the crops shown were suspended in 1996 and were replaced by the new production flexibility contracts described in the previous section. Because of the formulas used in the new program, it is possible that CCC outlays in 1996 could rise above the relatively low levels of 1995, and above what they would have been in 1996 had the old program been continued.

The likelihood of reducing further this component of the budget seems promising until one considers the amazing resiliency of these programs, most of which were authorized by the Agricultural Adjustment Act of 1938 or the Agriculture Act of 1949. As was stated earlier, support is not universal even in the farming sector. The list of subsidies is conspicuous in what it omits—tree crops, meats, grapes (wine)—so only a minority of farmers receive subsidies and little support is forthcoming from those sectors that do not. The new production flexibility contracts are capped at $40,000 per person ($75,000 for commodity loan subsidies), although some farming operations make multiples of this because of family and similar corporate arrangements. The subsidies do not really benefit large-scale agriculture (although keeping prices artificially high does), and there is extensive lobbying *against* subsidies by the purchasers of commodities. However, key elected representatives from the farm districts have been loath in the past to let agriculture move to the free market. In all fairness to the supporters of these programs, subsidies are not an American innovation—they are in place throughout the industrialized world and on a scale larger than that seen in the United States. They seem likely to stay in place, although they will possibly diminish in scale over time.

Transportation

Transportation presents a simpler picture than any of the agency budgets seen so far. Table 5.8 summarizes budgetary function 400, transportation, and the budget of the Department of Transportation. As can be seen

Table 5.8

Transportation Outlays ($ millions)

	1994	1995	1996e	Comments
400 Transportation Function	38,134	39,350	39,769	
Grants to state & local govts	23,633	25,995	24,256	Above 60% of the total.
Department of Transportation	37,228	38,777	38,994	
Highways	19,052	19,502	19,924	
Federal Railroad Admin.	833	1,035	912	
Amtrak subsidy	491	806	550	This is only the subsidy.
Federal Transit Admin.	4,119e	4,436	6,363	Public mass transit.
Federal Aviation Admin.	8,784	9,207	9,912	
Operations	2,363	1,967	2,478	
Airport grants in aid	1,620	1,826	2,983	
Facilities & equipment	2,378	2,639	1,996	
U.S. Coast Guard	3,739e	3,671	3,631	
Maritime Administration	542	447	465	Mostly merchant marine subsidies.

Notes: Only major programs are shown.

Because of reorganization of Department of Transportation, some 1994 values (e) are rough estimates.

these figures are similar, so most federal spending for transportation is within the departmental budget.[10]

About 60% of that budget is in the form of grants to states and local governments. The $20 billion spent for highways (more or less the budget of the old Federal Highway Administration), for example, is almost entirely in the form of federal grants to earmarked highway or bridge projects for construction or repairs. For such projects the federal government typically funds 80% of the expenses. The Federal Transit Administration provides about $6 billion annually in support for mass transit projects, mostly for capital investments and, again, largely through grants. The typical transit subsidy pays 80% of capital costs and 50% of operating *deficits* for targeted transit projects.[11]

The often controversial Amtrak subsidy, which for some reason is right in the thick of partisan fights over subsidies every few years, absorbs

[10]The Department of Transportation was going through a major reorganization in 1995 and 1996, so the classification of budgetary categories from one year to the next (from FY 1995 to FY 1996) is difficult.

[11]CBO, "Reducing the Deficit . . . ," March 1994, p. 141.

about $550 million of the budget. It likely gets a lot of attention while other subsidies that are much larger are ignored and unthreatened because Amtrak has no solid regional nor political constituency to defend it. Nonetheless, the subsidy has not only survived nearly a decade of attacks during the Reagan era but it has grown somewhat. The maritime subsidy at the bottom of Table 5.7 is nearly as large, yet seldom does one hear of it.

Budget reduction of any significance would be difficult to achieve because most of these programs are popular and in some cases they are probably badly underfunded. This is certainly the case with highway funds. A dollar saved here merely means that one dollar less is spent on the nation's deteriorating bridge and highway system.[12] The FAA is at least partially funded by heavy aviation use taxes and, again, cutbacks there would be gravely felt. Both categories fund economic infrastructure, and financial neglect in the name of budget austerity can impose a far higher economic toll than the original savings. Certainly, not everyone supports public transit, but if this funding category were substantially reduced, modern public transit would probably cease to exist in the United States.

Education

The budget of the Department of Education provides an interesting example of federal spending because it allows us to explore the issue of grants to state and local governments, which comprise more than 70% of all spending for budgetary function 500, education, training, employment of social services. The budget for this function and for the Department of Education is shown in Table 5.9. Once again, the funds associated with the budgetary function far exceed the budget of the department that is most strongly associated with the budgetary category. Spending for this category is scattered throughout many agency budgets. A considerable chunk of it is found in the Employment and Training Administration of the Department of Labor, which had outlays of $4.4 billion in 1994, a figure that increased to $6.4 billion in 1995 because of the emphasis on job training by the Clinton administration.

---

[12]*Scientific American*, in a grim article discussing the state of highway bridges in the U.S., claims that more than 200,000 are deficient and that between 150 and 200 spans suffer partial or complete collapse yearly. The authors blame the problem on poor maintenance, and estimate the repair bill at about $90 billion. See "Why America's Bridges are Crumbling," by Kenneth F. Dunker and Basile G. Rabbat (engineers), *Scientific American*, March 1993, page 66.

Table 5.9

Education Outlays ($ millions)

	1994	1995	1996est	Comments & primary spending targets
500 Education, Training, Employment and Social Services Function	46,307	54,263	54,131	
Grants to state & local governments	32,744	34,125	36,561	63% of total in 1995.
Grants for education only	15,577	15,955	17,830	65% of education budget in 1995.
Department of Education	**24,699**	**31,322**	**30,404**	Primary Targets
Elementary & Secondary Education	**9,226**	**9,145**	**10,153**	General academic achievement and school-to-work transition.
Education reform	2	61	538	
Education for the disadvantaged	6,846	6,808	7,113	Migratory families, neglected and delinquent children.
Impact aid	830	808	830	Schools impacted by "federally connected children."
School improvement programs	1,461	1,391	1,587	Wide range of specific educational objectives.
Indian education	79	71	78	Native Americans.
Bilingual Educ & Minority Language	**222**	**225**	**239**	Bilingual education.
Special Education & Rehabilitation	**5,349**	**5,647**	**6,230**	
Special education	2,980	3,177	3,511	Children with disabilities.
Rehabilitation & disability research	2,244	2,333	2,593	Disabled students rehabilitation programs.
American printing house for the blind	6	7	7	Students below college level who are blind.
National Institute for the Deaf	42	46	41	Employment training for the deaf.
Gallaudet University	77	84	78	College prep and related training for the deaf.
Office of Vocational & Adult Ed	**1,341**	**1,482**	**1,513**	Vocational and adult education.
Office of Postsecondary Education	**7,962**	**14,113**	**11,368**	
Student financial assistance	7,118	7,047	7,395	Direct need-based college financial aid.
Higher education	796	871	898	Black and Hispanic-serving colleges & universities.
Howard University	204	208	191	Matching endowment grant for Howard University (17 sites).
Student loan subsidies, default, writeoff	2,697	3,509	3,838	See text. 1994 numbers not comparable with 1995 and 1996.
Educational research	**419**	**396**	**505**	
Educational research	277	279	336	General research, technology development.
Libraries	142	117	169	Public library services & construction.
Departmental management	321	404	464	General administrative expenses of Department of Education.

Despite the large numbers seen in Table 5.9, the U.S. government contributes relatively little to education in the United States and almost nothing to the cost of education for elementary and secondary students who are neither indigent nor disabled. Total spending for elementary and secondary schools in the United States is estimated to have been about $230 billion in 1993.[13] Of that amount, the federal government provided about $15 billion, or less than 7%. Primary and secondary education is financed generally by state and local governments, and higher education, which has a much greater percentage of private institutions, by state governments and private sources.

A close review of Table 5.9 shows that the Department of Education tends to target educational projects oriented toward low-income students, toward students with disabilities or who suffer from other disadvantages, and toward vocational training. Most of the contribution to higher education is in the form of direct need-based financial aid (about $7 billion in 1995) and in the subsidy cost of student loans for higher education (shown near the bottom of Table 5.9).

The dollar values shown for the latter category (student loan subsidies)—more than $3.5 billion in 1995—are not reliable figures. Unlike most figures shown in the budget, they are not cash outlays. The government is obliged under current law to subsidize some of the interest expense on most student loans and it must also cover the cost of loan defaults and collection costs.[14] Between $25 billion and $30 billion in loan commitments are expected to be made each year for the next few years under current legislation; about half of these will be subsidized. A budgetary account that authorizes loans (typically as entitlements) is called a **credit account;** the student loan programs are good examples of these. Budgetary outlays for credit accounts do not reflect cash disbursements entirely—they include subsidy cost estimates based upon, among other things, estimated loan default rates.

The Department of Education began phasing in their new direct loan program in 1994, supplementing an older loan program that relied upon

[13]Sources for nonfederal expenditures come from *Statistical Abstract of the United States, 1994*, Tables 223-227, published by the Department of Commerce, whose source for the data was largely the U.S. National Center for Educational Statistics, *Digest of Educational Statistics* and *Projections of Educational Statistics*.

[14]For example, a freshman entering college with financial need in 1995 was entitled to borrow $2625 on a subsidized Stafford Loan under the new direct loan program as long as the money is spent for educational expenses. The student would not need to begin payment on the loan until after graduation. While the student is in school and during any grace and deferment period interest payments on this loan are fully subsidized.

guaranteed loans from private lenders. This sudden program shift required an adjustment in the credit accounting for student loan subsidies, hence the strange and unreliable entry for 1994. The effective cost of student loan subsidies and related administrative expenses should be between $5 and $6 billion in during the next few years under current legislation.

At a time of moderate spending reduction elsewhere, the higher levels of spending shown for both the education, training, employment and social services budgetary function and the budget of the Department of Education show the priority given to such spending by President Bill Clinton. There were many assaults on some of these programs—especially on the one we discuss below, but the President used his veto power (and the threat of a veto) to preserve the programs and to even increase the funding on some of the more favored programs.

An Example of Federal Grants: The School-to-Work Opportunities Act of 1994

As was stated earlier, the budget of the Department of Education provides a good example of direct financial grants from the federal government to state and local governments. Under such programs, the federal government specifies an objective that can be met in part by federal funding. The programs are then managed and maintained at state and local operational levels. The federal government does little more than target an objective and set rules, limits, and procedures, and it pays for some, most, or all of the program through direct grants to state and local agencies. In the case of education grants, typically guidelines are established for soliciting grant requests and some funding is provided to pay for grant requests.

An example is provided by the School-to-Work Opportunities Act of 1994, promoted by the Clinton administration and passed in 1994 as HR 2884 by the 103rd Congress. This legislation authorized $300 million in expenditures for a new program in 1995 (reduced later in appropriations). The fiscal impact of this legislation, which involved outlays less than appropriations in 1995 (not an uncommon feature—appropriations can be carried forward into future years) is shown in Table 5.9 under the spending title "Education Reform." Here it is combined with another large program. As can be seen, spending in that category went from virtually nothing in 1994 to $61 million in 1994, and the Clinton administration desired to expand it to its full budget authority by spending $538 million in 1996.

To give a sense of what is involved in this legislation, Table 5.10 contains excerpts from the actual text of the legislation, including the language of

Table 5.10

Sample Excerpts from HR 2884, 103rd Congress
School-to-Work Opportunities Act of 1994

SEC.2. FINDINGS. Congress finds that—(1) three-fourths of high school students in the United States enter the work force without baccalaureate degrees, and many do not possess the academic and entry-level occupational skills necessary to succeed in the changing United States workplace; [followed by nine other findings]

SEC.3. PURPOSES AND CONGRESSIONAL INTENT. (a) Purposes: The purposes of this Act are—(5) to promote the formation of local partnerships that are dedicated to linking the worlds of school and work among postsecondary educational institutions, private and public employers, labor organizations, government, community-based organizations, parents, students, state educational agencies, local educational agencies, and training and human service agencies; [the fifth of 14 stated purposes]

SEC.102. SCHOOL-BASED LEARNING COMPONENT. The school-based learning component of a School-to-Work Opportunities program shall include— (4) a program of instruction and curriculum that integrates academic and vocational learning (including applied methodologies and team-teaching strategies), and incorporates instruction, to the extent practicable, in all aspects of an industry, appropriately tied to the career major of a participant; [the fourth of six components]

SEC.103. WORK-BASED LEARNING COMPONENT. (a) Mandatory activities: The work-based learning component of a School-to-Work Opportunities program shall include—(2) a planned program of job training and work experiences (including training related to preemployment and employment skills to be mastered at progressively higher levels) that are coordinated with learning in the school-based learning component described in Section 102 and are relevant to the career majors of students and lead to the award of skill certificates; [the second of five components]

SEC.605. AUTHORIZATION OF APPROPRIATIONS. (a) In General: There are authorized to be appropriated to the Secretaries to carry out this Act $300,000,000 for the fiscal year 1995 and such sums as may be necessary for each of the fiscal years 1996 through 1999.

Source: HR 2884 Enrolled, obtained via Internet Library of Congress Web server.

the authorization of appropriations (originally for $300 million), which appears at the bottom. This law is intended to elicit cooperative arrangements between schools and businesses for the purpose of training students for "high-skill, high-wage careers" as, essentially, an educational bridge program. HR 2884 solicits development grant applications (and offers up to $1 million in funding for each application), then it offers substantially more (an amount not specified by the legislation) to "local partnerships" (a formal school-to-work alliance of employers and educational agencies) to operate the bridge program.

The law is rather specific in its targets and is detailed in its proposal for implementation. It also has many restrictions; students enrolled in the program, for example, may not "displace any currently employed worker," nor may students be employed via the program unless they are "afforded adequate supervision by skilled adult workers" [SEC. 601]. The "block grants" that are sometimes proposed as alternatives to these highly restrictive grants would likely be less restrictive in both goals and program execution, allowing more latitude for program definition at the local level.

Because this law provides a good example of how programs are created, we will return to it in later chapters when we discuss authorizations and appropriations (or, in other words, future funding).

Funds Appropriated to the President

This final budget category is chosen for review not because of its fiscal importance but because of the curious mix of classifications that are found here. Generally, these are funds over which, in some cases (but not all) the President has some discretional authority for spending.

Table 5.11 show the general spending categories authorized under funds appropriated to the President, but these bland titles understate some of the more peculiar and telling features of the individual programs. As can be seen by the titles, the vast bulk of the roughly $11 billion authorized is spent for international programs as part of U.S. foreign policy. Most of it, though, is not really at the discretion of the current president, but instead is tied up by previous commitments. To illustrate this point, it is worth quoting directly from the budget where the text explains expenditures for International Security Assistance:

> Economic Support Fund—For necessary expenses to carry out the provisions of chapter 4 of part II, [$2,349,000,000 to remain available until September 30, 1996: *Provided,* that of the funds appropriated under this heading, not less than $1,200,000 shall be available only for Israel, . . . *Provided further,* that not less than $815,000,000 shall be available only for Egypt, . . . , with the understanding that Egypt will undertake significant economic reforms which are additional to those which were undertaken in previous fiscal years . . . *Provided further,* that it is the sense of Congress that the recommended levels of assistance for Egypt and Israel are based in

Table 5.11

Funds Appropriated to the President ($ millions)

	1995	1996est
Total funds appropriated	11,161	10,494
Federal drug control programs	31	86
International security assistance	4,951	5,025
International development assistance	5,297	5,065
Agency for International Development	3,248	2,901
Peace Corps	235	226
International monetary programs	−265	19
Military sales programs	1,811	184
Special assistance for Central America	26	3
Unanticipated needs	1	1

great measure upon their continued participation in the Camp David Accords and upon the Egyptian-Israeli peace treaty. . . .][15]

This passage demonstrates that peace—or more precisely, being the peacemaker, can come at a price. The Camp David Accords, a 1978 summit meeting of the leaders of Egypt and Israel sponsored by President Jimmy Carter, ended decades of war between these belligerents and it resulted in the Israel-Egypt Peace Treaty, signed in March 1979. Although the treaty resulted in a lasting peace, which is surely desirable, a provision of the treaty has cost the taxpayers of the United States, not a party to the war, billions of dollars every year, including the $2 billion spent in fiscal year 1996, some 17 years after the settlement.

Financing the 1995 Loan Bailout Package for Mexico

One of the more controversial budgetary matters of 1995 arose when the Mexican peso plunged in value and the Mexican financial markets collapsed not long after the completion of the North American Free Trade Agreement which liberalized continental trade in North America (the cause of the collapse, though, was not linked to NAFTA).

President Clinton first asked Congress for a multibillion loan package to help the beleaguered neighbor to the south (not an unusual request), but was spurned. Then in February 1995 the President unilaterally ex-

[15]*Budget of the U.S. Government, Appendix, FY 1996*, p. 64.

tended a $20 billion loan package without the sanction of Congress. He did not draw from funds appropriated to the President. Instead, he drew the lending authority from an obscure and little-used fund in the agency budget of the Department of the Treasury. The exchange stabilization fund, as it is called, has the following purpose:

> The Secretary of the Treasury is authorized to deal in gold and foreign exchange and other instruments of credit and securities as deemed necessary, consistent with U.S. obligations in the International Monetary Fund (IMF), regarding orderly exchange arrangements.[16]

In other words, this was a fund authorized to be used by the U.S. Treasury in foreign currency transactions in order to help stabilize exchange rates; presumably (though not explicitly stated by law) those that strongly impact the U.S. dollar. To use the fund's entire lending authority (the fund had a net equity position of slightly more than $19 billion in 1995) to redeem Mexican *Tesobonos* (bonds of the Mexican government) amounted to a generously imaginative interpretation of the fund's purpose.

On the other hand, the loan bailout seemed to work, and it certainly did help bolster Mexico's economy. Equally important, Mexico repaid the loan obligation in its entirety and ahead of schedule.

What's Next?

A discussion of the larger and more important programs, like Social Security, Medicare, and many of the entitlements programs, is still ahead, although not every federal program can be discussed in a book like this. For that reason, the reader interested in some of the smaller programs might now refer to Appendix D: Outlays by Function, Subfunction, and Major Program, which lists the outlays for 1995 and 1996 (estimated) for every federal program with outlays exceeding $100 million.

In the next chapter we begin to explore some of the more complex entitlement budgets—harder to explain but inherently more interesting and troublesome. We will look first at the concept of entitlements, then we will examine need-based (welfare) entitlements spending, and finally we will examine the largest and most endangered of them all: social security and the medical trust funds.

---

[16]*Budget of the United States Government, Appendix, FY 1996*, p. 784.

6

Entitlements, Social Security, and Medicare

I n 1993 *Nebraska Senator Bob Kerrey* introduced a new word to the popular American lexicon: **entitlements.** Concerned about the long-range trends emerging in such areas as Social Security and health care, Kerrey convinced President Clinton to form the Bipartisan Commission on Entitlements and Tax Reform, which eventually issued an alarming report warning that the growth of entitlements would impose an unbearable burden upon government and the economy. Among other things the commission concluded that by the year 2012, "projected outlays for entitlements and interest on the debt will consume all tax revenues collected by the federal government," and that by the year 2030 expenditures for Medicare, Medicaid, Social Security and federal employees' retirement would absorb all tax revenues and that federal spending would exceed 37% of GDP, as opposed to 22% in 1993.[1] The commis-

[1] The Bipartisan Commission on Entitlements and Tax Reform, "Interim Report to the President," obtained via the Internet at Web site http://www.charm.net/~dcarolco/.

sion made some rather casual assumptions in reaching these conclusions, but the general cause for concern, the projected growth of entitlements programs, is worrisome and is in need of eventual reform. As the report points out, "current trends are not sustainable."

This chapter surveys and discusses the need-based entitlements and the large entitlements programs, with particular emphasis on the three largest: Social Security, Medicare, and Medicaid. At issue is not only the present size and composition of these programs but trends in their growth, because they are driven by demographic forces over which we can exercise very little control. Because most of the large entitlements programs are operated as federal trust funds, Chapter 7 describes how these trust funds work, which we need to know before we are able to explore the long-range issues. These two chapters, therefore, should be seen as a unit.

Entitlements: What Are They?

Let us begin our exploration of this controversial topic by drawing a definition from the glossary (slightly modified):

> **entitlements:** Spending, typically in the form of a benefit payment, mandated by federal law that extends benefits to those who qualify under the provisions of law. Most entitlements payments go to individuals, but some also go to corporations or to state and local governments. Entitlements programs include Social Security, Medicare, Medicaid, federal pensions, federal need-based public assistance (welfare) of all forms, and agricultural subsidies. Entitlements payments are legal obligations of the U.S. government. The only way an entitlement can be changed or the fiscal requirements altered is by amending the authorizing legislation that extends the benefit.

In other words, an entitlement begins with authorizing legislation that determines qualifications and identifies the benefits that are to be extended to those who meet the qualifications. For example, the Medicare program, discussed in more detail later in this chapter, was created as part of President Lyndon Johnson's Great Society Program authorized in 1965 under Title XVIII of the Social Security Act. The program offers a full range of medical benefits to people who qualify for Social Security. Medicare expenditures were equal to nearly $160 billion in 1995.

Entitlements are controversial for two reasons: they now comprise the majority of federal expenditures, and they are growing very rapidly, and are projected to continue growing at an alarming rate for generations to come.

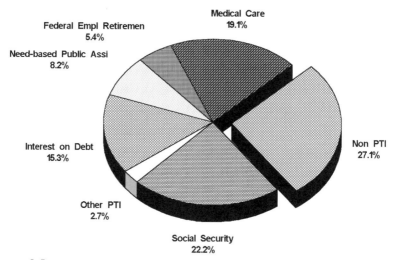

Figure 6.1
The Government as Check Writer, Payments to Individuals (PTI), FY 1995

The Government as Check Writer

The author William Greider once wrote that "the most important function of the federal government is mailing checks to citizens."[2] By that he meant Social Security checks, pension, welfare, and veterans' checks, checks to hospitals and doctors for medical care, and checks sent for a host of other reasons.

When Greider wrote that in 1981, such disbursements equaled 48% of federal outlays. That figure is now 58%. See Figure 6.1, where the major entitlements categories are shown as a percentage of total federal outlays. Interest on the federal debt technically is not an entitlement, but of course interest payments are merely another form of check writing, and when that is included in the tally, more than 72% of federal spending is in the form of direct or indirect payments to individuals!

Table 6.1 breaks down the payments more completely and it shows their amounts for fiscal year 1995. As can be seen, some of the payments are disbursed indirectly in the form of grants to state and local governments,

[2]Greider's comment is from an article he wrote about David Stockman, director of the Office of Management and Budget in the Reagan administration, "The Education of David Stockman," *The Atlantic Monthly*, December 1981, p. 33. This article provides an excellent overview of how the budget got out of control in the early years of the Reagan administration. Stockman was a zealous promoter of the balanced budget but was effectively steamrolled by the political process.

Table 6.1

The Government as Check Writer:
Payments to Individuals (PTI) FY1995, ($ billions)

Category	St & lo gov grants	Direct	Subtotal	Total
Social Security				337.0
Social Security OASI		292.7	292.7	
Social Security Disability		40.3	40.3	
Railroad retirement		4.0	4.0	
Medical Care				289.7
Medicare Hospital (A)		113.6	113.6	
Medicare Supplementary (B)		63.5	63.5	
Medicaid	89.0		89.0	
Veterans care	0.3	16.3	16.6	
Other	3.9	3.1	7.0	
Federal Employee Retirement				82.2
Civil Service		38.3	38.3	
Military		27.8	27.8	
Veterans service-connected		14.8	14.8	
Other		1.3	1.3	
Public Assistance				61.8
Supplemental Security Income		23.6	23.6	
Family support payments	17.1		17.1	
Earned income tax credit		15.2	15.2	
Veterans non-service-connected		3.0	3.0	
Low income home energy	1.4		1.4	
Other	1.0	0.4	1.4	
Food, Nutrition & Housing				63.0
Housing	17.2	8.3	25.5	
Food Stamp Program	2.7	22.8	25.6	
Child Nutrition & Milk Program	7.4	0.1	7.5	
Supplemental Feeding	3.4		3.4	
Other	1.0		1.0	
Unemployment compensation		21.9		21.9
Student assistance	0.1	14.7		14.8
All other	1.3	2.9		4.2
Total Payments:	145.8	728.6		874.6
Memo:				
Total PTI as % of total outlays				57.6%
Net Interest Payments (NIP)				232.2
Total PTI plus Net Interest				1,106.8
Total PTI & NIP as % total out				72.9%

Source: Budget of the U.S. Government, FY1996, Historical Tables, Table 11.3.

typically in some kind of funds-matching arrangement. For example, Medicaid, the government's need-based medical plan, uses a funds-matching arrangement with participating states (in California, for example, the state's component of the plan is called MediCal), with Medicaid paying about 60% (on average—the percentage varies widely from state to state) of total costs. The total of all such payments equaled $875 billion in 1995, and when interest payments are included the sum substantially exceeds $1 trillion. All of the programs included in Table 6.1 are entitlements.

The growth rates of some of the larger programs are discussed later in the chapter when we look at long-term issues, but we can anticipate them by noting that the medical programs are projected to grow at ranges approaching double digits each year. Not only are the programs, large but under present legislation they are destined to get much larger.

Large Need-Based Entitlements Programs

The entitlements programs that benefit individuals can be roughly grouped into the following categories: (1) retirement benefits (Social Security, Railroad Retirement, and federal pensions; (2) medical (Medicare and Medicaid); (3) unemployment; (4) and need-based entitlements. Table 6.2 summarizes the features of the large need-based entitlements programs (except for Medicaid)—programs that people generally think of as welfare programs.

Most need-based welfare programs in the United States are administered and partially paid for at the state and local level. Federal agencies nonetheless perform three very important roles: 1.They finance most of the costs of these programs (when Medicaid, which is need-based, and smaller entitlements programs not shown in Table 6.2, such as those for student financial aid, are added to the tally, federal expenditures for need-based entitlements exceed $200 billion), funding about 65% of total public-aid costs; 2. Much more important, federal legislation often *creates* the programs, and state and local governments are encouraged or even required to participate; 3. State and local government participation is typically required under terms, conditions, eligibility requirements or mandates that are to some degree controlled by a federal agency. This condition has for years bred some resentment at the state level because federal control is often seen as inflexible or excessively bureaucratic. As can be seen in the table, state participation in these programs, including partial funding, is pervasive.

In recent years the states have agitated for considerably less federal control or restrictions, and they have appealed to Washington, with limited success, to transform more of these programs into direct block grants. These have the effect of passing federal money directly to the states with fewer strings attached (in other words, with fewer direct demands on how the money is to be spent). As will be described in the next section and in Appendix G, the Aid to Families with Dependent Children (AFDC) was converted to a block grant program in the summer of 1996.

Related to the issue of grants and block grants, state governments (typically through their governors) in recent years have insisted that the federal government create fewer **unfunded mandates,** which are programs mandated by federal law to be applied at the state or local level, but without federal funding or with only partial federal funding. In response, in 1995 Congress passed a law curbing unfunded mandates, but the effectiveness of the law remains to be seen.[3]

It is clear that the large federal programs are oriented toward nutrition assistance, housing subsidies, energy subsidies, and programs to help children or the disabled. Interestingly, aside from the earned income credit on federal taxes, there is no direct federal payment to families or to individuals of direct poor relief (a cash payment made simply by virtue of low income), except for payments to families (including single parents) with children. The earned income credit on taxes allows families (not individuals) with some earned income reported on IRS Form 1040 to earn a tax credit if the income reported is less than $24,396 (in 1995) for a family with two or more children. At very low incomes a tax "refund" in excess of withholdings can be earned. This is the closest equivalent to federal direct poor relief.

The absolute levels of expenditures on these programs are large, but they are a relatively small part of the overall budget picture. The combined programs shown in Table 6.2 have outlays equaling less than a third of either Social Security or defense, and are less than half of net interest paid each year. Had the programs not even existed in 1995, the budget deficit still would have been $50 billion.

---

[3]Like many of the laws passed in 1995 and 1996, the law restricting unfunded mandates was tall on political enthusiasm and short on content. Even the Welfare Reform Act passed only one year later, discussed on p. 114 and in Appendix G, seemed to include many unfunded mandates. There will be many gray areas in the interpretation of unfunded mandates, and the 1995 law will not likely make the issue go away.

Table 6.2

Large Need-Based Entitlements Programs (Excluding Medical)

Program (name, depmt, bud func)	Originating legislation & state participation	Beneficiaries & eligibility	General benefits	Program cost (1995)
Supplemental Security Income (SSI); Health & Human Services; 609	1935 Social Security Act, present program established in 1972 with creation of SSI program; states supplement the program.	Blind, disabled, or aged with income below $5,352 per year (Jan. 1994). Disability qualifications almost the same as Social Security.	Direct cash payment; maximum federal single $458, married joint $687 (1994), average $354 (1994).	$26.488 billion
Aid to Families with Dependent Children (AFDC)—discontinued in 1996, replaced with Temporary Assistance for Needy Families (TANF) program; 609	AFDC: 1935 Social Security Act, TANF: Welfare Reform Act of 1996 (see text).	Families with dependent children, eligibility set by states with some federal guidelines. See text.	Cash assistance, under TANF federal contribution to state capped by block grant. Average family payments vary by state.	$17.133 billion (AFDC program)
Food Stamps; Department of Agriculture; 605	Food Stamp Act of 1964; all states required to participate, though U.S. government covers full cost of program.	Households with gross income below 130% of poverty guidelines and net income (after mandated deductions) below 100% of poverty guidelines.	Food stamps redeemable for food where food is sold; average benefit in FY 1994 was $69.	$25.6 billion
National School Lunch and State Child Nutrition programs; Department of Agriculture; 605	1946 National School Lunch Act, 1966 Child Nutrition Act; subsidy for participating state programs.	Reduced-price subsidy scale beginning for family incomes below 185% of poverty guidelines to free meals if below 130% of same.	Direct cash payments to participating schools.	$7.499 billion

Table 6.2 *(continued)*

Program (name, depmt, bud func)	Originating legislation & state participation	Beneficiaries & eligibility	General benefits	Program cost (1995)
Supplemental Food Program for Women, Infants, and Children (WIC); Department of Agriculture; 605	1966 Child Nutrition Act; grants made to states that in turn pass funds to qualifying health and welfare agencies.	Pregnant and postpartum women and children up to 5 years, diagnosed as having nutritional disorder, income up to 185% of poverty level.	Vouchers or checks allowing purchase of nutritious food at participating retail grocery stores. Average monthly benefit worth about $30.17 in FY 1992.	$3.404 billion
HUD Public Housing Agency (PHA) and Indian Housing Agency (IHA) low-rent public housing projects; Section 9 subsidized public housing and Section 8 rental assistance; Housing and Urban Development; 604	1937 Housing Act; plans often administered locally.	Typically, families with income no more than 50% of area median.	Section 9 public housing built by HUD, rental charges subsidized. Section 8 homes rented from qualified private sources. Rent restricted to specified percentage of income, remainder subsidized.	$27.524 billion
Low-Income Home Energy Assistance Program (LIHEAP); Health and Human Services; 609	1981 Omnibus Reconciliation Act; grants to states, administered by states, payments made by states.	Households with income under highest of 150% of poverty guidelines or 60% of state median income.	Cash, vouchers, coupons, or prepaid bills paid directly to household or energy supplier.	$1.419 billion

Notes: The primary source for this information was "Social Security Programs in the United States," *Social Security Bulletin*, Winter 1993, Vol. 56, No. 4, and *Annual Statistical Supplement 1995*, to the *Social Security Bulletin*. Other sources were *Budget of the United States Government Fiscal Year 1996, Appendix, Analytic Perspectives, and Historical*

On the other hand, the need-based programs show remarkable resiliency. Most have been around for decades. They come under scrutiny every few years and they are trimmed here and there (some were attacked with great fanfare in the early Reagan years), but the core programs prevail with surprisingly little alteration, with the salient exception of the old AFDC program, an entitlement program that provided cash relief to the poorest families with children. That program was substantially modified in 1996, and is discussed in the next section.

The programs that fall under the jurisdiction of the Department of Agriculture, which include the nutrition programs and the huge Food Stamp program, are very stubbornly protected by the extremely powerful and politically complicated agriculture coalition (for lack of a better word) in Congress. Representatives of rural areas and farm states and districts, Democrats and Republicans alike, are as protective of these programs (many of which do have the indirect effect of subsidizing agriculture) as they are of direct farm programs. Future reform in these areas will likely consist of curbing program growth rates (in other words, slowing them down) rather than substantially reducing or eliminating programs. Of course, merely curbing program growth can have a beneficial budgetary impact over many years, so long as the discipline is maintained. It is for these reasons that the substantial welfare reform of 1996 left these programs relatively unaffected.

Changes Made by the Welfare Reform Act of 1996

The 104th Congress made some substantial changes to one of the larger welfare programs, the old Aid for Families with Dependent Children (AFDC) by passage of the Welfare Reform Act of 1996 (also called by the sponsors the Personal Responsibility and Work Opportunity Reconciliation Act). Although the bill, HR 3734, was signed into law by a reluctant President Bill Clinton (it probably would not have been signed after the presidential election) it did not have true bipartisan support. It was largely a Republican law, although did have some support among Democrats, who split on the issue.

The law made very substantial changes to some components of the federal welfare system, while leaving others relatively unchanged. To understand what was and what was not changed, it is useful to categorize the federal welfare programs for the poor that existed prior to the reform. These can be divided roughly into five categories (refer back to Table 6.2 for more specifics and funding levels for these programs):

1. the Supplemental Security Income (SSI) program that provides benefits for the blind, disabled, and aged who are not covered by Social Security programs;

2. the various nutrition programs, mostly under the jurisdiction of the Department of Agriculture (see Table 5.3), such as the Food Stamp, National School Lunch, and Supplemental Food Program for Women, Infants and Children (WIC);

3. the Medicaid program, described later;

4. subsidy and public assistance programs for housing and energy,

5. and the old cash support program for impoverished families with children, the program of Aid to Families with Dependent Children (AFDC), which was authorized with Social Security in 1935 and has been operating ever since as a matching grant program administered by the states. The old AFDC program was a true entitlements program, but unlike Social Security and Medicare, the necessary qualifications and level of benefits offered was determined in part at the state level and varied considerably from state to state. In fiscal year 1993, for example, average monthly family cash benefits ranged from $121 in Mississippi to $751 in Alaska. The federal component of program costs in fiscal year 1995 equalled $17.1 billion.

With one very salient exception descibed below, almost all of the major change affects the old AFDC program, which was eliminated and replaced with a new Temporary Assistance for Needy Familes (TANF) program. TANF is still a cash assistance program administered by the states, so in that respect it is similar to the AFDC program that it replaced. Here are the three primary changes made to AFDC/TANF by the 1996 law:

1. The old AFDC program was an entitlements program, but the new TANF program is not, at least at the federal level. The TANF program is a block grant program subject to annual appropriations and a budgetary cap.

2. TANF benefits are discontinued after 60 months of benefits have been extended to any family (the 60 month allowance need not be continuous).

3. Adult parents and guardians of dependent children who qualify for TANF benefits must find work after receiving benefits for 24 months.

In addition to the replacement of the AFDC program with the TANF program, the law also denied Supplemental Security Income and Food

Stamp benefits to *legal* alien immigrants (generally all benefits were denied to illegal aliens), and it restricted some others.

Because of the desire to avoid a confrontation with President Clinton and possibly a veto, Medicaid and other medical benefits for the poor were largely unaffected by the law. They await special treatment through medical reform, if that happens.

The Welfare Reform Act of 1996 was complex and there are many small features that we have not discussed and there are many qualifications and exceptions to those issues that were discussed. More important, the actual impact of the law upon those affected is very controversial and deserves some treatment. For that reason, the law is described and discussed in much more detail in Appendix G.

Social Security[4]

The Social Security program, created in the heart of the Great Depression and a true American institution, has been described by some as the "crown jewel" of federal government programs. Certainly no program is more far-reaching. More than 43 million people receive Social Security benefits of one kind or another, and more than 140 million pay taxes into the program. An overview of the system is provided in Table 6.3.

The original legislation created the retirement program, now called Old Age Survivors Insurance (OASI), and the original federal unemployment program, a joint cooperative arrangement with state governments that is now separate from Social Security. In 1956 Disability Insurance (DI) was added to the program, and the combined program is now called the Old Age Survivors and Disability Insurance (OASDI) program.

Social Security is clearly an important element of the unified budget. We saw in Table 4.2a that the Social Security budgetary function, with outlays of $335.8 billion, or 22% of the total, is now the largest function, having passed defense in 1992. Because system administrative costs come to less than 1% of outlays for the OASI retirement plan (a remarkably efficient system) and to less than 3% for disability insurance, the vast bulk of this

[4]Much of the information here comes from various editions of the quarterly *Social Security Bulletin* and the *Annual Statistical Supplement,* published by the Social Security Administration. The actuarial status of the Social Security and medical trust funds are reviewed every year in the *Social Security Bulletin.* An especially detailed summary of the various social insurance programs, including Social Security OASI and Disability Insurance, Medicare, Medicaid, and Supplemental Security Income is found in Volume 56, No. 4, Winter 1993, of the *Social Security Bulletin* and in *The Annual Statistical Supplement, 1995, to the Social Security Bulletin.*

Table 6.3

The Social Security System at a Glance

Statistics (1995)

Total beneficiaries . . . . 43.4 million
Total retired workers . . . . 26.7 million
Total retired workers, spouses, children. . . . . 30.1 million
Disabled workers. . . . . 4.1 million
Disabled workers, spouses, children . . . . 5.8 million
Total who pay OASDI taxes . . . . 140.9 million
Ratio of taxpayers to beneficiaries. . . . . 3.25 to 1
Average monthly benefits, retired $700
Average monthly benefits, disabled $663
Employee/employer tax rate (each) 6.2%
Maximum cap 1996 (no tax above this income) $62,700
Total tax at cap $7,774.80

Major milestones

August 14, 1935	Social Security Act signed by F.D. Roosevelt, creating the retirement and unemployment insurance programs.
1937	First social security taxes paid.
1939	Benefits extended to spouses and children.
1940	First monthly benefits paid.
1956	Disability insurance program created.
1972	A one-time 20% benefit increase enacted by Nixon administration (in an election year), thereafter, benefits indexed to inflation.
1983	Because of fears of insolvency of fund, tax increases accelerated and some benefits became taxable.

Sources: Social Security Bulletin, Winter 1995, The 1996 Annual Report of the Board of Trustees of the Federal Old-Age and Survivors Insurance and the Federal Disability Insurance Trust Funds, 1996 Annual Report, and various historical sources cited elsewhere in the text.

cost was for benefit payments to the 43 million recipients of the program. Taxes received from nonfederal employers and employees totaled $351 billion, so on net, the system brought in $15.3 billion more than it paid out in fiscal year 1995. The system ran an external surplus of that size.

OASDI (the combined program for retirement and disability) is funded from the FICA payroll tax of 6.2% of gross income (the remainder of the 7.65% is for Medicare), and this amount is matched by the employer. The taxable amount is capped ($62,700 in 1996—the payroll tax is not levied for income above this amount). Of the 6.2%, 5.26% is dedicated to the retirement account (OASI) and 0.94% goes to the disability account (DI).

The Social Security System is essentially a funds in–funds out system that runs a small surplus. The expression "funds in–funds out" means that payment obligations in any given year are met by receipts in the same year. From the standpoint of the taxpayer, this means that taxes paid into the system in any given year are generally used to finance disbursements in that same year. Social Security is *not* a sinking-fund system, where payments are invested or in some way set aside to earn interest until needed. This implies that the *funding requirements of the system through the years must generally be met with tax receipts from those same years.* This qualification will not really change even when we take into account the Social Security Trust Funds.

Most of the controversy surrounding Social Security, including the viability of the system in the next century, involves long-range issues and therefore requires a discussion of the status of the trust funds. We will return to Social Security in the next chapter.

Health Care

Health care in the United States continues to move on and off the primary crisis agenda in American politics. Given the stature of projections for future program requirements, it is certain to be the frequent topic of debate for years to come. Social Security financing may become the crisis of Generation X (as we will see) but the health-care financing crisis is taking place here and now. Resolution may be ahead but so far it has proceeded in jerks and starts. President Bill Clinton's banner program proposal for the 103rd Congress was radical health-care reform, promoted aggressively and relentlessly, only to sputter to nothing when it became apparent that the few congressional supporters originally enlisted by the President were balking at the risk of such potentially dangerous radical reform.[5] There was no element of the plan that was not strongly

[5]The Clinton health plan was projected to cost about $400 billion by the year 2000; this would have been offset partly by costs in the private sector. As it stands in the 1996 budget, Medicare, Medicaid, and other health costs are projected under *current* legislation to be about the same amount, although changes made in the future *might* reduce that total. A quick review of the original health proposal can be found in "Reforming the Nation's Health Care System to Provide Health Security for All Americans," *Budget of the United States Government, Fiscal Year 1995*, Chapter 4, or "Health Care Reform," *Economic Report of the President, February 1994*, Chapter 4.

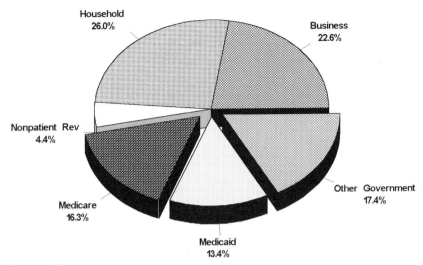

Figure 6.2
Health-Care Financing, 1991

opposed by some large constituency. The early 1990s will probably for-ever be remembered as the age of angry voter discontent. Cool-headed reform, which may have been possible in another era, was not even a re-mote possibility in the 103rd Congress. And because the problem was not resolved it resurfaced in the form of proposed changes to Medicare and Medicaid in the Republican-dominated 104th Congress; these also stalled very quickly.

Health care in the United States is extremely expensive and it absorbs a disproportionate share of our national production when compared to that of other industrialized countries. Figure 6.2 shows how we funded the $751.8 billion spent on health care in 1991, or $2868 per person. This is 13.4 percent of GDP, which is by far the highest percentage in the world, as shown in Figure 6.3. Health care *inflation* reached alarming proportions in the 1980s, averaging 8.1% compounded each year. This was the highest average for any major category in the Consumer Price Index and it was much higher than the average for all items, which was 4.7% over the same period. Fortunately, in the last five years because of the emphasis on managed care at least the *inflation* rate is slowing down to more tolerable levels.

The debate continues to rage about the *quality* of health care in the United States, but there is little to debate on one issue—it is expensive.

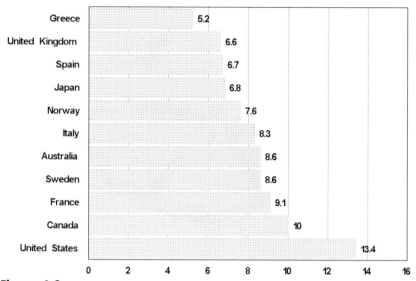

Figure 6.3
Health-Care Expenditures as a Percentage of GDP, Select Countries, 1991

And given that the federal government is the major player in this arena, it will be expensive at the federal level as well, and until the Social Security crisis comes along in about 20 years, health-care expenditures will continue to be the problematic area of concern in the federal budget.

Federal expenditures for health care can be classified in three general categories, two of which are summarized in Table 6.4:

1. Medicare, the inclusive health-care program for retired people, costing $160 billion in 1995;

2. Medicaid, the need-based health-care program of grants to state and local health care providers, costing $89 billion;

3. all other federal health programs, including research and development (such as the budget for the Centers for Disease Control and Prevention), and medical programs for federal employees, defense personnel and veterans, totaling to an estimated $26 billion in fiscal year 1995.

These three categories sum to the impressive figure of $275 billion. More important, under current entitlements laws, these figures, as large as they are, are slated to grow at nearly double-digit ranges past the year 2000, making them the fastest growing components of the budget. The

Table 6.4

Medicare and Medicaid at a Glance

Medicare

Originating legislation . . . . 1965 Title XVIII of the Social Security Act
Administrative agency . . . . Health and Human Services (func 571)
Primary beneficiaries . . . . Recipients of Social Security benefits
Number of beneficiaries . . . . . . Approximately 36.5 million
State & local involvement. . . . . Virtually none
Financing . . . . 1.45% payroll tax, employer and employee (2.9% total), for Hospital Insurance; small monthly premium ($42.50 in 1996) for Supplementary Medical Insurance (SMI); the rest from general revenues.
Projected annual growth rates
 to year 2002 . . . . 9.35% annually
Program outlays (1995) . . . . . . $159.9 billion

Medicaid

Originating legislation . . . . 1965 Title XIX of the Social Security Act
Administrative agency . . . . Health and Human Services (func 551)
Primary beneficiaries . . . . Recipients of Temporary Aid for Needy Families (TANF) and Supplemental Security Income (SSI)
Number of beneficiaries . . . . . . Approximately 35 million (1994)
State & local involvement. . . . . . Medicaid is a funds-matching grant program administered by states; states fund between 17% and 50% of total costs
Financing . . . . General revenues (at federal level)
Projected annual growth rates
 to year 2002 . . . . 9%
Program outlays (1995) . . . . . . $89.1 billion

Sources (for statistics): 1996 Annual Report of The Board of Trustees of the Federal Hospital Insurance Trust Fund, 1996 Annual Report of the Board of Trustees of the Federal Old-Age and Survivors Insurance and Disability Insurance Trust Funds, Annual Statistical Supplement, 1995, to the Social Security Bulletin.

sum total for the three in fiscal year 2002 is projected at more than $430 billion under current legislation (meaning if current law is not changed). The new millennium may usher in an era of promise, but the health-care component will carry a hefty price tag.

Medicare

Contrary to popular belief, the United States has socialized medicine, but only for that segment of the population that is retired and earns Social Security benefits. Social Security OASI recipients are eligible for Medicare, the government's comprehensive health-care program. Created in 1965 as part of President Lyndon Johnson's Great Society program, Medicare and its companion program, Medicaid, created at the same time, have loomed to huge proportions and they dominate the government role in health care. The generous benefits provided by the Medicare program is shown in two parts in Table 6.5.[6] Medicare is divided into Part A, Hospital Insurance, which as the name implies, covers hospitalization, and Part B, Medical Insurance, also called Supplementary Medical Insurance (SMI), which covers visits to the doctor and the other services listed. As can be seen coverage is exhaustive and deductibles are low—open heart surgery, possibly costing more than $80,000 in a state like California, would likely cost the Medicare patient less than $1,000.[7] Virtually all kinds of health care are covered, except for one conspicuous exception—nursing home care for the infirm elderly. This *is* covered in Medicaid as we will see later, but only if the patient is poor (although, of course, one of the fastest ways to become poor is to require extensive, long-term nursing care).

And what does the program cost the beneficiary? Aside from the Medicare taxes deducted from our paychecks, which entitle us to benefit from the system upon retirement (again, generally, one is entitled to Medicare if also entitled to Social Security OASI benefits), there are no premiums at all for Part A coverage, and premiums of only $42.50 per month for Part B (although visits to the doctor include a $100 deductible per year). This premium is supposed to increase slightly each year, but it was actually reduced in 1996, a presidential election year, from $46.10 the previous year.

The popularity of Medicare and the 37 million votes that go along with that popularity are easy to understand. Many of the current beneficiaries of Medicare grew up in the Great Depression, and are acutely fearful of poverty and ill health in their retirement years, and they dread the

[6]The information presented in both parts of Table 6.5 and in much of the rest of the material included here is taken from *Your Medicare Handbook 1996*, Health Care Financing Administration Publication 10050, April 1996.
[7]This example was based upon the recent experience of an individual known to the author.

thought that the one will lead to the other. Most have worked industriously through their lives (otherwise they would not qualify) and in an age that many see as indolent, they feel, perhaps rightly so, that they deserve the peace of mind that comes from secure health care.

Therefore, any effort to tamper with Medicare benefits, or to raise deductibles or the monthly premium, is politically hazardous, to say the least. On the other hand, the retired population, inherently conservative and interested in deficit reduction, has been more sensitive in recent years to appeals for protecting the long-range health of these programs. This group might show more willingness through the 1990s to contribute some share of the sacrifice.

Regardless, the focus of the debate may not revolve around whether any reform program is actuarially sound, but may instead focus on emotive and ethical issues that reach across many generations.

Medicare Financing

Medicare is partly financed by a tax earmarked for the purpose (approximately 55% of outlays), by the premiums paid for Plan B (15%), and by general revenues (30%). The special tax dedicated to Medicare (technically, to the Plan A Hospital Fund only) is, of course, the 1.45% component of the 7.65% FICA payroll tax (the rest is for OASDI—Social Security). But unlike the Social Security component of the FICA tax which in 1996 was capped at an income level of $62,700, the Medicare tax is not capped. Present beneficiaries of Medicare benefits believe that they are entitled to the generous benefits of the program because they paid these taxes prior to retirement (but only since 1965, and at lower rates than presently, of course) and they pay a small premium presently for Plan B Supplementary Medical Insurance coverage.

Medicare Reform

Medicare becomes a serious budgetary problem if, given present benefits, the earmarked tax and the small premium cover less and less of the cost of the program over time. This is certain to happen if there are no changes in the program. Medicare financing is presently deemed to be in trouble. As will be explained in the next chapter, the Hospital Insurance Trust Fund, which is responsible for funding the Medicare Part A benefits shown earlier in Table 6.5, is expected to have all trust fund reserves depleted as early as the year 2001 under current program assumptions. Because the program cannot continue its operations if the trust fund is

Table 6.5a

Medicare Part A Benefits: 1996

Services	Benefit	Medicare pays	Patient pays
Hospitalization Semiprivate room and board, general nursing and other hospital services and supplies.	First 60 days	All but $736	$736
	61st to 90th day	All but $184 a day	$184 a day
	91st to 150th day	All but $368 a day	$368 a day
	Beyond 150 days	Nothing	All costs
Skilled nursing facility care Semiprivate room and board, skilled nursing and rehabilitative services and other services and supplies.	First 20 days	100% approved amt.	Nothing
	Additional 80 days	All but $92 a day	Up to $92 a day
	Beyond 100 days	Nothing	All costs
Home Health Care Part-time or intermittent skilled care, home health aide services, durable medical equipment and supplies and other services.	Unlimited as long as patient meets Medicare conditions.	100% of approved amount; 80% of approved amount for durable medical equipment.	Nothing for services; 20% of approved amount for durable medical equipment.
Hospice Care Pain relief, symptom management and support services for the terminally ill.	For as long as doctor certifies need.	All but limited costs for outpatient drugs & inpatient respite care.	Limited costs for outpatient drugs and inpatient respite care.
Blood When furnished by a hospital or skilled nursing facility during a covered stay.	Unlimited if medically necessary.	All but first 3 pints per calendar year.	For first 3 pints.

1995 Part A Medicare Premium: Ordinarily (if qualified for Social Security or equivalent), none.

Source: This is a slight modification of a table of the same title in Your Medical Handbook 1996, published by the Health Care Financing Administration of the Department of Health and Human Services. There are some qualifications on benefits and premiums discussed in that document. This table above should not be consulted for actual Medicare benefits, since it is not being provided for that purpose.

Table 6.5b

Medicare Part B Benefits: 1996

Services	Benefit	Medicare pays	Patient pays
Medical Expenses Doctor's services, inpatient and outpatient medical and surgical services and supplies, physical and speech therapy, diagnostics tests, durable medical equipment and other services.	Unlimited if medically necessary.	80% of approved amount (after $100 deductible).	$100 deductible, plus 20% of approved amount and limited charges above approved amount.
Clinical laboratory services Blood tests, urinalysis, and more.	Unlimited if medically necessary.	Generally 100% of approved amount.	Nothing for services.
Home health care Part-time or intermittent skilled care, home health aide services, durable medical equipment and supplies and other services.	Unlimited as long as Medicare conditions are met.	100% of approved amount; 80% of approved amount for durable equipment.	Nothing for services; 20% of approved amount for durable medical equipment.
Outpatient hospital treatment Services for the diagnosis or treatment of illness or injury	Unlimited if medically necessary.	Medicare payment to hospital based on hospital cost.	20% of billed amount (after $100 deductible).
Blood	Unlimited if medically necessary.	80% of approved amount (after $100 deductible and starting with 4th pint).	First 3 pints plus 20% of approved amount for additional pints (after $100 deductible).

1995 Part B Medicare Monthly Premium: $42.50

Source: This is a slight modification of a table of the same title in Your Medical Handbook 1996, published by the Health Care Financing Administration of the Department of Health and Human Services. There are some qualifications on benefits and premiums discussed in that document. This table above should not be consulted for actual Medicare benefits, since it is not being provided for that purpose.

depleted, this program will require a major overhaul before the turn of the century.

The combative 104th Congress began a review of Medicare, but efforts at significant reform stalled completely as the 1996 presidential elections approached—the topic was just too controversial and politically dangerous to explore in an important election year. Leading up to the election in November 1996, reform efforts were as moribund as the original 1993 Clinton health-care reform initiative.

For the leery politician a strong precedent for the dangers of tampering with Medicare has already been established. Congress in 1988 passed the Medicare Catastrophic Coverage Act, which appeared to most to be a veiled attempt to raise Medicare premiums. It did provide a new benefit, protection from "catastrophic medical bills" in Part A. Given that Part A covers hospital stays up to 150 days, the new coverage extended benefits beyond that. But it came at a cost—a new monthly premium on Part A. After the legislation was signed into law by President Reagan, it met with a firestorm of opposition from organized voting groups. When Congress returned in 1989 with a new President (George Bush) their hottest priority was to pass the Medicare Catastrophic Coverage Repeal Act of 1989, which overturned all reforms of the 1988 legislation and returned everything to the status quo.

Legislators are not likely to forget that in the 1994 election 62.2% of white eligible voters above age 65 voted, compared to 44.7% for all voters. Only 34% of the age group 18–44 bothered to go to the polls. No legislator can afford to be cavalier about issues affecting the elderly.[8]

Medicare reform is clearly a political minefield. It might be worth considering the following statement of beneficiary rights from the 1996 Medicare Handbook to see why:

Fee for Service or Managed Care?

One important decision you may have to make is how you will receive your Medicare hospital and medical benefits. . . . You can receive your Medicare benefits either through a fee-for-service system or through a managed care plan such as a Health Maintenance Organization (HMO).

If you choose fee-for-service, you can go to almost any doctor, hospital or other health care provider you want to. Generally a fee is charged each time a service is used. Medicare pays its share of the bill. You are responsible for paying the balance.

In managed care, you usually get all of your care from the doctors, hospitals, and other health care providers that are part of the plan, except in emer-

---

[8]Voting statistics are easily obtained from the U.S. Census Bureau Internet Web site at http://www.census.gov/.

gencies. Depending on the plan, you may have to pay a monthly premium and a copayment each time you go to the doctor or use other services.[9]

The fee-for-service option is, of course, the patient's dream, the doctor's delight, and the accountant's nightmare. No matter how spurious or grave the illness, there is no obstacle to office visits, medical tests, examinations, and medical procedures. And although caps are put on what is charged for the services provided, there are very few constraints on trying to bring patients into offices as frequently as possible. Unfortunately (from the standpoint of program cost control), in 1996 only about 10% of Medicare beneficiaries were using the managed care option.

Although many issues will arise in the continuing debate over Medicare, the seemingly innocuous menu of fee-for-service versus health maintenance organizations (or managed care in general) will be the focal point. In that debate, a terrible (from the politician's point of view) dilemma arises. Medicare costs cannot be brought under control, and the system itself may not be able to survive unless a strong majority of beneficiaries is convinced or is forced to switch from fee-for-service to managed care. Present evidence seems to indicate that fee-for-service is strongly preferred by a majority of Medicare recipients, and any political effort to force them into managed care would not bode well for the politicians involved. This is the primary reason why the issue was entirely dormant in the summer leading up to the 1996 elections.

Medicaid

The federal Medicaid program provides medical coverage to low-income beneficiaries, although it does so on a very selective basis.[10] Because Medicaid, unlike Medicare, is partially state-funded and generally administered at the state level, eligibility requirements vary from state to state (a person who is eligible in one state may not be in another). The program is primarily oriented toward needy children and their mothers, pregnant women, and the disabled. Generally, program benefits are extended to families who are eligible for the old Aid for Families with Dependent Children (AFDC) program (now called the Temporary Assistance for Needy Families (TANF) program), which consists mostly of low-income single mothers with children, and to the disabled or elderly

[9]*Your Medicare Handbook, 1996,* Health Care Financing Administration, p. 5.

[10]Most of the information on Medicaid is taken from the *Social Security Bulletin,* Vol. 56, No. 4, Winter 1993, and from the *Annual Statistical Supplement, 1995, to the Social Security Bulletin.*

recipients of Supplemental Security Income (SSI). Eligibility requirements have been loosened in recent years to allow marginal exceptions; families and individuals who fail to qualify for these other programs but who come close to qualifying are sometimes eligible for Medicaid.

Like other need-based programs, Medicaid is conspicuous for whom it omits. Single individuals, unless disabled, are not entitled to Medicaid benefits, but more importantly, neither are the medical facilities that treat them. The cost of trauma care at some inner-city hospitals, which frequently involves young, single men who are the victims of everything from auto accidents to gunshot wounds, forces the hospitals that bear these costs to rely upon state and local sources or private charity for their funding (or by overcharging private insurers as compensation—apparently a common practice in the 1980s, but less tolerated presently). As a result the federal provision of health benefits ranges from extremely generous for the elderly to adequate for needy mothers and their children, to nothing at all for angry young men from the inner cities. But then angry young men do not vote.

Unlike Medicare, which is entirely a federal program in both its funding and its administration, Medicaid is a state funds-matching program, requiring the active participation of state governments for partial funding and administration. States must pay no less than 17% and no more than 50% of total program costs that are generated by the requirements of the Medicaid program. The federal average of costs absorbed in 1994 was 57.7%.

One area of Medicaid coverage that is growing in expense is likely to become more controversial in the 1990s. As mentioned earlier, the old-age health-care program, Medicare, does not cover the cost of long-term nursing-home care. Medicaid does offer such coverage—nationally, 45% of such fees are paid for by Medicaid—but only after the beneficiary has exhausted all wealth and most income. In other words, Medicaid will pay the fees of someone on Medicare after that person has become indigent because of the inability to meet high nursing home costs. In fact, since 1993 states are required to recover from the estates of the deceased any of the costs of nursing homes or related long-term coverage provided by Medicaid. Given that nearly 5% of those over age 65 and 22% of those over age 85 are in nursing homes presently,[11] this might become a contentious issue if substantial cutbacks in Medicaid are proposed.

---

[11] "Trends in the Health of Older Americans: United States, 1994" *Vital and Health Statistics,* Centers for Disease Control and Prevention, Publication # 95-1414, April 1995. Anyone who wonders why elderly Americans are concerned about their health care should consult this publication.

Aside from the financial contribution made by the states, the Medicaid program, like most federal programs is financed through general revenues. There is no Medicaid trust fund. The federal component of Medicaid cost $89 billion in 1995. The same program cost $14 billion in 1980, and only $2.7 billion in 1970. Partly because of the growing costs of care in nursing homes, Medicaid is projected to continue to grow at about 9% per year for the rest of the century (assuming there is no change in entitlements). At this pace, combined federal and state spending on Medicaid programs would exceed $230 billion by the year 2000. That is an unacceptable number in an era of responsible budget management and deficit reduction. Like Medicare, Medicaid must undergo a substantial revision.

Medicaid Reform

Medicaid reform, if it happens, will most likely be tied to welfare reform. Alhough they did not get very far, proposals sponsored by the Republicans in the 104th Congress emphasized making Medicaid into a huge block-grant program, using a formula to turn over to each of the 50 states a given amount of money to use at their discretion for their individual need-based medical programs. This would remove the program's entitlement status at the federal level, although entitlements would likely be preserved at the state level. Such an approach is very attractive when the goal is outlay and deficit reduction. Block-grant budgets are very easy to control by simply appropriating each year the amount of money needed for spending and the passing on that amount to the states. If the goal is to cut outlay growth rates from 9% projected to 3% actual, it is very easy to do with block grants. Simply pass the appropriations laws and inform the states that they will receive 3% increases in their grants each year.

There is, of course, one clear drawback to this approach. It gives the federal government substantial budgetary control over medical spending for the poor while removing entirely any accountability or responsibility for the consequences of the cutbacks. None of the hard decisions will be made at the federal level—no services will be denied at the federal level, decisions to close hospitals or reduce trauma care will not be made at the federal level, so national politicians will be held less accountable for such decisions. Instead, the financial and political burden will be foisted on the state governments, potentially provoking crisis after crisis at that level.

In summary, blocks grants are an excellent solution if the goals are strictly budgetary, but they become problematic if the ultimate concern instead is to provide suitable and humane health care to the indigent at reasonable cost. And as was the case with Medicare, the concerns of the elderly, especially with respect to the funding of long-term nursing-home care, are likely to strongly influence the tone of the debate.

What's Next?

Our discussion of Social Security and Medicare is incomplete. The real controversies surrounding both of these programs concern their financial integrity going into the twenty-first century. The financing of these programs is the ultimate issue. Given the present status of the programs, their costs are destined ultimately to rise above revenues, depleting trust fund reserves and jeopardizing the financial integrity of the overall budget.

Social Security, Medicare, and many other federal programs are financially managed as trust funds. Therefore to understand the long-range financial issues, the peculiar and complicated rules that govern federal trust-fund financing must be probed. The next chapter, which should be seen as a continuation of this chapter, will begin with a discussion of trust-fund financing, using the Aviation Trust Fund as a simple example. Once the essentials of trust-fund financing are covered, we will explore the more detailed accounting of the four major trust funds that comprise the Social Security and Medicare systems. That will finally enable us to explore some of the more controversial (and disturbing) twenty-first century issues.

Trust Funds and the Emerging Issues of the Twenty-First Century

From the previous chapter we know that presently both the Social Security and the Medicare programs extend benefits to around 40 million people and are therefore immensely popular and important. Yet the media in recent years have entertained us with dark and gloomy forecasts about the financial viability of these programs as we approach the twenty-first century. The Social Security retirement program is sometimes described as virtually doomed and eventually bankrupt, and Medicare is characterized as hopelessly under-funded.

Are the modern-day critics of these huge programs being unnecessarily alarmist? Is there any merit to their dark and depressing prophesies?

Unfortunately, the answer to the second question is yes. Social Security and Medicare may work reasonably well right now, but for reasons to be explored in this chapter, the funding of these systems becomes increasingly problematic as the years go by.

The Social Security and Medicare systems, or at least their financial aspect, are represented on the books as four large trust funds. Therefore, to understand their financial status, we must begin by exploring the arcane world of federal trust funds.

Trust Funds: What Are They?

A **trust fund,** represented schematically by Figure 7.1, is very little more than an accounting procedure used by the federal government. It is a series of bookkeeping entries that keeps a tally of funds available for some designated purpose. Incoming receipts that are intended for the trust fund are credited to the account and outlays are deducted. If the account runs a surplus over the fiscal year—if receipts exceed outlays, the fund's balance grows by the amount of the difference. If the account runs a deficit where outlays exceed receipts, then the fund's balance drops by the amount of the deficit. It works exactly like a checkbook, except it is more like a checkbook within a checkbook, where funds are being moved around internally to some extent.

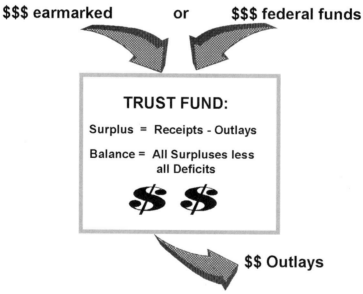

Figure 7.1
Federal Trust Funds

Table 7.1

The Aviation Trust Fund
FY1995 ($ millions)

ID 20-8103-0-7-402		Rec & out	Balance
Starting balance			12,386
Receipts			
Ticket tax	+	4,768	
Waybill tax	+	361	
Fuel tax	+	211	
International departure tax	+	233	
Interest earned	+	757	
Other receipts	+	33	
Total receipts	+	6,363	
Outlays			
Trust fund share FAA operations	–	2,546	
Grants-in-aid for airports	–	1,826	
Facilities and equipment (net)	–	2,572	
Other outlays	–	440	
Total outlays	–	7,384	
Net change	–	1,021	<1,021>
Ending balance			11,365

Source: Budget of the U.S. Government, FY 1997, Appendix, p. 747.

The Aviation Trust Fund and the Federal Civilian Employees Retirement Trust Funds

The best way to see how a trust fund works is by example. Table 7.1 shows the fiscal year 1995 status of a relatively simple trust fund, the Aviation Trust Fund which is found in the budget of the Department of Transportation. (This trust fund is not an entitlements trust fund.) This fund began the fiscal year with a balance of $12.4 billion, and ended the year with $1 billion less. Receipts for this fund mostly came from special taxes earmarked for the fund, including nearly $4.8 billion in ticket taxes on airline travel. Some outlays by this fund were included in general outlays by the Federal Aviation Administration, which was seen in Table 5.7. Because outlays exceeded receipts, producing a deficit within the fund of almost exactly $1 billion, the fund's balance declined by that amount during the fiscal year.

As a note of interest, this fund's strength was substantially weakened in fiscal year 1996. Many of the taxes shown in Table 7.1, including the

Table 7.2

Federal Civilian Employees Retirement Funds FY 1995 ($ billions)

		Rec & out	Balance
Starting balance			346.4
Receipts—federal funds			
Transfer from other agencies	+	33.6	
Interest earned from Treasury	+	28.7	
Receipts—other	+	4.5	
Total receipts	+	66.8	
Total outlays	–	38.9	
Net change (surplus)	+	27.9	27.9
Ending balance			374.3

Source: Budget of the U.S. Government, FY 1997, Analytic Perspectives, p. 264. This is a composite of more than one trust fund.

ticket tax, expired on December 31, 1995, and were supposed to be renewed. But because of the legislative gridlock at the time (this was the period when the government was being shut down every few weeks) this did not happen, so the trust fund was slated to lose somewhere between $3 and $4 billion in revenues, severely reducing its balance.

The aviation trust fund is an example of a fund that earns its receipts by special taxes earmarked for the fund. The Social Security Trust Fund also works this way, as we will see later. Most federal trust funds, though, gain their receipts from funds merely transferred from other federal accounts. All funds in federal budgets are classified either as trust funds or as federal funds[1] (essentially, all outlays that are not from trust funds are classified as "federal funds"). Therefore, to be precise, many trust funds gain their receipts in the form of federal funds transferred as a bookkeeping entry from some other federal account.

A good example of the latter is the Federal Civilian Employees Retirement Fund, summarized in Table 7.2, which had a balance of $346.4 billion at the beginning of fiscal year 1995. Of this fund's $66.8 billion in receipts in 1995, almost all were in the form of federal funds transferred from other government accounts. Each federal agency is required to transfer federal funds to this retirement account trust fund as a provision

[1]This budgetary term has no connection whatsoever to the benchmark interest rate called the "federal funds rate" targeted by the Federal Reserve System. The terms are coincidental.

Table 7.3

U.S. Public Debt
Total Interest-Bearing Debt of the U.S. Government as of December 1995 ($ billions)

Instrument	Maturity	Interest category	Amount
Marketable debt			3,307.2
U.S. Treasury Bills	13, 26, 52 week	Discount	760.7
U.S. Treasury Notes	1–10 years	Coupon	2,010.3
U.S. Treasury Bonds	10 + years	Coupon	521.2
Non-marketable debt			1,657.2
U.S. government accounts			1,299.6
Foreign governments			40.8
U.S. Savings Bonds			181.9
Other			134.9
Total debt			4,964.4

Source: Treasury Bulletin, March 1996.

for the eventual retirement of civilian employees employed by that agency. These payments are included in the totals for outlays by that agency. That this fund has a $374 billion balance does *not* mean that this amount of cash is set aside or is available to fund future retirement liabilities—not even close.[2]

Trust Funds and Nonmarketable Treasury Debt

In both the aviation trust fund and the retirement trust fund there are two rather large entries for "interest earned," in the former case contributing $757 million dollars to the fund's receipts and in the latter about 40% of the total. This is evidence of yet another complication of trust-fund financing: federal trust funds hold their balances in the form of yield-bearing Nonmarketable U.S. Treasury Debt. To explain this, a summary of the U.S. public debt shown in Chapter 1 as Table 1.3 is reproduced here as Table 7.3 (it has exactly the same information). In Chapter 1 we explained that the debt category labeled U.S. government accounts

[2]The aggregation of most of these federal funds transferred to the retirement accounts shows up in the unified budget under the large negative entry labeled *undistributed offsetting receipts*, which was discussed in Chapter 4 (see also the definition of the term in the glossary).

(equal to approximately $1.3 trillion in December 1995) was technically debt of the U.S. Treasury to government trust funds. Therefore, the aviation and retirement trust funds—their approximate balances—and all other trust funds constitute this category of treasury debt. The aviation fund owns about $11 billion of it, for example (some tiny amount of a trust fund's balance is typically in some other form), and earns interest on those securities.

Again, though, it must be stressed that this is merely an internal bookkeeping convention used by the federal government. Because the U.S. Treasury is the fiscal agent for all branches of the federal government, the federal government is, in effect, issuing debt and paying interest to itself. For each financial asset created, a matching liability is generated. The accounting entity called the trust fund gains the asset and the U.S. Treasury gains the offsetting liability. On *net,* there is no change in the fiscal stature of the government as a whole. In the use of this accounting convention, the government is neither richer nor poorer, more indebted nor less, *nor more able to nor less able to* meet future funding commitments for programs linked to trust funds.

The payment of interest into these trust fund accounts is also an arbitrary accounting convention. These interest payments, typically classified as federal funds, are *not* included in the amounts for net interest in the unified budget, nor should they be. Interest payments to trust funds such as the aviation fund alter the surplus or deficit generated by the fund (reducing the deficit or increasing the surplus). A surplus is funded by the bookkeeping transfer to the fund of yet more nonmarketable U.S. Treasury securities.

A Summary of Trust Fund Financing

Because this relationship is sometimes hard to understand (and to explain) the points made above will be summarized:

1. A federal trust fund is like a checkbook: if receipts exceed outlays, the balance in the fund will grow by the amount of the difference; if outlays exceed receipts, the balance in the trust fund will decline by the difference;

2. In some trust funds, most receipts come from taxes earmarked for the trust fund, whereas in other trust funds most or all receipts come from federal funds transferred as outlays from elsewhere in the federal budget or simply from general Treasury revenues;

3. When a trust fund runs a surplus, the U.S. Treasury issues to the trust fund nonmarketable interest-bearing securities equal to the amount of the surplus, such that over the years the trust fund's balance consists of these securities. Interest paid on these securities becomes part of a trust fund's receipts;

4. When a trust fund runs a deficit, total securities held on the books by the trust fund are reduced by the amount of the deficit;

5. Although this point has not been demonstrated, it will be shown later when we look at the financing of the Social Security Trust Fund. We will see that when a trust fund using earmarked taxes for receipts runs a surplus, *the overall deficit of the unified budget is reduced by the amount of this trust fund's surplus.* This important feature of trust fund financing will be explored in detail later in the chapter.

The accounting convention for trust funds used by the federal government is somewhat arbitrary, but to recognize that does not necessarily invite criticism of the procedure. Corporations use internal accounts and budgets to help estimate the true costs of the many programs that might be administered by the corporation. For example, a corporation might have a large internal equipment maintenance fund to smooth out the infrequent but high costs of large-scale equipment failure, or they might have a fund that reflects future pension obligations. Nor would it be unheard of for one of the funds to pay interest as a bookkeeping entry to another, especially if the funds transferred were a true loan from one agency to another (possibly made to avoid borrowing from an external source and having to pay actual interest to the outside lender). In the case of federal procedures, to require an agency like the Department of Defense to reflect funding for future military retirement is a sound good accounting practice, because to fail to do so would understate the true cost of defense.

The real problem arises not in the fact that the trust funds are managed this way, but rather in the interpretation, and especially in the interpretation provided in political debates that describes what these funds actually *are*!

Again, as stated above, these funds do not represent the means for the U.S. Treasury nor for anyone else to fund future obligations of the federal government. They represent internal debts of one agency of government to another, and all federal programs *on net* must be funded ultimately from *external* sources through either taxes or through borrowing from the private sector. In no sense are they like money set aside by an individual into a family of mutual funds. The balances in the trust funds (and the nonmarketable debt that represents those balances) cannot be *raided* or used by the Treasury for other purposes, such as to balance the budget. The nonmarketable debt that makes up the trust funds is, by definition, a *liability* of the U.S. Treasury, the fiscal arm of the government, and the Treasury can no more raid its own liabilities than the owner of a credit card can "raid" the balance due and payable to the bank on the credit card bill.

Trust-fund financing, though, does have one very important implication for the program the trust fund represents: under current law a trust-fund balance guarantees *long-range financing for the program.* This is because federal law (with some exceptions, as always) limits allowable spending by a trust fund *to the amount of receipts collected by the trust fund* over the years. Therefore, if receipts in the early years of a program vastly exceed outlays, as is the case for the Social Security Trust Funds and for the federal retirement trust funds, and those trust funds grow even more with interest earned over the years, the upper limit on the amount the program can spend is stretched into the distant future. Receipts (from any source) realized in 1996, if not used in 1996, can be turned into nonmarketable Treasury securities earning interest and can be used in 2024, or in any other year. This is *not* the case for programs funded out of federal funds.

There is a contrary feature of this trust-fund financing arrangement as well: if the trust fund's balances are depleted, spending by the program financed by the trust fund is no longer allowable. There is no automatic provision that would continue a depleted program with financing taken from federal funds.

The issue of trust funds is complicated and easily misunderstood. It is difficult to discuss entitlements without understanding them, because most of the largest entitlements accounts are trust funds. (There are some significant exceptions, including the huge Medicaid need-based medical program discussed in the previous chapter, which is not operated as a trust fund.)

Now that the groundwork has been laid, it is appropriate to look at the trust funds for the two largest entitlements programs, Social Security and Medicare.

The Social Security and Medicare Trust Funds

College students graduating in 1997 will begin paying, as soon as they find work, 7.65% of their earned income into three federal trust funds, and their employers will make a matching contribution. These students will be expected to make at least this contribution, and possibly more, throughout the 45 years or so they are employed. One of these trust funds, the Medicare Hospital Insurance Trust Fund, ran a deficit for the first time in 1995 and is expected to run out of funds in the year 2003. Another, the Social Security *Disability* Trust Fund had been running deficits for years and saw its reserves nearly exhausted in 1994, provoking an immediate crisis and a dubious solution, which is described below. But the largest share of taxes goes to the third, the Social Security *Retirement* Trust Fund, currently running a small surplus that contributes to a large fund balance at this time. For these college students the present-day status of this fund is not very important. What for them matters is the condition of the fund around the year 2040. Unfortunately, the outlook is not good. By current projections the retirement fund will begin running a deficit around the year 2018, and the fund's reserves are expected to be exhausted in the year 2031, about the time these students turn 55.

In other words, young people today are paying very high taxes into trust funds that are projected by reliable actuarial standards to be hopelessly bankrupt by the time these same contributors are eligible to receive their benefits. And the dire projections are not being made by polemicists or zealous politicians hell-bent on wrecking the system—they are being made by the actual trustees of the systems, the Boards of Trustees for the Social Security and Medicare Trust Funds. Their projections and warnings are published every year in the *Social Security Bulletin* and in their annual reports.[3]

The Social Security Trust Funds (OASI and DI)

To understand these doomsday predictions we have to look at the present status of the funds. Table 7.4 shows the two Social Security Trust funds. The two Medicare Trust Funds will be shown in the next section.

The 7.65% (employer and employee) payroll tax, called the FICA (Federal Insurance Contribution Act) tax or SECA (Self-Employed Contribution Act) tax (if one is self-employed and pays the immensely unpopular

---

[3]The titles of the most recent annual reports of the trustees of the large trust funds are: *1996 Annual Report of the Board of Trustees of the Federal Old-Age and Survivors Insurance and the Disability Insurance Trust Fund* (hereafter *OASDI Trustees' Report*), *1996 Annual Report of the Board of Trustees of the Federal Hospital Insurance Trust Fund* (hereafter *HI Trustees' Report*); and *1996 Annual Report of the Board of Trustees of the Federal Supplementary Medical Insurance Trust Fund* (hereafter *SMI Trustees' Report*).

Table 7.4
The Social Security Trust Funds Funds Status, FY 1995 ($ millions)

Federal Old Age and Survivors Insurance Trust Fund (OASI)

ID 20-8006-0-7-651	Rec & out	Totals	Balance
Starting Balance			416,335
Receipts			
FICA taxes	272,848		
SECA taxes	16,815		
Income tax on benefits	5,115		
Interest earned	31,417		
Other	2,127		
TOTAL RECEIPTS		328,322	
Outgo			
Benefits	288,624		
Administrative costs	1,798		
Other	6,289		
TOTAL OUTGO		296,711	
SURPLUS	31,611	31,611	
Memo:			
Surplus less interest	194		
Ending Balance			447,946

Status: The trust fund is running a small surplus presently, is expected to go to deficit around FY 2018, and is expected to be exhausted around FY 2031.

Federal Disability Insurance Trust Fund (DI)

ID 20-8006-0-7-651	Rec & out	Totals	Balance
Starting Balance			6,370
Receipts			
FICA taxes	64,339		
SECA taxes	3,580		
Income tax on benefits	335		
Interest earned	1,888		
Other (incl. refunds)	73		
TOTAL RECEIPTS		70,215	
Outgo			
Benefits	40,201		
Administrative costs	1,070		
Other	109		
TOTAL OUTGO		41,380	
SURPLUS		28,835	28,835
Memo:			
Deficit less interest		26,947	
Ending balance		32,205	

Status: This trust fund was running a deficit in 1994. Some receipts from the FICA tax were transferred to OASI to ensure solvency, but this will now exhaust OASI Trust Fund earlier than was projected two years ago. Expected to be exhausted around FY 2015.

Notes: FICA taxes are ordinary payroll taxes. SECA are payroll taxes for the self-employed.
Sources: Budget of the United States Government, FY 1997, Appendix, and 1996 Annual Report of the Trustees of the Federal OASI DI Trust Funds. Data are not identical from these sources because Appendix uses fiscal year, trustees use calendar year.

15.3% tax), is broken into three parts and allocated to three of these four trust funds: 5.26% to OASI (the retirement fund), 0.94% to DI (the disability fund), and 1.45% to HI (the Plan A Hospital Insurance Trust Fund of Medicare, shown in the next section).[4]

The huge OASI Trust Fund, with a balance of almost $448 billion at the beginning of fiscal year 1996, is *presently* the healthiest of the funds. The fund pulled in receipts of $328 billion in fiscal year 1995, of which $290 billion were the tax receipts described above. Given outlays, mostly for benefits (program administration costs are remarkably low—not much of this elusive "government waste" to be found here), the fund ran a surplus of about $32 billion.

As described earlier in this chapter, the balance in these funds is held in the form of interest-bearing, nonmarketable U.S. Treasury securities issued by the Treasury as the funds balances grow (if running a surplus; deficits are financed by, in effect, cashing them in). The importance of the interest earned on these balances can be seen in the OASI Trust Fund—it contributed $31.4 billion in revenues, nearly equal to the surplus. This surplus can have the effect of *reducing* the deficit of the overall unified budget. Again, this is essentially a "funds in–funds out" system that self-finances each year, and when dedicated tax receipts exceed outlays for a trust fund like this, the excess cash goes to U.S. Treasury balances and is disbursed for other purposes, reducing the net *external* borrowing needs of the Treasury. Technically, the Treasury has borrowed funds (the surplus) from the OASI Trust Funds, used them for something like defense or justice, and has shown evidence of that borrowing by issuing nonmarketable securities to the trust fund and thereafter paying interest on them. However, the deficit of the unified budget and hence net external borrowing needs are reduced by *only the surplus less interest earned,* just $194 million in the case of the OASI Trust Fund, and *not* by the full amount of the surplus. Interest earned is not a receipt from outside the government, so it does nothing to reduce the external deficit. When the surplus-less-interest total of the Disability Insurance Trust Fund shown in the bottom half of Table 7.4 is added, the total net surplus of the two funds equals $27.1 billion, so the external deficit is reduced by about this amount.

In summary, the Treasury issues nonmarketable debt to these two trust funds equal to the size of their surpluses ($60.4 billion in our example),

---

[4]The OASDI allocations will change slightly in FY 1997, to 5.35% OASI and 0.85% DI, which will cause the OASI Trust Fund to run a larger surplus and the DI Trust Fund to run a smaller surplus.

and the deficit of the unified budget and hence external borrowing needs are reduced by the size of the surplus *less interest earned* (about $27.1 billion).[5]

The 1994 Solution to the Crisis in the Disability Trust Fund

According to the 1993 trustees report for the Social Security and Medicare Trust Funds, the DI (disability) Trust Fund was "projected to be exhausted in about 2 years" (in 1995), a warning that was repeated in the 1994 report. The 1993 report also projected that the OASI Retirement Trust Fund would "be able to pay benefits for about 50 years."

In contrast, in the *1996 Trustees' DI Report,* a year after the disability fund was supposed to be depleted, instead of being broke the disability fund was projected to run surpluses well past the turn of the century with fund balances remaining positive until 2015.

On the other hand, in the *1996 Trustee's OASI Report,* the retirement trust fund had more than a decade shaved off of its life. Whereas in the 1993 report it was expected to last another 50 years, in the 1996 report it was projected to have funds exhausted in the year 2031, for a remaining lifetime of 35 years.

Where did the lost years go?

The answer is summarized in Table 7.5, and is explained by a law entitled Public Law 103-387, passed with remarkably little fanfare on October 22, 1994, a few days before the end of the legislative session and just prior to the midterm election. Given the public's concern over the health of the Social Security Trust Fund, to the extent that the fund has ever been "raided" (to borrow a term from the emotional debates over the balanced budget amendment that were to follow six months later), it was raided by this legislation.

Prior to this fix, the Disability Insurance Trust Fund was in dire straits, with funds projected to be exhausted by 1995. With the exhaustion of the fund's balances there would have been no legal means for the fund to continue to meet its obligations. As was explained earlier trust fund spending is normally capped by the receipts of the fund (including interest earned), with spending authority carried over by the fund's balance.

---

[5]This is a *97% definition:* for complicated reasons that are not discussed here and mostly concern inter-agency transfers, the amount of deficit reduction would be a little different than this figure. Additionally, what has been said above does *not* apply to those trust funds, like federal employee retirement funds, that draw their receipts internally from federal funds. Their impact is deficit neutral.

Table 7.5

The 1994 Fix to the DI Trust Fund
Public Law 103-387
October 22, 1994

	1993	1995
FICA allocation (%)		
HI (hospital)	1.45	1.45
DI (disability)	0.60	0.94
OASI (retirement)	5.60	5.26
Total	7.65	7.65
Exhaustion of OASI trust		
fund predicted in	2043	2031
Exhaustion of DI trust		
fund predicted in	1995	2015

Note: Rates shown are employee only. Employer makes matching contribution.

Sources: The Boards of Trustees of the Social Security and Medicare Trust Funds Annual Reports, 1993, 1995, 1996, Public Law 103-387.

When the balance disappears, normally so does the spending authority unless special legislation allows this to be circumvented.

As Table 7.5 makes clear, the fix, recommended in the 1994 trustees' report, was easy. Of the 6.2% (employee portion) payroll tax, the allocation between OASI and DI was changed: OASI was reduced from 5.60% to 5.26%, and DI increased from 0.60% to 0.94%. The change in allocation was made retroactive to January 1, 1994. The problem was solved overnight—the Disability Insurance Trust Fund gained 20 years of life. Of course, it all came at a cost. Billions of dollars each year that previously were earmarked for the retirement fund are permanently lost, shortening the projected life of the fund by more than a decade. This change also impacted substantially the surplus of the OASI Retirement Trust Fund. As seen in Table 7.4, this trust fund had a fiscal year 1995 surplus of $31.6 billion, about equal to the interest paid into the trust fund by the Treasury. In fiscal year 1994, the same fund generated a surplus of $60.7 billion, more than double the interest income for the same year. This is the primary reason that the trust fund is now projected to be depleted much earlier than predicted in the 1993 forecasts.

In summary, this "solution" has had three important effects: 1. it caused a more rapid depletion of the OASI retirement fund; 2. it rendered unnecessary a thorough review of a program known to be abused, mismanaged, and faced with spiraling costs, and 3. the public did not notice.

Emotional public debates in the following spring about how future legislation might "raid" the Social Security fund (to reduce the deficit or to balance the budget) sounded rather hollow after Public Law 103-387. One would hope that future financial reform will provoke solutions that are a little more courageous than this.

The Medicare Trust Funds

The status of the two Medicare Trust Funds are shown in Table 7.6. The Hospital Insurance (HI) trust fund (Plan A of Medicare, as described in Table 6.5) is funded primarily from the 1.45% FICA/SECA payroll tax, plus some premiums paid by those who only marginally qualify for the program. Under federal law income taxes paid on OASI benefits must be dedicated in the budget to the OASI, DI, and the Hospital Insurance Trust Funds as program receipts, so that when combined with interest earned on the fund's nonmarketable securities they constitute most of the rest of the receipts.

This fund is in terrible shape. The fund suffered a deficit in fiscal year 1995, and full depletion of the fund is expected in the year 2003. The 1996 HI Trustee's Report declared that the fund "remains severely out of financial balance," and that the "long-range outlook also remains extremely unfavorable." Given the data presented by the trustees, the last comment would have to be regarded as remarkably upbeat given the actual fiscal data they present on the condition of the fund, which is close to hopeless. In fact, to overcome the long-range imbalance, they point out that the current 2.90% payroll tax (counting employer's contributions) would have to be *immediately* increased to 7.42%. This, of course, is not even an option in the political sense.[6]

The same report more cheerfully describes the Supplementary Medical Insurance (SMI) Trust Fund (Plan B of Table 6.5) as sound, but only because this one is mostly financed by transfers from federal funds rather than earmarked revenue sources, unlike the OASI, DI, and HI trust funds. Additionally, these subsidies from federal funds (that is, transfers from general Treasury receipts) ". . . are established annually at a level sufficient to cover the following year's expenditures."[7] Although the trust

---

[6]These quotations and tax estimates are from the *FY 1996 HI Trustees' Report*, pp. 14 and 15.

[7]*FY1996 SMI Trustees' Report*, p. 9. Data on the decline of the premium ratio are from Figure I.E2.

Table 7.6

The Medicare Trust Funds Funds Status, FY 1995 ($ millions)

Federal Hospital Insurance Trust Fund (HI)

ID 20-8005-0-7-571	Rec & out	Totals	Balance
Starting balance			129,555
Receipts			
FICA & SECA taxes	98,054		
Income tax on OASI	3,913		
Premiums	998		
Interest earned	10,833		
Other	1,049		
Total receipts		114,847	
Outgo			
Benefits	113,402		
Administrative costs	1,246		
Other	235		
Total outgo		114,883	
Deficit		36	<36>
Memo:			
Deficit less interest		−10,869	
Ending balance			129,518

Status: This trust fund ran a deficit for first time in 1995. The fund is expected to be exhausted in 2003, severely out of balance thereafter.

Federal Supplementary Medical Insurance Trust Fund (SMI)

ID 20-8004-0-7-571	Rec & out	Totals	Balance
Starting balance			20,919
Receipts			
Premiums collected	19,243		
Fed funds transferred	36,988		
Interest earned	1,935		
Other	1,938		
Total Receipts		58,169	
Outgo			
Benefits paid	63,482		
Administrative costs	1,704		
Other	27		
Total outgo		65,213	
Deficit		7,044	7,044
Memo:			
Deficit less interest		−8,979	
Ending balance			13,874

Status: The trust fund is running a large deficit, but because it receives most receipts from federal funds and is financed year by year, it is not considered endangered. On the other hand, federal funds transfers will have to grow substantially over the years.

Sources: "Actuarial Status of the Social Security and Medicare Programs," Social Security Bulletin, Vol. 57, No. 1, Spring 1994, and Budget of the United States Government, FY 1997, Appendix.

fund is technically sound, the program's growth at about 10% annually is unsustainable, with most of the growth financed by general tax revenues. In the first 7 years of SMI's operation (after 1967), premiums equaled half of expenses. This balance is declining rapidly. Of the fund's $58 billion in receipts, only one-third came from the monthly SMI premium ($42.50 in 1996) paid by the elderly. In yet another alarming projection, the trustees warned that without a sizeable increase in premiums and assuming no change in coverage, premiums will cover less than 10% of outlays by the year 2020. Despite such warnings, the premium was actually *reduced* in 1996, an election year, from $46.10 to $42.50.

In summary, these large trust funds and the programs they represent, amounting to about $520 billion in outlays yearly, do not have a very strong net impact on the present deficit or on the issue of immediate deficit reduction. As a group, they clearly help the situation somewhat. Because of the large surplus of the Disability Insurance Trust Fund, their net effect is to reduce the deficit. Together they ran in 1995 a gross surplus of $53.8 billion and a net surplus (less interest earned) of about $17 billion. Given the relatively small size of the net surplus, deficit reduction is not really helped much by these programs (far less than public debates on the matter would lead one to believe), but they are more or less paying their way as a group on a cash basis. Here is the problem: they will not do this for much longer and, more important, projections show the programs gravely underfinanced in a generation or so. Down the road a decade or two, we may face a crisis of profound proportions. Its earliest manifestation is with us now, mostly in the form of the projected insolvency and then the quick fix of the Disability Insurance Trust Fund and the emerging deficit in the Hospital Insurance Trust Fund.

Long-Term Issues

The Social Security retirement and medical programs are threatened partly because they pay fairly generous benefits, at least from an accounting or an actuarial perspective, given the lifelong contributions made to these programs by the present beneficiaries, especially in the case of health care. Medicare is financed largely by a substantial intergenerational subsidy.

Contributions made for the Social Security retirement program by those now retired were relatively low up until the 1980s, as is made apparent by Table 7.7, which shows tax rates, earnings caps, and average and maximum contributions for selected years. Even in the early 1980s, the average wage earner was contributing less than $1500 per year

Table 7.7

Schedule of FICA Tax Rates for Social Security and Medicare Select Years: Employees Rate and Employers Matching Contribution

Year	Total FICA	TRUST FUNDS			Earnings cap (OASDI only)	Average annual wage	Average OASI contribution
		OASI	DI	HI			
1937	1.00	1.00			$ 3,000		
1950	1.50	1.50			3,000	2,715	81
1960	3.00	2.75	0.25		4,800	4,007	220
1970	4.80	3.65	0.55	0.60	7,800	6,186	452
1980	6.13	4.52	0.56	1.05	25,900	12,513	1,131
1981	6.65	4.70	0.65	1.30	29,700	13,773	1,295
1982	6.70	4.575	0.825	1.30	32,400	14,531	1,330
1983	6.70	4.775	0.625	1.30	35,700	15,239	1,455
1984	7.00	5.20	0.50	1.30	37,800	16,135	1,678
1985	7.05	5.20	0.50	1.35	39,600	16,823	1,750
1986	7.15	5.20	0.50	1.45	42,000	17,322	1,801
1987	7.15	5.20	0.50	1.45	43,800	18,427	1,916
1988	7.51	5.53	0.53	1.45	45,000	19,334	2,138
1989	7.51	5.53	0.53	1.45	48,000	20,099	2,223
1990	7.65	5.60	0.60	1.45	51,300	21,028	2,355
1991	7.65	5.60	0.60	1.45	53,400	21,812	2,443
1992	7.65	5.60	0.60	1.45	55,500	22,935	2,569
1993	7.65	5.60	0.60	1.45	57,600	23,133	2,591
1994	7.65	5.26	0.94	1.45	60,600		
1995	7.65	5.26	0.94	1.45	61,200		
1996	7.65	5.26	0.94	1.45	62,700		
1997	7.65	5.35	0.85	1.45	Higher		

Notes: (1) Self-employment taxes (SECA) are generally double rates listed for FICA.

(2) For FICA, each rate shown is the employees only; the employer makes a matching contribution.

(3) There is no earnings cap on the HI tax for either employer or employee, though there was between 1963 and 1993 (not shown). The cap in 1993 was $135,000.

(4) The annual average contribution is to OASI only (excludes DI and HI) and includes the employer's contribution; calculated by the product of double the OASI rate times average annual wage.

(5) OASI, DI, and HI taxes are all earmarked receipts for the trust funds of the same names.

Sources: Table 2.A3, Social Security Bulletin, Annual Statistical Supplement, 1994, Table 1, Factors for Indexed Earnings, Social Security Bulletin, Vol. 58, No. 1, Spring 1995, Board of Trustees of the Social Security and Medicare Trust Funds 1995 Annual Report and author's estimates.

(counting the employers matching contribution) to the fund. A person retiring in 1996 after 45 years of service earning the average wage would have contributed about $45,000 over a lifetime of work. Nonetheless, given the life expectancy of slightly more than 17 years for a person just turning 65, and given the current average monthly benefit for a retired person of $700 per month, the Social Security retirement system (OASI) is paying the rough equivalent of a 5.5% worklife annuity. In other words, if this person who retires in 1996 had placed an amount equal to Social Security contributions (including employers' portions) into a bank account or an investment fund paying slightly less than 5.5% annually, compounded over the last 45 years, the annuity today based upon remaining life expectancy and presuming this same yield would pay out a monthly pension that is roughly equal to the present average benefit paid by OASI for retired workers. Given that this payout will rise with inflation over the next 17 years, the true annuity value of such a "contract" would be very close to 5.5%. This number, of course, falls slightly each year as the program matures.

A survey article published in the *Social Security Bulletin* cited 1993 research that showed that retirees now in their seventies who were born before 1922 earned inflation-adjusted rates of return of 5.9 to 12.5%, depending upon how old they were (the older their "birth cohort," the higher their rate of return from Social Security).[8]

We must remember that Social Security retirement contributions did not actually earn anything at all because it was largely a funds in–funds out system. The yield-equivalent calculation demonstrates that present payouts are not outrageously high and are by most reasonable standards quite fair.

The long-term problem really has its origin in another area: demographics, or more specifically, the *aging of America*. Mostly because of declining birthrates and longer life expectancy, America is getting older. Figure 7.2, which shows the median age of the U.S. population and the percentage of the population above age 65 projected into the future, reflects this aging very well. The median age in 1970, a little before today's college population was born, stood at 28 years. Some 60 years later cen-

---

[8]Leimer, Dean R. "A Guide to Social Security Money's Worth Issues," *Social Security Bulletin*, Summer 1995. This article surveys a large number of cohort studies that are concerned with this issue, and it should be consulted by anyone who is interested in the subject. The data referred to in the text are from one study cited: Duggan, James E., Robert Gillingham, and John S. Greenless, "Returns Paid to Early Social Security Cohorts," *Contemporary Policy Issues*, October 1993, Vol. 11, pp. 1–13. The earlier estimates (5.5%) were the author's own.

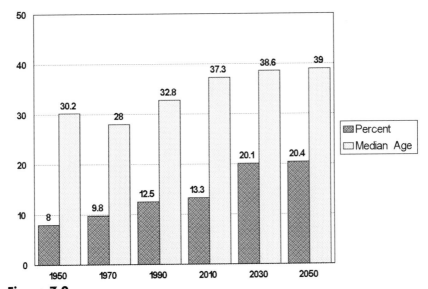

Figure 7.2
Percent of Population above Age 65

sus bureau projections place the median age nearly 11 years higher.[9] Even more revealing is the percentage of the population above age 65, which is projected to double, from below 10% to more than 20% of the population between 1970 and 2030.

More important to the issue of program funding is the projected ratio of contributors to beneficiaries for the two Social Security programs, shown in Figure 7.3, as made by the trustees of the Social Security Trust Funds.[10] In both ratios the numerator reflects the number of people projected to be

[9]The historical data shown here and the projections shown in this figure and in Figure 6.6 are from the U.S. Census Bureau and were retrieved from a series of files on Internet http://www.census.gov/. The projections reflect the so-called "middle series." Projections are made assuming various fertility rates and other population variables. This "middle series" is typically cited as the best guess.

[10]The source for these projections is Table II.F19 of the *1995 Annual Report of the Board of Trustees of the Federal Old-Age and Survivors Insurance and Disability Insurance Trust Funds, House Document 104-57*, April 3, 1995, p. 122 (this is the detailed report). The projections shown are the "intermediate cost" projections—the middle of three ranges used for estimates, one projecting a more favorable picture and the other a worse picture under different assumptions. All projections discussed in this chapter are "intermediate cost" (middle estimate) projections. Not all researchers agree with the trustees' projections. For a more positive outlook, see Richard Sutch in Section 8 of the Bibliography.

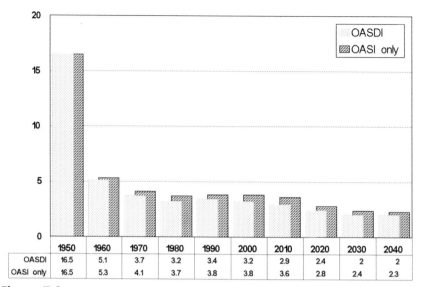

	1950	1960	1970	1980	1990	2000	2010	2020	2030	2040
OASDI	16.5	5.1	3.7	3.2	3.4	3.2	2.9	2.4	2	2
OASI only	16.5	5.3	4.1	3.7	3.8	3.8	3.6	2.8	2.4	2.3

Figure 7.3
Ratio of Contributors to Beneficiaries, OASI (retirement) and OASDI (combined) Trust Funds

paying taxes into the system for the year shown; that figure is divided by the number of projected beneficiaries. The larger of the two figures is for the retirement system alone (OASI only), and the smaller figure includes disability insurance (OASDI). For example, whereas in 1960 5.3 people were paying into the retirement fund for every 1 person drawing retirement benefits, by 2040 that number is projected to fall to 2.3. For what is ultimately a funds in–funds out system, the burden of support on the taxpaying generations is projected to grow very sharply over time.

This is the primary reason why the trust fund will move into deficit status within the next 15 or 20 years; this is why the trust fund is projected to be exhausted. Two other implications quickly become apparent: for the retirement trust fund to continue to meet its obligations either benefits will have to be reduced or taxes will have to be raised substantially, probably through a much higher payroll tax.

To some extent, a reduction in benefits for future generations is already phased in. Under present Social Security law, the normal retirement age is 65, and an early retirement plan with reduced monthly benefits allows retirement as early as age 62. Present law increases the normal retirement age in two steps, first to age 66 then age 67. Present taxpayers who reach age 62 by the year 2000 will not be entitled to full retirement benefits until they reach age 66. Finally, to add insult to injury, those young contributors to the system today, who pay very high tax rates, will not be eligible to retire with full benefits until age 67, if they reach 65 after the year 2020. Additionally, there has been some discussion in recent months of raising the full retirement age to 70.[11]

The Japanese Solution

In the discussion in Chapter 3 on international comparisons we saw that Japan faces the same kind of problems with their social security system as we do with ours. Their primary social security retirement system is remarkably like our own. The Japanese system is financed with a payroll tax where employer and employee pay the same rate (higher than ours), and the normal retirement age is 65 years. Early retirement is possible at age 62 with reduced benefits, as in the United States.[12]

Prior to October 1994 Japanese men paid 7.25% of earnings and women paid 7.225% for their primary pension insurance program with, in both cases, matching employer contributions (by comparison, for the same year, employees in the U.S. paid a payroll tax of 5.6% with a matching employer contribution). Also like the U.S. system, there is an earnings cap (530,000 yen per month, which is about $5300 per month at an exchange rate of 100 yen to the dollar—because of the volatile instability of the dollar, such comparisons are not very meaningful).

The birth rate in Japan is lower than in the United States so the Japanese population is aging more rapidly. For example, by the year 2025, 26% of the Japanese population is projected to be above age 65, compared to only 20% of the U.S. population by 2030. The Japanese are already beginning to face problems that will arise for the U.S. Social Security System in another generation. In effect Japan is simulating our future and we might, to some extent, learn from their experience. However, the solution that they have chosen recently is not likely to find many supporters for an equivalent solution in the United States.

---

[11]In these years under present law, one can still take early retirement at age 62, but with reduced benefits compared with what is paid now.

[12]A general description of the Japanese social security system is included in the 1993 edition of *Social Security Programs Throughout the World*, available on the Internet at http://www.ssa.gov/statistics/ssptw.html. Discussion of the changes made in the system in 1994 are found in *International Updates, Social Security Bulletin, Vol. 58, No. 1, Spring 1995*, pp. 88–89.

In November 1994 the Japanese government decided to properly fund the pension obligations of their retirement system by simply raising taxes year after year. As stated above, the rate prior to October 1994, counting the employer contribution, was 14.5% of earnings (for men), compared to 11.2% in the United States. That rate was increased to 16.5% in October 1994 and to 17.35% in October 1996. The tax rates will continue to rise by an average of about one-half percent per year, and they are projected to reach a ceiling of an astonishing 30% by 2025! And, of course, this rate does not include contributions for health, nor disability, nor ordinary income taxes. Thirty percent is the rate for the retirement program alone!

To be sure, the Japanese approach is a "solution," but clearly it is not a solution that is likely to be very popular in the United States. It is discouraging to see that a country as innovative as Japan finds relentlessly higher tax rates as the only solution.

Are There Any Other Solutions?

Because the Social Security Trust Funds and medical trust funds largely finance their outlays from receipts taken in the same year (funds in–funds out), it is very hard to wean away from such programs, even if they are unpopular. People presently receiving benefits have paid into the systems throughout their working lives, as have others destined to receive benefits in the near future, and they rightfully look upon their benefits as an unqualified obligation of the U.S. government. Any effort to divert revenues away from the system toward some other option, such as private annuities, will leave the systems more underfunded than they are presently, and dollar-for-dollar this will add to the budget deficit. Nonetheless, neglect is not an option. The program is unsustainable as presently structured and it must be changed, and the sooner the change is initiated, the higher its likelihood of success.

New and creative proposals are beginning to surface for Social Security reform, although none of them have had much impact upon legislators. A good representative sample is provided by the 1994–1995 Advisory Council on Social Security, a group or researchers who met and prepared for Congress some suggestions for reform.[13] Reviews like these tend to consist of four possible elements or some combination of the four:

[13]The full report of the Advisory Council and other supporting documents, including minutes of meetings and hearings, can be accessed on the web at http://www.ssa.gov/policy/adcouncil_intro.html, or by following instructions from the SSA home page at http://www.ssa.gov/.

1. raise taxes;
2. reduce benefits;
3. allow the Social Security System to invest some portion of its trust fund into private financial assets that are likely to have a higher return than nonmarketable treasury securities (and more important, come from an outside source rather than from another branch of government);
4. allow contributors to the system to invest some portion of what is now their FICA tax privately, like an IRA.

The first option, effectively what has been described as the "Japanese solution," is not likely to be very popular in the United States, at least in the immediate future. Fortunately, if this option is chosen (even as a partial solution), taxes would not have to be raised nearly so much in the United States as in Japan. According to one projection made in the 1995 OASDI Trustees' Report, a payroll tax of about 9% (or double that if it includes the employer's contribution) as compared to 5.6% now might be sufficient to fund the system. Such a tax increase would be unpopular (and is certainly contrary to the *current* trend), but if phased in slowly over time and explained carefully, it *might* be politically possible. On the other hand, to rely upon this as the only solution might naively underestimate voter discontent.

The second option, a slow reduction in benefits, will certainly be attempted to some degree. It is probably the least equitable solution, because benefits for those who are presently retired or for those who are approaching retirement will not be reduced much, if at all. Instead, the real candidates are younger people who are not expected to retire for many years—in other words, those now supporting the system with record high taxes. In summarizing the most commonly considered options benefits can be reduced by:

1. tampering with the complicated benefits formulas, which would effectively lower payouts given the contribution history, and phasing that in slowly over time (watchdog groups would expose it immediately if it were attempted with current retirees);
2. adjusting cost-of-living formulas or even the cost-of-living index itself to slightly lower the growth rate of outlays over time;
3. increasing income taxes on Social Security benefits and rolling the proceeds back into the Social Security System (this is already being done—what is being proposed is a reduction in the present income exemption);

4. raising the retirement age, which, again, has already been done as discussed earlier in the text—new proposals suggest age 70 as appropriate—which effectively tells young people today that the problem of their retirement is going to be solved by not letting them retire quite so early.

The third option, the investing of surplus funds by the system itself into private financial assets, currently has little support for two good reasons. First, given the amount of money involved and the possibilities for favoritism and even corruption, who would decide where the money would go? Far more important to our theme, a diversion of these funds away from their present disposition would severely compound the deficit problem, at least in the early years of any new program. These surplus funds currently reduce the overall deficit as discussed earlier, and their diversion to another purpose would eliminate this beneficial effect.

The fourth and final option, allowing current taxpayers to divert some portion of their FICA payroll tax to private investments, such as IRA-type mutual funds or bank deposits, has received considerable attention in recent years and is probably the option that is most attractive to those who would benefit from it. Such a program would allow contributors, as an option rather than as a requirement, to divert some percentage, such as 5, 10, or 20%, of the OASI component of their FICA payroll tax to a tax-deferred mutual fund or bank deposit. Although there might be fund-switching privileges, early withdrawal could not be an option no matter what the purpose. If as much as 20% of the OASI contribution could be deferred, the fund could conceivably pay such contributors an annuity greater than their Social Security retirement benefits.

There are two large drawbacks to this option. Most importantly, this option does absolutely nothing to improve the financial integrity of the Social Security Trust Fund; in fact, it undermines it even further. The option is posed more as a *substitute* for an ailing fund than as a solution for the fund's problems. Secondly, as was the case for third option above, this solution, because it would cut back on tax revenues, compounds the deficit problem.

To wean away slowly to true annuity-type options is possible and might prove to be the ultimate twenty-first century solution, but to try to do so and achieve deficit reduction would amount to a nearly impossible combination. If deficit reduction remains the goal, then trust funds and their present method of financing must remain largely in place. For the funds to remain viable over time, taxes must be raised gradually—the

"Japanese solution"—or benefits must be sharply reduced, or both. By the year 2020 or so, the desired triad of a small deficit or no deficit, benefits at present levels, and taxes at present levels, is a virtual impossibility. And what is being said here applies not only to the retirement fund, but also to the disability fund and, without question or qualification, to the medical funds.[14]

What's Next?

Despite the dire prognosis for the future, presently we must concern ourselves with prospects for fiscal moderation and deficit reduction over the next few years. It is hard to imagine that we could ever get our financial house in order in the year 2040 if fiscal prudence escapes us in the year 2000.

There is in place presently a corpus of legislation that is intended to enforce budgetary discipline. In the next chapter we explore the budget enforcement apparatus.

[14]For more information on Social Security the reader is encouraged to consult some of the literature in Section 8 of the Bibliography or an excellent newly-published book by Kingson, Eric R. and Schulz, James H., ed. *Social Security in the 21st Century,* New York: Oxford, 1997.

The Legal Framework for Budget Enforcement[1]

E *fforts to promote fiscal responsibility* do not proceed in a legal
vacuum. Numerous laws exist to guide the conduct of our
elected legislators when it comes to federal finance, and these
laws have a history that goes back to the nation's founding. *The United
States Constitution,* for example, has many sections regulating the right

[1]Much of the material in this chapter was taken from the various books of *The
Budget of the United States Government* (see the list in Table 4.1) for various years;
especially *Analytical Perspectives* for *FY1996.* Two especially useful books on the
same subject are those written by Stanley E. Collander and Allen Schick. See section
2 of the bibliography.

of the government to tax, spend, borrow, and coin money. Most people know that there is a ceiling on the U.S. debt, but few people know that the ceiling goes back to 1917, and since 1941 there has been an upper limit on gross federal debt that is routinely revised upward as the need arises. Since 1960 the limit has been revised upward 64 times. From this example alone it is clear that the best of intentions (or perhaps mendacious politics) can at worst lead to utterly ineffective results. (The ceiling was set at exactly $300 billion in March of 1962, for example. It was last increased to $5.5 trillion in March 1996).

More recent legislation has produced better results than the old debt ceiling, now something of a national joke. In this chapter we will explore the modern legal environment for budgetary enforcement.

The Modern Budget Laws: The Congressional Budget Act of 1974, Gramm-Rudman-Hollings, and the BEA

The Congress and the President now follow a budgetary timetable and they are expected to follow a general framework for reaching agreement on budgetary decisions. The first modern budgetary guidelines were established by the Congressional Budget and Impoundment Act of 1974 and by subsequent amendments. The important budgetary timetable, which establishes a calendar and sets important deadlines for both the President and the Congress, is discussed later in this chapter. The corpus of rules that now govern budgetary decisions has its origin in the 1974 legislation. It now includes provisions contributed by:

1. The Gramm-Rudman Act, formally known as the Balanced Budget and Emergency Deficit Control Act of 1985;
2. a revision of this legislation called the Gramm-Rudman-Hollings Act, formally known as the Balanced Budget and Emergency Deficit Control Reaffirmation Act of 1987 (the original act and its revision will hereafter be referred to as GRH);
3. the Budget Enforcement Act of 1990;
4. and a revision and extension called the Omnibus Budget Reconciliation Act of 1993.

The later two acts were extensions of GRH, and this composite legislation of five major laws, which provides the legislative umbrella for modern budgetary decisions will hereafter be referred to as the Budget Enforcement Acts, or BEA. Most of this chapter will concern itself with the BEA.

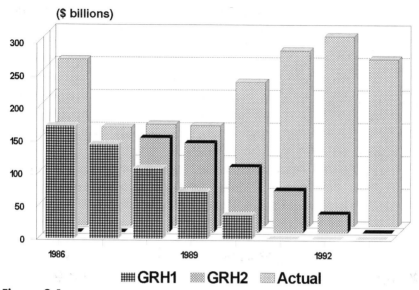

Figure 8.1
GRH Compliance Deficit Targets

The Failure of Gramm-Rudman-Hollings

The GRH legislation, first introduced in 1985 and revised in 1987, was an unqualified failure (except to the extent that it finally influenced the more effective Budget Enforcement Act in 1990). GRH set targets on the deficit, mandating in the 1985 law that it be reduced to zero (a balanced budget) by 1990. It reset the balanced budget target in 1987 to be accomplished in 1993. Figure 8.1, which shows the GRH deficit targets (two sets) and the actual deficit, indicates the extent to which the intent of this legislation was circumvented. In 1992, for example, by the terms of the 1985 law the budget was to be balanced, and by the terms of the 1987 law, the deficit was to be $28 billion. The actual deficit in 1992 was more than $290 billion, the highest ever recorded. The failure of GRH was so significant and conspicuous (the law was initially introduced with the flourish and fanfare typical of legislators who are long on promises and short on results) that it provoked an image of cynicism and incompetence in the public. Each fiscal year would typically end on a wild note in the GRH years, with extraordinary partisan acrimony (although no worse than that seen in 1995), hysterical claims that the government was "out of money" and was "going to go bankrupt" (effectively impossible in both cases), accompanied by newspaper and TV interviews with federal employees (park rangers were popular) who "do not know if they will have jobs on Monday!" One could always tell when October 1st was approaching by the bizarre surge in the political cacophony, followed by silence after the start of the new fiscal year, with a $250-billion-plus deficit as the only lasting residual.

The reason for the failure of GRH and for the year-end circus was both technical and political. The technical weakness will be explained later in the chapter when we discuss how it was fixed. The political component can be explained now: it was due both to lack of will and of nerve, probably with a dash of duplicity thrown in.

The BEA

The two pieces of legislation from 1990 and 1993, referred to here as the Budget Enforcement Acts (BEA),[2] set goals that differed in a very significant way from GRH. The BEA does not mandate deficit reduction, nor does it set deficit targets. In effect, it puts a cap on certain types of spending while maintaining a sort of deficit neutrality on the rest. To explore how budgetary discipline through BEA is now supposed to work, we need to explore how spending and taxing are authorized by law.

The Legislative Path of Spending

Table 8.1 briefly summarizes the legislative path that begins with an idea for a federal program and ends with both **budget authority** and **outlays.** Budget authority (a better term might be *spending authority*, because that is what is being granted) extends permission to undertake financial obligations, including contracts, that will eventually result in **outlays,** or spending.[3]

From Authorizing Legislation to Outlays

There are two potential paths from program proposal (or amendment) to outlays. Both begin with **authorizing legislation,** which must be introduced as a bill in at least one of the houses of Congress, enrolled[4] by both,

---

[2]Stanley Collender, *Guide to the Federal Budget, Fiscal 1995,* tells his readers that whereas the 1974 legislation passed only after months of debate, the GRH and BEA legislation was passed after "extraordinarily limited public discussion." (p. 19).

[3]We are using the 97% *definitions* here; for more detailed and technically correct definitions, see the Glossary.

[4]A bill that is passed by one house of Congress is said to be "engrossed" (by that house), and one passed by both is "enrolled" for the President's signature.

Table 8.1

The Legislative Path of Federal Spending

1. Authorizing legislation

Congress passes and the President signs legislation that authorizes an agency, such as the Department of Education or the Department of Defense, to undertake a designated task or program. The authorizing legislation generally places an upper limit on appropriations.

Example: HR 2884, 103rd Congress, School-to-Work Opportunities Act of 1994, which created a grant program to develop an educational bridge between schools and the workplace for selected students, authorized appropriations of $300 million for FY 1995 (see Table 5.10 in Chapter 5 for specific language).

2a. Permanent budget authority	2b. Appropriations acts
By extending financial rights by law to those who qualify, certain authorizing legislation, typically entitlements, does not require appropriations and is not reviewed annually, although it may be reviewed every few years. **Examples:** Social Security, Medicare	Originating in the House of Representatives but approved by both houses of Congress, appropriations acts provide to agencies with programs that do not have permanent budget authority, the annual **budget authority** to undertake financial obligations that will result in **outlays.** Appropriations may be made for one year or for longer periods of time. Some spending, such as defense, the EPA and NASA also requires annual **authorization bills.** **Example:** HR 4606, Departments of Labor, Health and Human Services, and Education, and Related Agencies Appropriations Act, 1995, which authorized outlays for the School-to-Work Opportunities Act.

3. Outlays

Budget authority and outlays will seldom coincide in any fiscal year. Typically some budget authority is earmarked for outlays in future years, and some portion of outlays are authorized by unspent budget authority from prior years. Program administrators at the agency level are sometimes given some latitude for determining the timing of outlays; in other cases annual deadlines are strictly enforced.

and signed into law by the President. This legislation authorizes an agency like the Department of Education to undertake some program or task to fulfill a governmental mandate. The authorizing legislation typically evaluates the financial requirements of a new or altered program and it can impose financial constraints or provisions, such as an upper limit upon annual appropriations. HR 2884 The School-to-Work Opportunities Act of 1994, introduced in Table 5.9, is a good example of authorizing legislation. Sponsored by President Bill Clinton, it created the School-to-Work Opportunities Program offering grants-in-aid to qualified state and local agencies and it authorized appropriations of up to $300 million for 1995. The funding history of the program thereafter depends upon whether the authorizing legislation requires **appropriations** or creates **permanent budget authority.** The latter typically is used for entitlements-type programs.

If the program requires appropriations, as is shown in Table 8.1, the budget authority to undertake actual financial obligations, including outlays or contracts that will lead to outlays, must be provided in one of the 13 **appropriations acts** that are initiated annually in the House of Representatives and are passed by both houses of Congress. Refer to Table 8.2 for detailed information. Again using the example of the School-to-Work Opportunities Act (HR 2884), the actual appropriations of funds for that program was included in HR 4606, The Departments of Labor, Health, and Human Services, and Education, and Related Agencies Appropriations Act, 1995. The actual language of appropriations is quoted in Table 8.2.

If, on the other hand, the program extends certain financial rights, as is typically the case for entitlements programs, such as federal pensions, health care, or Social Security, then annual budget authority and outlays are determined by those factors that determine entitlements payments, as discussed in Chapter 6 (mostly the nature of the entitlement extended by law and the number of people or agencies who qualify). They do not require annual appropriations nor any other form of annual financial review. For example, the old Aid for Families with Dependent Children (AFDC) program was an entitlements program. The section of public law that authorized spending for the AFDC program, Title 42, Section 601 of the United States Code, which is labeled *Authorization of Appropriations,* first outlined in detail the purposes of the AFDC program, then declared, ". . . there is hereby authorized to be appropriated for each fiscal year a sum sufficient to carry out the purposes of this part." Such language in an authorization bill means that program needs dictate spending, and that whatever funds are necessary to feed those needs are automatically authorized. Annual appropriations for this program are

Table 8.2

Example: The Language of Authorization and Appropriations for the School-to-Work Opportunities Act of 1994

First, legislation must be passed **authorizing** an agency to undertake a designated task or program. That authorizing legislation often includes the authorization of appropriations. Reproduced below is the language from the authorization of appropriations for HR 2884, the School-to-Work Opportunities Act of 1994 [see Table 5.10 for more text from HR 2884]:

SEC. 605. **Authorization of Appropriations.** (a) In General: There are authorized to be appropriated to the Secretaries to carry out this Act $300,000,000 for the fiscal year 1995 and such sums as may be necessary for each of the fiscal years 1996 through 1999.

Second, if the authorizing legislation does **not** create **permanent budget authority** (typically entitlements, such as Social Security) that does not require appropriations, then the agency must receive permission to undertake financial obligations for the program in an **appropriations act.** The appropriations may be for one year or longer. Appropriations will often earmark less money than the maximum allowed by authorizations. In some cases, programs can be combined in appropriations acts. The 1995 act that appropriated funds for the School-to-Work Opportunities Act combined funds with the related **Goals 2000: Educate America Act.** Appropriations were granted for 1995 under **HR 4606, the Departments of Labor, Health, and Human Services, and Education, and Related Agencies Appropriations Act.** The text of the bill granted appropriations with the following language:

Be it enacted by the Senate and House of Representatives of the United States of America in Congress assembled, That the following sums are appropriated, out of any money in the Treasury not otherwise appropriated, for the Departments of Labor, Health and Human Services, and Education, and related agencies for the fiscal year ending September 30, 1995, and for other purposes, namely: [two other titles listed] . . .

TITLE III—Department of Education

Education Reform For carrying out activities authorized by titles II, III, and IV of the Goals 2000: Educate America Act and titles II, III, and IV of the School-to-Work Opportunities Act, $528,400,000 of which $503,670,000 shall become available on July 1, 1995, and remain available through September 30, 1996.

Sources: HR 2884 enrolled, 103rd Congress, and HR 4606 enrolled, 103rd Congress, obtained via Library of Congress Thomas Web server, http://www.loc.gov/.

not required. When AFDC was eliminated by the Welfare Reform Act of 1996 (described in Chapter 6 and in Appendix G), this section of the United States Code was superseded by the new law. AFDC was replaced by a program (Temporary Assistance for Needy Families—TANF) that requires annual appropriations and disburses the proceeds through block grants, thus ending the entitlements status of the federal government's oldest and largest welfare cash-support program.

Some agencies or programs, including defense, NASA (for at least part of their budget), and the Environmental Protection Agency (EPA) require annual **authorization bills** in addition to appropriations bills. Though these overlap considerably, the authorization bills often address long-range contracts, such as those for weapons systems in the defense budget, that will involve outlays years into the future. Many other programs require separate authorization bills every few years, but not annually. Such authorization bills provide the Congress a periodic format for reviewing established programs.

Tax legislation normally has the same status as **permanent budget authority,** and is treated in the same way. Like most entitlements, tax legislation is not subject to annual review, although tax legislation can be considered and reviewed in any congressional session. Tax legislation formally originates in the House Ways and Means Committee. Article I, Section 7, of the U.S. Constitution requires that all bills for "raising Revenue shall originate in the House of Representatives" (although the Senate may propose amendments to existing legislation), and jurisdiction within the House is determined by the current Rules of the House of Representatives (which can be modified at the beginning of any congressional session), which refer all "revenue measures generally" to the Ways and Means Committee. Again, though, this is a legal formality and the true origin of tax legislation (meaning the de facto proposal and promotion) can come from any sponsor in either house. If it is a new law, at some early juncture it will be channeled through Ways and Means.

Some tax legislation is passed with time limits that require renewal of the tax after a few years have passed. In the absence of such renewal, the tax automatically expires. For example earlier we saw that the 10% aviation ticket tax expired on December 31, 1995, at the time when the Republican Congress and Democratic President Bill Clinton were engaged in a rancorous battle over the budget. The failure to immediately restore the tax caused a drop in receipts for the Aviation Trust Fund of more than $3 billion, which meant that general tax revenues had to be used for portions of programs that are normally financed by the trust fund.

Who Does What?

In Table 8.3 we see a summary of the role played by the President and many of the key committees and bureaucracies.[5] Even though certain committees have clearly stipulated responsibilities, taxing and spending matters can originate anywhere in the Congress, or they can come from the President. The political forces that shape such legislation can be more strongly influenced by the chair of a key Senate committee or by a political leader, such as the Speaker of the House, than by a budget committee or an appropriations subcommittee. For example, the real source of legislation affecting farm subsidies might come from the Senate Agricultural Committee; for Medicare, from a health subcommittee in the House; for education, from the President in a legislative proposal with financial implications.

The role played by the two bureaucracies listed, the **Office of Management and Budget (OMB)**, part of the executive branch of government and answerable to the President, and its Congressional counterpart, the **Congressional Budget Office (CBO)**, is very significant, as we will see. Of the two agencies, the OMB now wields the most power and plays the most significant role.

BEA Rules: Restrictions on Spending and Taxing

As was earlier the case with GRH, present legislation does not set deficit targets nor does it mandate deficit reduction. BEA now does establish a complicated mix of spending and taxing limits. We have seen that programs are financed either by appropriations, like defense, or by permanent budget authority, like most entitlements. We will now see that the limits imposed by BEA depend upon whether the affected program requires appropriations or is authorized by permanent budget authority.

BEA classifies all federal spending under three general categories:

1. net interest on the debt;
2. **discretionary spending**; and
3. **mandatory spending**, also called **direct spending.**

These categories of spending are outlined in Table 8.4, which show the values for fiscal year 1995. As can be seen, the three components total to

---

[5]Some of the rights or duties listed, such as the right to sequester will be explained later in the chapter. It might be useful to review some of the summary tables after the chapter has been completed. Some will be more understandable the second time around.

Table 8.3

The Major Players in the Budgetary Process

President of the United States: Presents the advisory budget to Congress in early February (the documents listed in Table 4.1) for the following fiscal year. All budgetary legislation, including appropriations and authorizing legislation, requires his signature (which implies veto power). Can use power of **sequestration** if BEA provisions are violated (see text).

House and Senate Budget Committees: Responsible for producing (by April 15) Congress's version of the budget, called the **Congressional Budget Resolution.** Both committees monitor and contribute to general BEA enforcement.

Senate and House Appropriations Committees (and 13 subcommittees): Make recommendations to their respective houses on **appropriations,** which translate into **budget authority** and finally **outlays** (spending). Appropriations bills are initiated in the House Appropriations Committee, beginning on May 15, and are then sent to the Senate.

House/Senate Conference Committees: The House and Senate usually pass different versions of bills dealing with the same subject, then they send it to a conference committee where representatives from both houses work out a compromise bill, which is sent back to both houses for final passage.

House Ways and Means Committee: All revenue (including tax) measures are supposed to originate in this committee. (Article I, Section 7 requires that "All Bills for raising Revenue shall originate in the House of Representatives; but the Senate may propose or concur with Amendments as on other Bills.")

Note: Although these committees have the duties and privileges listed, *the primary political pushing and tugging* that results in spending and taxing occurs at all levels and in various committees and it *culminates* in full floor discussion in each house.

Office of Management and Budget (OMB): Part of the executive branch, the OMB aids the President in the preparation of his budget. The OMB is also ultimately responsible for the important economic assumptions in making baseline estimates and in the preparation of the **current services budget** (see the text and glossary). OMB issues the **sequester previews** (see the text) and is therefore potentially instrumental in initiating **sequesters** (although the actual exercise of sequester is reserved for the President).

Congressional Budget Office (CBO): The congressional counterpart of the OMB that answers to Congress. The CBO aids in the preparation of the **Congressional Budget Resolution** and it makes baseline estimates to compare to those made by the OMB (they often disagree substantially). CBO is required by BEA to annually compile a report that lists spending and revenue options for reducing the deficit.

Table 8.4

Discretionary and Mandatory Spending, 1995 ($ billions)

Category	1995	% of total
Discretionary	545.7	35.9
Defense	273.5	18.0
Nondefense	272.2	17.9
Mandatory	741.3	48.8
Social Security	333.3	21.9
Medicare	156.9	10.3
Means-tested entitlements	92.5	6.1
Medicaid	89.1	5.9
Federal retirement	65.8	4.3
Unemployment	21.3	1.4
Undistributed offsetting receipts	−44.5	−2.9
Deposit insurance	−17.9	−1.2
Other	44.8	2.9
Net interest	232.2	15.3
Total outlays	1519.0	100.0

Sources and Notes: Budget of the United States Government, FY 1997, Historical Tables, Tables 8.1 and 8.5. Undistributed offsetting receipts are mostly agency contributions to retirement programs—see Glossary.

outlays of $1.519 trillion, with 36% for discretionary spending (about half of that for defense), 49% for mandatory spending, and the remaining 15% accounting for net interest.

Net interest on the debt is placed in a separate category because the expenditure is not really an entitlement. But like an entitlement, the annual outlay cannot be directly controlled because it is determined by the size of the net debt outstanding, the effective interest rate paid on that debt, which in turn depends upon market rates and the composition of the debt (low-yield bills versus high-yield bonds, for example) when new debt is financed or old debt is rolled over.

Generally, mandatory (direct) spending consists of entitlements and is financed via permanent budget authority, while discretionary spending does not consist of entitlements (it includes virtually all other spending) and it requires appropriations.

As always, there are exceptions. The large food stamp program, for example, which spends about $25 billion annually and is found in the budget of the Department of Agriculture, is an entitlements program but requires annual appropriations. The deficit of the U.S. Postal Service, although not an entitlement, is classified as mandatory spending. The BEA rules that govern spending for these two categories differ substantially and require separate explanations.

Discretionary Spending and Caps

Discretionary spending is controlled by **discretionary spending limits**, or **caps** as they are usually called, set in the BEA legislation of 1990 and 1993, subject to certain annual adjustments that are required to be small and technical in nature. The caps apply to both budget authority and to outlays for discretionary spending. The original caps and the adjusted caps are shown in Table 8.5.[6] The cap of $548.0 billion for 1996 means that if aggregate discretionary spending exceeds that amount then an automatic cutback called a **sequester** (to be described in more detail later in the chapter) might be initiated. These caps apply to the total of discretionary spending and not to the individual agencies, although individual agency budgets can be strongly affected by these caps.

The uncomfortable impact of certain unanticipated "emergency" expenditures becomes apparent when looking at the caps. The increasing reliance on federal emergency relief (now mostly through the agency created to manage and provide that relief, the Federal Emergency Management Agency, or FEMA), cost more than $30 billion between 1993 and 1996, and the brief but expensive war with Iraq which lasted about two months cost an additional $60 billion. The allowable emergency waiver on caps is truly a loophole, but so far it has been used exclusively for emergencies.

As can be seen, the caps are stringent and they represent a real effort to achieve austerity. They are nearly the same for 1998 as they were in 1993, and although they represent only about 36% of total federal spending, this is core spending on traditional government programs: defense and most spending on transportation, education, energy, housing, justice, State, NASA, and so forth. And it appears that so far there has been a

[6]Some of the adjustments shown are very technical in nature and cannot be explained in this book. The interested reader can find a valiant effort to explain the adjustments in the *Budget Enforcement Act Preview Report*, pp. 201–205 of *Analytic Perspectives, FY 1996*.

Table 8.5

Original and Adjusted Discretionary Spending Limits (Caps) 1991 to 1998 ($ billions)

	1991	1992	1993	1994	1995	1996	1997	1998
Original statutory outlay caps as set in BEA 1990, 1993	514.4	524.9	534.0	534.8	540.8	547.3	547.3	547.9
Adjustments								
Changes in concepts & defns.		1.0	2.4	0.6	1.0	-2.9	-2.6	-2.7
Inflation adjustment		-0.3	-2.5	-5.8	-8.8	0.6	1.8	3.2
Emergency requirements	1.1	1.8	5.4	9.0	10.1	5.4	3.9	1.4
Operation Desert Storm	33.3	14.9	7.6	2.8	1.1			
Other	2.8	3.4	3.5	4.5	2.5	-2.3	-1.8	-1.3
Total adjustments	37.2	20.8	16.4	11.1	5.9	0.8	1.3	0.6
Adjusted outlay caps	551.6	545.7	550.4	545.9	546.7	548.0	548.7	548.5
Adjusted budget authority caps	537.1	536.6	535.7	525.1	511.0	523.0	530.3	534.4

Source: Table 12.1, page 202, of Analytic Perspectives, FY 1997. Adjustments shown for outlays only.

The relief for emergency requirements applies to relief from domestic natural disasters.

The figures for Operation Desert Storm (the war with Iraq) includes operation Desert Shield.

The inflation adjustment reflects the difference between the inflation assumptions made when the caps were enacted and actual inflation rates. A negative number means that initial inflation estimates were too high.

good-faith effort to enforce the caps. To the credit of the legislators who promoted and passed the 1990 and 1993 BEA restrictions, the caps seem to be a budgetary restriction that works, at least for the time being.

Mandatory Spending and PAYGO

The regulatory picture becomes much more complicated when we look at efforts to constrain mandatory spending. An immediate problem arises because almost all mandatory spending is for *entitlements*. This guarantees that spending will rise, possibly a great deal, as ever larger numbers of people become eligible for entitlements payments. Congress can not just cap Medicare, Medicaid, Social Security or military retirement benefits because if it did, the complex authorizing legislation would have to be rewritten every year to squeeze off more and more benefits. In other words, it is much easier to restrict appropriations than it is to substantially amend authorizing legislation that goes back more than half a century for some programs. In addition, BEA provisions that affect mandatory spending are not so clear as those that influence discretionary spending, and they are much more open to interpretation. Having made these qualifications, we can now review the *essence* of the BEA restrictions on mandatory spending:

Given reasonable projections of entitlements (mandatory spending) based upon existing legislation, and given reasonable revenue estimates based upon existing tax code, a *deficit projection* can be estimated. Congress may not pass any new legislation that affects mandatory spending or taxation if the *combined* effect of such legislation increases the deficit beyond this projection in any year between the present and 1998.[7] Essentially, Congress can raise or lower spending in various entitlements programs and can change the tax code (including lowering certain taxes if they choose), so long as the *net* effect of such changes in any congressional session does not increase the projected budget deficit. If there is a violation of this rule a sequester—an automatic cutback in spending, can be triggered. This is similar to the penalty for a breach of discretionary spending caps.

The rules that govern mandatory spending and receipts are called pay-as-you-go rules, or **PAYGO**. Although our discussion captures the spirit of PAYGO, there are many complicated features that must be explained. To begin with, not all mandatory spending is subject to PAYGO restrictions. For example, Social Security, any deficit of the U.S. Postal Service, some types of emergency funding, and federal deposit insurance (used for

[7]Between, specifically, the 102nd Congress (1993) and 1998.

the savings-and-loan bailout), all classified as mandatory spending, are not subject to PAYGO provisions. This means that if Social Security legislation is changed in a way that increases the deficit or if there is a sudden surge in the Postal Service deficit, a PAYGO sequester (an automatic cutback in spending) will not be triggered. It must be understood that PAYGO does not substantially limit spending nor does it directly limit the size of the deficit. To make this point, consider the following question.

What if spending rises unexpectedly because of an unanticipated surge in qualified beneficiaries in a large entitlements program like Medicare? Or what if tax receipts fall because of a weak economy? Either case would increase the deficit beyond projections. Will a sequester be triggered?

The answer is no. PAYGO rules apply only to *new laws* or to *amendments to old laws* that affect mandatory spending (except for the categories excluded above) or taxes. The rule evaluates only the impact of legislative changes. Mistakes in assumptions, windfall gains, or unexpected losses, no matter how they impact the deficit, are not taken into account and will not trigger a sequester.

The BEA rules on mandatory spending and taxation clearly require that someone undertakes the task of making budgetary projections, including deficit projections. Both the Office of Management and Budget (OMB), which answers to the President, and the Congressional Budget Office (CBO), which answers to Congress, are responsible for the budgetary assumptions and projections, and for reconciling those projections and assumptions if they disagree.

BEA Rules: The Current Services Budget

The Office of Management and Budget is required by the BEA to compile a **current services baseline budget** as a benchmark for comparison as legislative changes are considered. The current services budget makes a 5-year budget projection based upon present-day assumptions about economic trends and the effects of *existing* spending and tax legislation.[8] In effect, the current services budget answers the following question: What will be the levels of spending, taxing, and the deficit over the next 5 fiscal years

---

[8]Five years is the convention, but because the Republican-controlled 104th Congress declared in 1995 that they wanted to balance the budget by FY 2002 and established their budgetary goals accordingly, the revised FY 1996 projection was for 7 years and the FY 1997 was for 6 (both ending in FY 2002).

given present economic assumptions and assuming no changes in present law? The latter assumption implies no change in existing entitlements, so the estimation of the current services budget must include a financial projection that reflects changes in the number of beneficiaries and the impact of their financial rights over the 5 year period of the projection.

Table 8.6 shows the **economic assumptions** used for the fiscal year 1997 current services baseline budget, which makes a forecast to the year 2002. As can be seen, real GDP is forecast to grow at 2.8% each year and the inflation rate was estimated at a little under 3%. Clearly, such assumptions strongly impact projections of tax receipts (higher values would result in forecasts of higher receipts, of course) and they affect certain entitlements.

The current services baseline estimates for FY 1997 (using historical data from 1994 and 1995, and current-services projections for 1996 to 2002) is shown at the bottom of Table 8.6. It should be remembered that the current services baseline budget is not a *forecast*—it is a baseline reference document that assumes no new legislation. It is used to monitor mandatory spending to comply with the BEA provision that the net effect of new legislation and taxing is deficit neutral. Loosely speaking, new legislation can not increase the deficit numbers shown in the current services baseline estimate. If it does, it can result in a sequester, or in automatic spending reduction.

The fiscal year 1996 current services projection of outlays by function is shown in Table 8.7. Estimates are shown for 1996 and 2002, along with projected annual growth rates. Total outlays are projected to grow at 4.4% compounded annually(about 35% overall), a little lower than the projected growth rate of nominal GDP. Compare the growth rates of the individual functions. It is easy to see which categories consist mostly of entitlements. The national defense category is projected to grow at less than 3% per year. Compare that to Medicare and Medicaid, both of which are projected to grow at around 9% annually *given the law as it applied in 1996* when the fiscal year 1997 current services budget was developed by the OMB. Such growth rates do *not* violate BEA (or, more properly stated, they will not violate BEA if realized). The growth rates shown can be reduced by amending authorizing legislation to alter entitlements (restricting or reducing certain Medicare benefits, for example). Under BEA, though, such a change might not result in deficit reduction—it can be used to fund spending increases elsewhere or to finance tax cuts. BEA does not require deficit reduction.

Table 8.6

OMB Current Services Estimates: FY 1977
Summary of Economic Assumptions & Baseline Receipts ($ billions unless otherwise indicated)

	1994a	1995	1996	1997	1998	1999	2000	2001	2002
Economic assumptions									
Real GDP growth rate	3.8	3.7	2.7	2.8	2.8	2.8	2.7	2.8	2.8
Real GDP (1987 dollars)	5,290	5,484	5,633	5,792	5,956	6,121	6,290	6,467	6,648
Estimated inflation rates (%):									
GDP deflator	2.0	1.9	2.0	2.2	2.2	2.3	2.2	2.2	2.2
Consumer Price Index (all urban)	2.6	2.8	2.7	3	2.9	2.8	2.8	2.8	2.8
GDP (current dollars)	6,634	7,004	7,336	7,708	8,101	8,517	8,946	9,405	9,881
Unemployment rate	6.3	5.6	5.7	5.7	5.7	5.7	5.7	5.7	5.7
Interest rates									
91-day Treasury Bills	3.7	5.5	5.0	4.6	4.3	4.3	4.0	4.0	4.0
10-year Treasury Notes	6.5	7.1	5.7	5.4	5.1	5.0	5.0	5.0	5.0
Estimated baseline receipts									
Individual income taxes	543.1	590.2	632.2	662.3	696.6	730.9	769.4	811.9	857.4
Corporate income taxes	140.4	157.0	167.0	181.6	197.0	207.3	219.9	231.3	240.4
Social insurance taxes	461.5	484.5	507.4	535.9	560.5	587.9	616.8	645.0	676.1
Excise taxes	55.2	57.5	53.2	52.0	52.4	53.3	53.8	54.5	55.5
Other	57.6	66.0	68.1	69.6	72.1	75.0	78.6	82.0	86.5
Total receipts	1,257.7	1,355.2	1,427.9	1,501.5	1,578.6	1,654.4	1,738.5	1,824.8	1,915.9
Total outlays	1,460.9	1,519.1	1,581.5	1,651.3	1,722.9	1,798.8	1,878.2	1,955.5	2,046.9
CS deficit estimate	203.2	163.9	153.6	149.8	144.3	144.4	139.7	130.7	131.0

Source: Tables 15.3, 15.5, and 15.7, Analytic Perspectives, FY 1997. Figures for FY 1994 and 1995 are actual, except for 1995 economic assumptions, and 1996 to 2000 are the estimates used for the current services budget.

Table 8.7

Current Services Budget Projections, Outlays by Function ($ billions)

Function	1995a	1996	% 2002	% annual absolute	average
Medicare	159.9	177.7	304.5	90.4	9.6
Medicaid	89.1	95.0	159.4	78.9	8.7
Justice	16.2	18.7	25.5	57.4	6.7
Social Security	335.8	350.8	466.8	39.0	4.8
Income security	220.4	228.5	294.6	33.7	4.2
Veterans benefits	37.9	37.7	46.6	23.0	3.0
Community & regn dev	10.6	12.8	12.9	21.7	2.8
General science	16.7	16.9	19.4	16.2	2.2
National defense	259.4	254.6	294.2	13.4	1.8
General government	13.8	13.6	15.6	13.0	1.8
Transportation	39.4	39.8	43.0	9.1	1.3
Net interest	232.2	241.1	248.4	7.0	1.0
Education, trn & empl	54.3	54.5	56.6	4.2	0.6
Natural resources	22.1	21.3	23.0	4.1	0.6
International affairs	16.4	14.3	16.8	2.4	0.3
Agriculture	9.8	7.7	8.2	−16.3	−2.5
Energy	3.6	1.8	1.8	−50.0	−9.4
Undistributed offs rec	−44.5	−40.3	−44.8	N/A	
Commerce & hou credit	−14.4	−3.6	6.1	N/A	
Total outlays	1519.1	1581.5	2046.9	34.7	4.4

Source: Table 15.12, Analytic Perspectives, FY 1997. Percentage calculations are by author. In this table, budgetary functions are ranked by projected growth rates.

The percentage absolute covers the period of the current services budget, from 1996–2000.

The percentage annual average is the compounded rate between 1996 and 2000.

The 1995/1996 Disagreement over Budget Assumptions

Although the primary task of projecting the current services budget falls with the OMB, the Congressional Budget Office (CBO) which, in a practical sense, answers to the dominant party in Congress, is required to make the same estimates. If the estimates differ, there is a vague mechanism for reconciliation, but the law in effect puts most power in the hands of the OMB, because the OMB has the final responsibility of recommending sequesters if PAYGO requirements have been violated.

A possibility for serious conflict arises if one party controls the presidency and the other controls Congress. Economic assumptions may vary, and over 5 years the final impact upon the estimate for the deficit can be substantial. This potential for disagreement became very apparent in preparation for the budgets of for fiscal years 1996 and 1997 after the newly elected Republican-controlled 104th Congress came into power in January 1995. Under the stewardship of the new Speaker of the House, Newt Gingrich, and guided by their new mandate, the Republican Contract with America (reproduced in Appendix E), the Republicans began work on a new plan to balance the budget, settling upon a gradual program that targeted fiscal year 2002 as the first surplus year. This zeal for deficit reduction caught the Clinton administration by surprise. The President's first official budget for 1996—the large one always released in February—made projections only until fiscal year 2000, as required by law, and projected a deficit for that year $194.4 billion. Although the Republicans did not come up with their budgetary numbers until late June 1995, once they did, they challenged the President to come up with a balanced budget of his own. So, after a little hesitation, he did.[9]

The new economic assumptions found in the President's version of his balanced budget looked a little "cooked" to the CBO. The original 1996 current services economic assumptions had projected real GDP growth at only 2.5% (up until fiscal year 2000). The new budget (and ultimately the current services budget for fiscal year 1997, as seen in Table 8.6) raised this number to 2.8%. The Republicans cried foul—higher GDP growth projection numbers reduce the deficit, making actual program cuts less necessary if the goal is to balance the budget. In their mind, the President's budget was growing its way out of the problem. The President's staff members retorted that the CBO numbers were far too conservative, forcing hard program cuts unnecessarily. For a few weeks, an uncomprehending public was treated to a CBO versus OMB war over economic assumptions. The issue was finally eclipsed by graver concerns, such as one government shutdown after the other due to the inability to raise the debt ceiling and the failure to pass appropriations bills.

---

[9]This was one of the numerous tactical blunders made by the Republicans in 1995—they gave the President a challenge that was very easy to meet. As both parties were to discover, coming up with new numbers for the unified budget by function, roughly equivalent to toying with the numbers on Table 4.2a and Table 4.4 for future years, is very easy to do, but passing legislation to make the numbers *effective* is a different matter entirely.

BEA Rules: Concurrent Budget Resolutions and Reconciliation

As discussed previously, each year the President, with the help of the OMB, is required to release his huge advisory budget, which includes current services estimates, in early February. Upon receipt of this document, both houses of Congress are required to formulate their own version of the budget, called the **Concurrent Budget Resolution.** The deadline for passage of the Concurrent Budget Resolution, is April 15.[10]

The congressional version of the budget is much simpler than the President's. It is similar to the current-services portion of the presidential budget (which, again, projects tax revenues and spending given current legislation). Generally, the heart of the Concurrent Budget Resolution sets limits for outlays, budget authority, and various loan commitments for major budgetary functions for 7 years.[11] For example, the FY 1996 Concurrent Budget Resolution passed by the 104th Congress in June 1995, House Concurrent Resolution 67, set spending, revenue, and deficit targets for the fiscal years 1996 through 2002. This budget resolution, as mentioned earlier, set a deficit target of zero for fiscal year 2002. This target that was roughly repeated the following year in House Concurrent Resolution 178, the 1997 congressional budget. The Concurrent Budget Resolution does not set spending targets by agency or by individual program. It sets them only at the level of major budgetary functions (like 050, national defense and 270, energy).

There is one important feature of the Concurrent Budget Resolution that must be understood by anyone reviewing the numbers; the Concurrent Budget Resolution uses only the **on-line** budget (sometimes expressed as **on-budget revenues** and **outlays**). In yet another weird feature of federal law, most taxes and outlays from the two Social Security Trust Funds and from the subsidy to the U.S. Postal Service are classified as off-line or off-budget. Nothing else falls under this classification. The off-line budget always has a surplus because of the Social Security surplus. The

---

[10]The 104th Congress in 1995 did not pass its budget resolution until June 29, more than 2 months late. However, the Congress was attempting substantial reform and given its goals, meeting the deadline would have been impossible. Congress missed again, though, in 1996.

[11]Though the budget resolution is formatted differently, the task of making the 7 year forecast is nearly identical to taking the values for the Unified Budget by Function, shown in Table 4.2a, and projecting them for seven years into the future.

off-budget surplus must be added to the congressional numbers for out-lays, revenues, and the deficit we compare the Congressional budget to ei-ther the President's or the historical unified budget. A demonstration of this is shown later in the chapter.

The procedure for passing a Concurrent Budget Resolution begins with each house passing their own version of the budget after they re-ceive the President's advisory budget. Although each side generally knows what the other is doing, typically the two versions will not agree. Therefore, both versions are then sent to a **Budget Conference Commit-tee** staffed by representatives from both houses of the Congress, where a compromise is worked out. The budget resolution is then sent back to the floor of each house for a vote. The Concurrent Budget Resolution is not signed by the President, and it cannot be directly vetoed nor overturned by the President. It is not a law.

The Next Difficult Step: Reconciliation

The passage of the Concurrent Budget Resolution is the beginning rather than the end of the congressional budgetary process. Unlike the President's budget, which is largely advisory, the Concurrent Budget Resolution is supposed to be an enforceable budget. Spending targets are expected to be met, especially if they directly or implicitly mandate changes, including cuts, to either appropriations or permanent budget authority, including entitlements. The difficult process of enforcement is called **reconciliation.**

It must be remembered that major entitlements programs, like Medi-care, do not normally go through appropriations. Instead, their spend-ing levels are determined by the benefits defined by the authorizing legislation. Therefore, if these programs are to change, the legislation ex-tending benefits must be modified. That procedure must begin in the House and Senate committees and subcommittees that are responsible for such programs.

What does this requirement have to do with reconciliation? Reconcili-ation "requires" (the word is used loosely) the various committees re-sponsible for the programs impacted by the targets set in the Concurrent Budget Resolution to pass the necessary legislation to alter their pro-grams (such as Medicare, for example) in such a way that the new targets are met. The budget committees responsible for developing the Concur-rent Budget Resolution "advise" the other committees on how to do this, though in the tangled world of politics, given jurisdictional wars and relentless power struggles, this "advice" can range from being regarded as a direct order to being blithely ignored.

In some cases direct budget authority and outlay authorizations for programs previously approved can be canceled altogether. Such an act is called a **rescission** and the bills that accomplish this objective are sometimes called **rescission acts.**

The deadline for reconciliation is June 15. Ideally, by that time appropriations legislation (for discretionary spending) and changes to program legislation for mandatory spending are completed and in rough compliance with the budget resolution.

In years when the Congress is roughly in agreement with the targets implicit in the President's current services budget and therefore only wants to adjust certain programs, developing the Concurrent Budget Resolution and the process of reconciliation are largely perfunctory. Such was the case in the 103rd Congress in 1994. But when the President and the Congress are in disagreement and the Congress is pushing for substantial change, as was the case with the 104th Congress, then reconciliation becomes difficult and politically divisive.

The Clinton, Congressional, and Current Services Budgets of the 1996 Presidential Election Year

In 1995, the first year of the bitter divisions between Republicans and Democrats in Washington, the effort to plan the 1996 budget ended in a complete breakdown. As deadline after deadline was missed, very few of the necessary appropriations bills were passed. More important, the process of reconciliation completely fell apart and was never accomplished. This was partly, but not entirely, because of presidential vetoes or threats to veto. Many legislative proposals never made it out of committee, and other bills that had versions passed in both houses never made it out of conference committees (where members of both houses and both parties attempted to prepare compromise versions acceptable to both houses and, in some though not all cases, the President). Although disagreements between the Republican Congress and the Democratic President (and his staff) were vocal and conspicuous, more subtle but equally destructive fissures were developing between various Republican factions. These occurred especially between some of the more experienced members, used to calm and deliberate negotiations, even with the enemy, and some of the more impertinent and tactless freshmen, and between the cautious Senate and bold House. These divisions were largely out of the public eye and were contained within committees, cloakrooms, and private meetings, but this contributed to Washington's near paralysis on the budget and virtually everything else as well. In the opinion polls for that year and on into 1996, the Republicans took a drubbing, getting most of the blame for one shutdown after another as President Bill Clinton calmly succeeded at responding to repeated Republican demands, giving the image of remaining aloof and in control while Republicans seemed to go out of their way to give every impression that they were running amok.

The first three quarters of 1996, an important election year (not only for the Presidential election, but also for all House members and one-third of all Senators) became a year of stalling, with no one daring to introduce controversial budget legislation—and certainly nothing that addressed Medicare reform, which was sorely needed. Even the sweeping farm bill (discussed extensively in Chapter 5) was a dubious accomplishment. Even though it reduced outlays of the Department of Agriculture overall, it effectively replaced the old subsidies with welfare payments without guaranteeing the phase-out of the old subsidy programs. The Welfare Reform Act of 1996 was a far-reaching law, but it did not have a great budgetary impact, reducing outlays by only about $10 billion per year.

To be sure, everyone had a balanced budget proposal (at least in the numbers) going into the 1996 elections. The early 1996 Clinton budget had proposals showing balance with *both* OMB and CBO projections (all bets covered), and Congress had passed House Concurrent Resolution 178, its version of the on-line budget. The comparisons between the two are shown in Table 8.8, which also shows the 1997 OMB current services budget. It should be remembered that the current services budget is a benchmark, or *baseline,* budget. This represents the best guess by the OMB of what the deficit will be assuming that there are no changes in legislation, that their economic assumptions are valid (these were shown in Table 8.6), and that discretionary caps and PAYGO rules continue to be enforced. In other words, the current services estimate concluded that if nothing happens, the deficit in fiscal year 2002 would be $131 billion.

The President's budget and the congressional budget are, of course, balanced. Some of the relative priorities become apparent when comparing some of the numbers (at first glance, the President appears to be more generous to defense, but only because defense takes such a massive hit in his first year—$22 billion below current services). The lower revenue numbers (compared to current services) for both budgets imply modest tax cuts.

The most ominous comparisons can be found in the numbers for Medicare. Being far below current services estimates, both numbers imply substantial changes to Medicare program benefits. To repeat a question from the confusing and misleading debates prior to the 1996 elections, are these Medicare proposals *cuts*? The answer, yes and no, exposes a bit of a dilemma. Clearly program spending is projected to rise— 5.61% in the Republican budget, 6.85% in Clinton's. This is not a cut in program costs. But given that the current services estimate pegged the same number at 9.18%, clearly reflecting a rise in the number of beneficiaries, neither plan has much chance of being realized unless there are *some cuts in individual program benefits* for the majority of recipients, or a change in privileges and rights, such as forcing recipients from fee-for-service to HMOs. Numbers like *these* show the difficulty that lays beyond the 1996 election. It is one thing to pencil in these lower numbers. It is entirely another matter to go through successful reconciliation and change programs sufficiently to turn these numbers into reality.

On one final note, by close inspection Table 8.8 it is clear that most of the deficit reduction for both of these election-year budgets was largely *backloaded*. In both cases nearly two-thirds of the deficit reduction is accomplished in the final two years (after the *next* presidential election year, in 2000). This is truer of Clinton's budget than the Republican budget. Neither budget really reduced the projected deficit for fiscal year 1997 (from FY 96).

These are ominous signs. On the other hand, even if the goal is only met halfway (for example, by reducing the deficit to around $60 billion) that would be a notable accomplishment.

BEA Rules: Sequestration

No legislation imposed by Congress upon itself (deficit reduction, balanced budgets, or spending limits) is likely to be effective unless there is some sort of enforcement provision. **Sequestration** is supposed to perform that role for budgetary enforcement. If BEA limits for either discretionary spending or the mandatory PAYGO provision is violated, a **sequester** can be triggered. A sequester will forcibly reduce federal spending in one form or another (depending upon the type of violation). Sequestration is a remarkably complicated procedure. Some elements of the guidelines are vague and are subject to interpretation, which has led to disagreements between the OMB and CBO about spending limits.

Table 8.8

Comparison of Clinton, Congressional, and Current Services Budgets, Presidential Election Year ($ billions)

	1997	1998	1999	2000	2001	2002	Annual % change
Defense							
Clinton	248.3	244.7	247.3	254.6	257.3	265.6	1.36
HCR178	264.1	263.0	266.3	270.0	269.0	269.0	0.37
Current Services	270.3	280.0	285.1	293.5	302.4	308.1	2.65
Medicare							
Clinton	189.2	203.9	216.7	231.9	250.9	263.5	6.85
HCR178	191.2	205.7	215.8	228.8	241.5	251.2	5.61
Current Services	196.3	215.3	235.0	256.3	279.5	304.5	9.18
Total Revenues							
Clinton	1,479.0	1,546.3	1,616.3	1,688.9	1,776.0	1,882.6	4.94
HCR178 (on-line only)	1,083.7	1,130.3	1,177.5	1,231.2	1,290.7	1,359.0	
plus off-line	388.0	406.3	427.8	450.0	471.2	494.6	
Total Congress	1,471.7	1,536.6	1,605.3	1,681.2	1,761.9	1,853.6	4.72
Current Services	1,501.5	1,578.6	1,654.4	1,738.5	1,824.8	1,915.9	5.00
Total Outlays							
Clinton	1,639.6	1,691.3	1,741.8	1,797.0	1,841.4	1,878.9	2.76
HCR178 (on-line only)	1,311.0	1,354.7	1,383.9	1,416.5	1,432.4	1,462.9	
plus off-line	317.7	329.0	342.0	357.8	372.3	388.5	
Total Congress	1,628.7	1,683.7	1,725.9	1,774.3	1,804.7	1,851.4	2.60
Current Services	1,651.3	1,722.9	1,798.8	1,878.2	1,955.5	2,046.9	4.39
Deficit							
Clinton	160.6	145.0	125.5	108.1	65.4	3.7	
HCR178 (on-line only)	227.3	224.4	206.4	185.3	141.8	103.9	
minus off-line surplus	70.3	77.3	85.8	92.1	98.9	106.1	
Total Congress	157.0	147.1	120.6	93.2	42.9	−2.2	
Current Services	149.8	144.3	144.4	139.7	130.7	131.0	

Sources: For Clinton budget, all except defense, FY 1997 Budget of the United States Government, Table 5, p. 19. Clinton Defense budget is from Budget Supplement, Table 4.2, page 47. Congressional budget numbers are taken from House Concurrent Resolution 178, enrolled (the 1997 Congressional budget), which had on-line budget numbers only. Therefore, total Congress revenues, outlays, and deficit are calculated by adding off-line figures from Table 20.1 of Analytic Perspectives, FY 1997. The Clinton budget uses CBO rather than OMB assumptions.

These disagreements are likely to increase in years where different political parties control the houses of Congress and the presidency. What is described below, therefore, is the *essence* of sequestration.

According to BEA, the OMB must monitor all legislation affecting budget authority (appropriations acts) for discretionary spending and all legislation affecting direct (mandatory) spending or revenues. Within five days of the enactment of any such legislation, the OMB must submit to Congress a report on the estimated budgetary impact of the legislation. These estimates are used in ongoing calculations to determine whether caps are being breached in the case of discretionary spending, or PAYGO provisions are being violated in the case mandatory spending. (The ongoing review of mandatory spending and revenue measures is called the **PAYGO scorecard.**) In both cases the estimates must be based on the economic assumptions used by the OMB in the projection of the current services budget estimates.

Both the OMB and the CBO are required to publish three sequestration reports throughout the year. The OMB is also expected to issue reports "explaining" the differences between their reports and the CBO reports. The first report, called the preview report, is published as part of the President's budget that is submitted to Congress in February (it is included in the document entitled *Analytic Perspectives*), and is mostly a summary of the previous years developments in budget enforcement. The middle report, issued in August, is effectively a progress report. It is the third report, the **final sequester report,** that and is at the heart of budgetary enforcement.

The third report is issued *at least* 15 days after the end of a session of Congress, when the legislators have left and returned home (which means that legislators are unable to react to the sequester report until a new session of Congress reconvenes—a rather important feature of the BEA, as we shall see). If in the opinion of the OMB (they have the final word) either the appropriations acts passed in the congressional session just ended will breach discretionary caps or the net effect of new laws subject to PAYGO rules increase the deficit *in the current fiscal year and the budget year combined,*[12] then the President is advised to issue a sequestration order, which would impose a direct reduction in spending.[13]

The sequester for a discretionary spending breach differs from that for a PAYGO violation. In the event of a discretionary spending breach,

---

[12]This is one of the confusing subtleties of the law; new authorizing legislation (or amendments) affecting direct spending or revenues is not supposed to "increase the deficit in any year through 1998." Yet under PAYGO rules, the sequester report evaluates the net impact of legislation upon spending and revenues only in the fiscal year underway (a couple of months old at the time the final sequester report is issued) and in the next fiscal year.

[13]The budgetary violation can involve either authorizations *or* outlays—either can trigger a sequester. Likewise, if an agency exceeds authorizations in its spending, that can also trigger a sequester.

the resulting sequester will force a uniform cutback in all categories of discretionary spending (not just in the area of offending legislation) until the breach has been eliminated. Some discretionary programs are limited to 2%, so if the sequester involves a greater percentage, the remainder is taken out of unrestricted discretionary programs. If the offending appropriations legislation is passed before July 1, then a "within-session" sequestration occurs, forcing cutbacks within the same fiscal year. If the legislation is enacted after July 1, spending cutbacks do not occur directly. Instead, caps for the next fiscal year are reduced by the amount of the breach. In other words, if appropriations legislation for defense is enacted on July 15 and exceed the current discretionary cap by $40 billion, then there is no automatic spending cutback. Instead, the discretionary caps for the next fiscal year are reduced (all categories) by $40 billion.[14]

In the case of PAYGO rules (the PAYGO scorecard for mandatory spending and revenues), any violation and requirement for sequester is usually exposed in the final sequestration report released after the congressional session has ended. If the net effect of all legislation governed by PAYGO increases the deficit above the amount projected by the current services budget, say by $30 billion, then the resulting sequester will uniformly reduce spending across a range of mandatory spending categories that have been identified by BEA as sequestrable (in other words, the spending restrictions are *not* imposed across all categories of mandatory spending—most are exempt!). Strangely, this subcategory of mandatory spending that can be sequestered represents only 1.7% of total outlays and 3.5% of mandatory spending. The total outlay for all sequestrable spending is less than $30 billion. It includes Medicare (but only up to 4%), student loan programs, and direct grants to local governments for social services and family support, but it excludes Medicaid, Social Security and most farm subsidies. Therefore, if there were a $30 billion violation on the PAYGO scorecard, Medicare would be reduced by 4%, certain small programs would be completely wiped out, and 96.5% of mandatory spending would be untouched.[15]

---

[14]If this seems like a potential loophole, it probably is. One has to wonder what would happen if all appropriations were passed after July 1 in each congressional session if caps were consistently violated.

[15]This is not a loophole so much as a bizarre arrangement. It is hard to imagine that it would be literally enforced if the PAYGO scorecard triggered a large sequester. The PAYGO rules essentially act as a good faith-measure that warns Congress, "let's not even find out what would happen if we break this rule."

Finally, there are even some exceptions to these rules. First, a small vaguely defined allowance is granted for error on the various limits as a concession to the looseness of the procedure, which, after all, relies heavily on a large number of OMB guesses. Sequesters also can be suspended in case of war or in the event of a recession.

Sequesters were introduced by the Gramm-Rudman-Hollings legislation and were the primary enforcement provision of GRH and the primary reason for its failure (see Figure 8.1). Like current law, GRH required a sequestration report (only one). However, unlike current law, which requires that the report be issued 15 days *after* the end of the congressional session, GRH required that the report be issued on October 15, before the end the session. This deadline was the Achilles's heel of GRH. In an attempt to avoid sequestration, Congress merely postponed final appropriations until *after* October 15, triggering off wild political firestorms at the end of the fiscal year, but avoiding sequesters and all effective limits on spending.

The BEA Calendar

Although we have already discussed most of the deadlines in their proper context, deadlines and other important dates set by the BEA are summarized in Table 8.9. Congress begins its new session in early January, and within a month the President submits his budget to Congress. The formal budgetary year ends with the release of the final sequester report by the OMB. In the interim are resolutions, appropriations, reconciliations, and new legislation creating or altering permanent budget authority.

A review of the timetable reveals yet one more odd feature of BEA: the President and the Congress never formulate, nor do they agree on a final budget document, nor are they required to do so. The President's February budget is largely an advisory document, although it does include revisions of economic assumptions, caps, the sequester preview report, and the current services budget, all of which strongly limit final budgetary decisions. Congress then tries to develop is own version of the budget, the **congressional budget resolution,** and attempts to enforce BEA provisions through **reconciliation** (as discussed earlier). If reconciliation in an era of change, as during the 104th Congress, involves a full array of new legislation that changes many programs, the resulting legislation might be packaged together in what is called a **reconciliation bill.** Such a tactical step forces the President's hand; he either accepts all changes or he vetoes the

Table 8.9

The Budgetary Timetable

First Monday in February: President submits his budget to Congress.
The President submits his full set of budgetary documents, listed in Table 4.1, to Congress. These budgetary documents are for planning and advisory purposes, generally for the following fiscal year (October 1). They effectively begin the budgetary debate. The documents include a preview sequester report. This deadline is usually met unless a new President is assuming office.

April 15: Deadline for **Congressional Budget Resolution.**
Relying upon cooperation and agreement between House and Senate Budget Committees, Congress formulates its own version of the budget called the **congressional budget resolution.** The resolution specifies the level of revenues expected and of the deficit, and includes budgetary authority and outlays for each budgetary *function*, but *not* by agency or program. This deadline was not met in 1995 or 1996.

May 15: House consideration of annual **appropriations** begins.

June 15: Deadline for **reconciliation**
If in the **Congressional Budget Resolution** Congress has decided to make changes in mandatory spending, which requires altering permanent budget authority in authorizing legislation (as is the case with entitlements, for example) or tax changes, all of which is subject to PAYGO limits, instructions are sent to the appropriate committees to contribute to an overall reconciliation that assures aggregate spending and taxing decisions from all committees meet BEA guidelines. The overall effectiveness of this requirement remains to be seen. Reconciliation was not accomplished in 1995 or 1996.

June 30: House deadline for completion of **appropriations.**
This deadline was not met in 1995 or 1996.

August 20: OMB issues **midsession sequester report.**
If the OMB judges that BEA provisions have been violated by appropriations or by changes in new or existing authorizing legislation, this report can serve as an early warning that funds might be **sequestered.**

October 1: New fiscal year begins.
Fifteen days after end of congressional session: OMB issues **final sequester report,** and if necessary (if BEA is violated), President issues a sequester order.

entire package. The Congress can choose how it presents its legislation to the President, but there never is a *formalized* final budget agreed to by all parties. Spending and taxing, although monitored and constrained by a host of BEA limits as we have discussed, are always the net effect of the myriad evolving legislative provisions.

What's Next?

BEA restrictions and the two primary channels of spending and taxing authority are summarized in Table 8.10. The budget enforcement provisions discussed in this chapter are complicated, vague, and ambiguous in

Table 8.10

BEA Enforcement: The Two Categories of Budget Authority and Outlays

1. Authorizing legislation ... leading to	
2a. Permanent budget authority	2b. Budget authority through appropriations
1. Classified as **direct spending,** also called **mandatory spending.** Includes but is not restricted to **entitlements. Taxes** are also created by permanent budget authority.	1. Classified as **discretionary spending.**
2. Not subject to appropriations (one exception: the food stamp program).	2. Final spending authority usually subject to annual **appropriations acts.**
3. Levels of outlays each year determined mostly by rights and benefits extended by authorizing legislation, demographics (who qualifies for what), and economic assumptions.	3. Level of budget authority each year determined by appropriations. Some categories, such as defense, NASA, and EPA also require annual authorization bills.
4. No direct restrictions on spending, but subject to **PAYGO** provision of BEA. Any net combination of budget authority or outlays created by permanent budget authority that increases the size of the deficit above OMB projections can trigger a **sequester.**	4. Aggregate spending restricted by BEA **caps.** A breach in spending caps can trigger a **sequester.**
5. Examples: Federal employee and military retirement programs, Social Security, Medicare, Medicaid, federal unemployment benefits, farm subsidies.	5. Examples: Defense, agricultural research, most direct educational programs, NASA, most energy expenditures.
6. Outlay amounts in 1995: $741.3 billion, 48.8% of total.	6. Outlay amounts in 1995: $545.7 billion, 35.9% of total.

Note: These are 97% definitions—as always, there are some exceptions. Net interest ($232.2 billion in 1995) is not included in either column.

some areas, and untested in others, subject to interpretation and sometimes difficult to understand. Yet in the last few years these restrictions seem to be working. The deficit has fallen since 1992 absolutely and as a percentage of the GDP. Moreover, both the President and the Congress appear to be making a good-faith effort to comply with budgetary enforcement, such as it is, even though it does not assure a balanced budget.

So far we have discussed a whole series of *internal* problems associated with large deficits and related issues. They include rapid debt accumulation, high interest payments, the substantial growth of entitlements, intergenerational income transfers, and the long-range endangerment of trust funds and programs like Social Security and Medicare that depend upon those trust funds for financing.

There is, however, another element of deficit spending and corrections to deficit spending that is equally important and must also be discussed: the *external* effects of fiscal policy upon the economy. This will be the subject of the next chapter.

The Economic Impact of Deficits and Deficit Reduction

· ·

· ·

Until this point our discussion has been restricted to the budget, the deficit, and the attendant matters as an *internal* issue—as though we were discussing an enormous *accounting* problem. But we can not dismiss the fact that a budget that spends more than $1.5 trillion per year and borrows between $150 and $200 billion annually is going to have a substantial impact upon the economy. In this chapter we will explore the economic impact of the deficit and of deficit reduction.

The subject entertained here is controversial, to say the least. There is certainly no consensus on theory when it comes to fiscal policy. For that reason a general overview of some of the fundamental theory is presented.

Economic theory in general often explores *tradeoffs* that must be considered when making policy decisions. This concept—tradeoffs—embraces the notion that the consequences of any major decision will include both gains and losses. Very seldom do we have the luxury of making choices that provide only benefits at no cost to anyone. Any policy that promises only comfortable solutions without hazards or drawbacks probably has unseen—or worse yet, undeclared—flaws. Politics and economics are controversial fields precisely because decisions made under their rubric will typically have a beneficial effect upon some and a negative impact upon others. Political and economic choices, therefore, involve making decisions that weigh the benefits of an option against the costs, with the hope that, on net, the former substantially outweighs the latter.

Economic Theory, Research, and Policy

Having made this concession to the duality of economic and political policy, in this chapter we will attempt to systematically present both sides of the issues. We will begin by discussing what many theorists regard as the positive side of large-scale government spending and budget deficits. Then we will present a critical view of the same subject.

Any scholar who is familiar with the field of economics and empirical economic research knows that the more controversial debates in the discipline are seldom settled to everyone's satisfaction by looking at the data. The modern policy analyst is obliged to make take a stand, even if tentative, on theories and ideas that are still hotly disputed. This book is not intended to be an exhaustive survey of contemporary opinion,[1] and although an effort is made to provide some representation for the full range of ideas, the final stance taken in this chapter and in the epilogue clearly reflect the theories most favored by the author.

It should also be stated that the more advanced research done in economics these days tends to focus on very well-defined areas that sometimes are mere subsets or important tangential issues to the more sweeping, general, and inclusive presentations found in undergraduate textbooks or survey texts like this.

---

[1] Other books do that. The free readings from the Federal Reserve Bank of Kansas City, *Budget Deficits and Debt* (Bibliography, Section 4) and the reader by James Rock (Bibliography, Section 7) are good starting points to get a variety of opinions.

It is partly for these reasons that an annotated bibliography has been provided at the end of this work following the epilogue. By the annotations one can plainly see that many contrary opinions to those offered here are alive and well and that some of the more general theories have numerous subsets of related issues that are equally controversial.

The Support for Large-Scale Government Spending and Occasional Deficits[2]

As we saw in Chapter 2, when we reviewed spending and deficits in the early part of the century, government spending has not always operated on the scale that we see today—at least not in times of peace. For example, federal outlays as a percentage of GDP was only 3.4% in 1930, in contrast to 21% in 1996.

Equally important, the large inclusive and expensive entitlements programs, such as Social Security, Medicare, and the various need-based programs, have slowly evolved and grown over time and have not always been part of American economic life. Social Security was a product of the Great Depression. Neither Medicare nor Medicaid existed prior to 1965. Today these programs are huge and controversial and, as we discussed earlier in previous chapters, their long-range financial health is in jeopardy. Program supporters, though, are quick to point out that these programs, affecting tens of millions directly, provide very substantial economic benefits.

Government Spending as an Automatic Stabilizer

Business cycle theory reminds us that although market economies enjoy relatively high growth and that growth is the norm, economic recessions are common, and depressions, although infrequent, always loom as a possibility. The entire decade of the 1930s was marred by the gloom of a terrible worldwide depression; since then there have been nine recessions in the United States. Supporters of activist fiscal policy, often in the Keynesian tradition, are quick to point out that the Great Depression was

[2]For ideas sympathetic to or consistent with those represented in this section (although these writers might still take exception to the way this material is presented here), a good starting point might be the book by Robert Heilbroner and Peter Bernstein (Bibliography, Section 4) and articles by Robert Eisner and James Tobin (Bibliography, Section 4) or Steven Fazzari (Bibliography, Section 7).

essentially cured by the robust government spending of the 1940s, not as conscious antirecession policy, but as an incidental effect of necessary war-related spending. As soon as the government spending started, the economy started to flourish—and it was, of course, deficit-financed.[3]

In the contemporary setting, high levels of government spending are said to provide an *automatic stabilizer* to an otherwise cyclical economy. Private spending is procyclical. In a business recession, the initial downturn might be caused by a slight drop in consumer spending for consumer durable goods, which shows up as disappointing sales from the perspective of the businesses that are affected. Eventually, that stimulus can have a spread effect through the economy, triggering more reduced spending, and impacting areas like business capital investment, inventories, and payrolls. These secondary effects have the potential to deepen and prolong a recession.

In contrast to slumping private spending, government spending and the income created by such spending remains stable or even rises during the recession because of unemployment insurance outlays and temporary programs tailored to ease the burden of the recession. This provides a floor of noncyclical spending that has the effect of dampening the downward phase of the cycle. Consequently recessions in the modern era—since World War II—have been shallower and less threatening economically than those prior to World War II.

The antirecessionary impact of federal unemployment insurance is obvious. Figure 9.1 shows what happened to the Unemployment Insurance Trust Fund during the last recession, which began in late 1990 and lasted through 1992. Unemployment benefits, which were extended somewhat beyond normal limits during the recession, directly replaced nearly $40 billion of lost income in the worst recession year, 1992. In that same year the trust fund ran a deficit of $16.1 billion. The fiscal impact of this is clearly countercyclical.

In this context, deficits during recessions, whether intentional or the unwanted byproduct of falling tax revenues, are generally seen as countercyclical. The recession-year deficit arises specifically *because* federal spending does not fall in a recession—it might even rise because of unemployment and other support programs. Yet, because of the erosion of income and hence the tax base, revenues fall. Therefore, the government is effectively able to preserve its role as automatic stabilizer specifically because it is able to maintain its level of spending by borrowing what it needs (because, again, the deficit is financed by borrowing).

[3]See J.R. Vernon (Bibliography, Section 6).

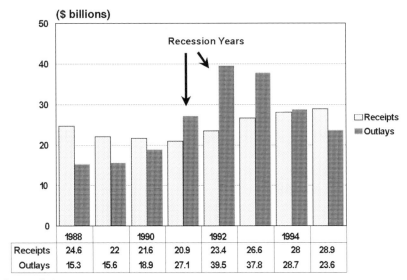

Figure 9.1
Unemployment Insurance, 1988–1995

The *composition* of federal spending, which over the years has strongly shifted in the direction of various support programs, has some bearing upon this issue as well. In 1960, the year in which John F. Kennedy was elected President, defense spending made up 50% of the federal budget, and entitlements programs constituted about a quarter of the total. Those two priorities have now been reversed entirely.

Supporters of the large entitlements programs point out that they provide, in an occasionally hostile and unstable economy, income to those social groups who are in most need of it—people with low income, the disabled, and the elderly. In the absence of such powerful government support programs, it is argued, these same groups would be victimized by an economy that favors people who are young, healthy, and, in the present period at least, well educated. Not only does this type of spending stabilize the economy, but it provides a very important *safety net.*

Federal Spending and the Multiplier Effect

Introductory economics textbooks typically introduce new students to the concept of the *multiplier.* The multiplier concept recognizes that any stimulus to income in a country or a region will have a greater final impact than the size of the initial stimulus. Consider, for example, the economic impact when a new company moves into a city, bringing with it a $10 million annual payroll. By how much will this stimulus increase income for the area? At first glance it might seem that the answer would be $10 million—the size of the new payroll. But it is clearly some amount greater than that. New employees hired by the company—employees perhaps attracted to the area from elsewhere—spend that income for rent, food, local entertainment, new car purchases, and so forth, and it is money that would not have been spent in the absence of a new payroll. This additional spending becomes new income for other parties, producing a secondary stimulus. That in turn is spent, producing a tertiary effect, and it continues until such time as the stimulus has run its course. By then the final net effect might be a multiple of the original stimulus by a factor of two to three, or more.

Final spending = (**k**) × Initial stimulus
where **k** is the multiplier.

This relationship is called the *multiplier effect*. For example, if the multiplier in a context like this is estimated to be about 2.5, the $10 million new payroll in a would raise annual income for the region by about $25 million (see Fig. 9.2). This example is called a *regional multiplier*, which measures the impact of a localized spending stimulus to the city or the region affected.

The concept of the multiplier can also be applied at the national level when federal spending is involved, especially spending that is deficit financed. The basic argument is this: If the federal government increases its outlays by some amount, the final impact upon national output, as measured by gross domestic product (GDP), will increase by some multiple of that amount. For example, if the multiplier is 2.5 at the national level, deficit-financed federal spending that increases by $10 billion it raise GDP by as much as $25 billion. It does so in exactly the same way as discussed in the example of the regional multiplier—jobs are created, the income is spent, which raises income at a secondary level, and so forth.

$$\Delta GDP = \mathbf{k}\ \Delta(\text{government outlays})$$

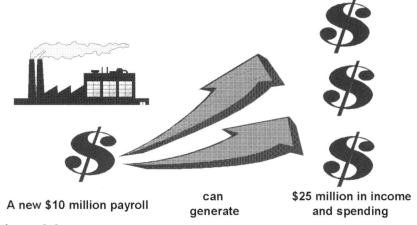

A new $10 million payroll   can generate $25 million in income and spending

Figure 9.2
The Power of the Multiplier: A Regional Example

According to the theory, deficit-financed spending has a much greater impact than spending financed by taxes. The latter reduces after-tax income, the ultimate source of consumer spending, so one tends to offset the other, substantially reducing the stimulating effect. Supporters of the concept of the multiplier are quick to point out that the stimulating effect of deficit-financed spending ultimately reduces the impact of the deficit because of the growth of GDP and, hence, the tax base. This proposition has some similarities to supply-side theories. And the multiplier works in both directions—cutbacks in spending go far beyond the initial amount impacted.

It would be a mistake to think that the power implied by the multiplier is always effective and that government spending is universally stimulating at all times and under all circumstances. The power of government spending working through the conduit of the multiplier will depend upon context.[4] When coming out of a depression or a severe recession, an easy monetary policy combined with a fiscal stimulus would likely be a very potent blend; the fiscal impact of war spending on the Great Depression

[4]Strange as it may seem, given the importance of the multiplier in college textbooks, advanced research is not really oriented toward estimating the size or even the validity of the multiplier at the national level. Most of the contemporary research is indirect on this subject, concerning itself more with such issues as "crowding out," discussed later in this chapter. See the annotation for the recent article by Julia Darby and Jim Malley (Bibliography, Section 3), which for the economics researcher at least, identifies one modern approach to this ages-old controversy.

provides a good example. But the same combination used in an inflationary environment, such as that in the late 1970s, would have disastrous consequences—the resulting excess demand could produce pure inflation. Additionally, the argument of the multiplier's potency cannot be used to justify *systemic deficits*—large deficits that endure year after year, whether or not the economy needs stimulus, nor can it be used to justify fiscal irresponsibility in general.

More relevant to the modern debate is the first concept discussed—that of the *regional multiplier*. Because the regional effects of federal spending are very powerful, even the most ardent budget cutters in Congress will often strive to protect programs that pump income into their own districts. Having a large federal program for defense, energy, or agricultural spending in one's district can stimulate a local economy as strongly as does a new business moving in. Equally important, because of the regional multiplier effect, program cutbacks that are diffused through the national economy can have a devastating effect in local economies that benefitted from the program. We will return to this point with examples when discussing the undesirable or harmful effects of budget cuts.

The Employment Effects of Federal Spending

The federal government, with more than 3 million civilian employees in 1995 (and with an additional 1.4 million military personnel), is by far the largest employer in the United States. In effect, then, federal spending is *directly* responsible for about 4.5 million jobs, and, again taking into account the regional multiplier effect and weighing the civilian impact of such labor intensive outlays as defense spending, it is indirectly responsible for many more. Effectively, when the government spends money jobs are created and maintained and when there are cutbacks, jobs are eliminated. Political supporters of high levels of government spending are very quick to point this out—what may be one person's tax burden is another's livelihood.

Equally important at the social and cultural level, the federal government has pioneered the creation of job opportunities for social groups that traditionally have been faced with limited employment opportunities because of racial, sexual, and other forms of discrimination. This is an ethical rather than a financial issue, but the government's large payroll has provided jobs that pay well and offer respectable social standing—jobs that may not have been available outside of the government.

Conservative critics of the employment effects of federal spending insist that these jobs are created only at the loss of opportunities in the private sector. They argue that the burden of taxes suppresses private spending and causes the loss of jobs, possibly having a net negative effect. Additionally, critics argue that government is hopelessly inefficient, and much federal work is little more than make-work that comes at taxpayer expense.

This argument, when generalized and carried to the extreme as it often is in political arguments, is somewhat unfair. Although one can find pockets of almost stupendous inefficiency in government (sometimes in small local programs supported by the most strident critics of government), some programs work with impressive efficiency. The U.S. Postal Service delivers 580 million pieces of mail *daily* at relatively low cost and with remarkable reliability (so much so that the old excuse "it was lost in the mail" has absolutely no credibility these days).[5] It does this with 790 thousand employees, most of whom appear to be working pretty hard, some under conditions of high stress. As discussed earlier, the retirement program in the Social Security Administration accomplishes its job spending far less than 1% of total outlays on administration.

Again the jobs argument is more strongly connected to debates over efficiency, the size of government, and issues of social equity, opportunity and fairness, and not the budget deficit. If it is the proper role of the federal government to create jobs or provide essential services that can only be met with a wide range of federal employment—and not everyone even agrees on this point—such a mandate does not justify waiving financial responsibility and prudence. Large systemic deficits cannot be justified merely because they create jobs.[6]

The Negative Economic Effects of Deficits

As was pointed out in the introduction to this chapter, in the eyes of the economist, typically no good thing comes without some cost. There are theories that laud the stimulating effects of deficits and the power of federal

---

[5]In fact, anyone doubting the efficacy and scale of operations of the U.S. Postal Service should visit their web site, http://www.usps.gov/ and find the section on "postal facts." The sheer scale of postal operations is impressive.

[6]Before moving to the next topic, it is appropriate here to bring attention to a popular modern theory, not discussed elsewhere in this text, that is critical of other theories that claim that deficits can have a stimulating effect upon the economy. The new theory, made popular by economist Robert Barro (Bibliography, Section 7) is called "Ricardian Equivalence." The theory states, in effect, that such short-term fiscal expedients as tax cuts are neutralized by the long-range view that they will have to be reversed or countered in the future. The best explanation and overview of this theory is provided by John J. Seater (Bib. Sec. 7).

spending. As might be guessed, these are counterbalanced by theories that warn of dangers arising from the excessive use of policies that involve high levels of government spending or deficits.

Although our topic is deficits, and not the level of federal spending or taxing, the two are not entirely separable. Earlier we reviewed certain tangential issues, such as the power of federal employment, from a liberal perspective. Therefore, in this section, before moving to the real subject at hand, we should review some of the general conservative criticism of large government.

Taxes and Disincentives[7]

Despite whatever benefits are conferred by large scale federal spending, it certainly has to be paid for, either with taxes or through borrowing. Borrowing only postpones the ultimate burden of taxes. The primary complaint against taxes is rather obvious—people do not like to pay and they are seldom convinced that they are getting their money's worth. While there is no way to be sure about a proposition like this, the American culture has probably reached its political limit on the tax burden that we are willing to absorb (meaning that no political platform that promotes tax increases has any chance of surviving more than one election cycle), even though the overall tax burden in the United States is far below that of most European nations.

In the United States, federal income tax rates are *progressive*—people with higher taxable incomes pay higher tax rates than do the middle-class or the poor. Table 4.5, which was presented earlier in the discussion of taxes, is reproduced here as Table 9.1. It shows that the highest marginal tax rate in 1995 was 39.6% for anyone with a taxable income greater than $256,500.

There is a strong conservative tradition that insists that these high levels of taxation produce a very substantial *disincentive* for economic growth and development. The argument proceeds from the premise that a market economy flourishes over the decades because *entrepreneurs* in the private economy accumulate capital, organize the resources, and take the risks that are necessary to make investments in ways that promote economic growth

---

[7]A good starting point for a more detailed overview sympathetic with the material that follows and suitable for the general reader might be the book by Douglas R. Slease and Tom Herman (Bibliography, Section 9). For the academic reader the text edited by Joel Slemrod, *Do Taxes Matter* (Bibl., Sec. 9) and other select articles in Section 9 of the bibliography are appropriate.

Table 9.1

Personal Income Tax Rates and Tax Brackets 1995 Tax Year

Marginal tax rates	Brackets for	
	Single	Married filing jointly
15%	$0	$0
28%	23,350	39,000
31%	56,550	94,250
36%	117,950	143,600
39.6%	256,500	256,500

Notes: (1) These rates apply to *taxable* income, after deductions, such as those for dependent children and mortgage interest, have been taken.

(2) Income earners must also pay FICA payroll tax for Social Security and Medicare at 7.65% of earned income, an amount that is matched by the employer.

Source: IRS form 1040, 1995 tax year.

and development and provide job opportunities. Supporters of the entre-preneurial theories are quick to point out that the United States is primar-ily a market economy, and because of opportunities for investment and the entrepreneurial spirit in the United States, the U.S. economy is the strongest and most prosperous in the world, and is the envy of other nations.

While this argument is sometimes taken to extremes and, as such, it glosses over some of the problems that we have in the United States, there is surely a strong element of truth present. Through the 1990s, U.S. en-trepreneurs have innovated at a blistering pace, introducing new tech-nologies and new companies in the pursuit of profit opportunities. Equally important, a considerable part of this momentum has come from small-scale entrepreneurs, rather than from large corporations, a devel-opment that would be far less likely to occur in the economic arena of our European and Asian competitors. This means that the prospects for upward—and downward—mobility are greater in the United States than in the other industrialized nations.

Taxes—or at least excessive taxes—and the entrepreneurial spirit do not mix in the eyes of free-market advocates. One of the primary motivating

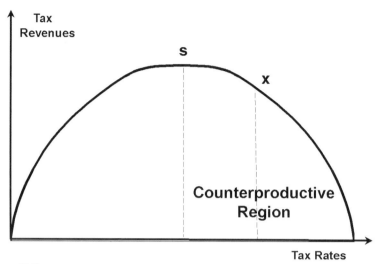

Figure 9.3
The Tax Rate/Revenue Tradeoff

forces behind entrepreneurial activity, and one that is necessary for its preservation, is the prospect of the financial reward that justifies taking the risk in the first place. Why bother taking the risk if, when successful, the reward is stripped away by taxes? In other words, high taxes discourage the entrepreneurial drive by removing the incentive, and the net effects are low levels of investment, slow job formation, and a stagnant economy.

Counterproductive Tax Rates

Linked to this argument was a theory that became popular during the era of supply-side economics in the 1980s. According to this theory, taxes can become such a disincentive to growth that when they are raised in the name of increasing federal revenues, tax receipts actually *fall,* making the policy counterproductive.[8]

This theory is represented in Figure 9.3. The effective tax rate is shown on the horizontal axis, and tax revenues are shown on the vertical axis. By general inspection of the relationship, an increase in the tax rate has the desired effect—an increase in tax revenues—only until it reaches a saturation point, represented as point s on the diagram. Thereafter, in-

[8]Made popular by Arthur Laffer (Bibliography, Section 9).

creases in the tax rate suppress economic growth to such an extent that tax receipts fall with each successive increase in tax rates. Tax receipts equal tax rates *times* the tax base, or income. The theory argues that if taxes go up, income goes down. What happens to the product, tax revenues, depends upon the relative degree of change. Finally, there is some point of taxation (point s) beyond which the drop in the tax base is sufficient to override the effect of the increased tax rate. The net effect is a reduction in tax receipts.

This theory is appealing and, indeed, self-evident. The United States is a market economy that relies upon private investment for much of its growth. Logically, there must be a point where taxes could be so high as to have the effect of crippling the private sector. This simple truth, which may apply only to extremes in tax rates, can be very dangerous when misinterpreted. It can lead to disastrous policies that can seriously compound the deficit problem.

The best way to expose this danger is through example. Suppose we were convinced that we had passed that counterproductive tax threshold represented by point s and that we were on the downside of the curve, as represented by point x. What, then, would be our solution if deficit reduction is the goal? Clearly *cutting taxes* provides the solution—one of the few cases in policy where there is no tradeoff, where there is only gain at no cost. Cutting taxes would raise revenues and it would cut the deficit by stimulating the economy.

So, what is the danger? This kind of no-pain theory becomes very attractive to politicians who want to tell their constituents that cutting taxes will *reduce* the deficit. The only voters inclined to vote against that would be those wary of the argument. Even though the theory may be appealing in its simplicity, an honest assessment of where we are actually *located* on the policy line is another matter altogether. If we are actually to the *left* of point s, which is almost certainly the case at present, and we cut taxes in the name of deficit reduction, the deficit will grow ever larger. This lesson has already been learned once.

All of this puts current tax policy somewhat in limbo. We are certainly still in the region where tax cuts will result in a loss of revenues, but we have no desire to move very much farther up the policy curve because of the inherent truth of the conservative argument. There is some point at which taxes become a severe disincentive.

Modern (1990s) versions of supply-side economics take a more subtle approach to tax controversies than the 1980s vintage theories. The contemporary variant of supply-side economics no longer necessarily promotes across-the-board tax cuts at a time when budget deficits are a problem. Instead reductions in the *highest* marginal tax rates and a movement to a flatter tax structure are advocated, again because of the disincentive effects of high taxes upon risk-taking and capital formation, as was discussed earlier.

Liberal defenders of the present tax structure remind us that our system of progressive stepped income taxes, as represented earlier in Figure 9.1, promotes more income equality in the United States. Taxes on the wealthy at high marginal rates help to fund entitlements programs that are marked for the elderly, poor, or disabled. This redistributes income nationally, and it substantially reduces poverty. (It should be noted that the FICA payroll tax, because of the fixed rate and the cap that exempts most of it from income above the cap, is regressive.) Wealth and income in the United States would be much more polarized than at present if income tax rates were substantially flatter. Ideologically therefore, this argument splits over equity versus efficiency. Liberals promote the distributional effects of progressive income taxes and high marginal rates for at least the upper tax brackets, and conservatives insist that these same tax rates stifle entrepreneurial initiative.[9]

Crowding Out: the Impact of Federal Borrowing upon the Credit Markets and Interest Rates[10]

Probably the most potent argument against budget deficits is found in the *crowding out theory*. This theory warns of the potential damage done

[9]This controversy over progressive versus flat taxes and the effects upon incentives and income distribution will likely rage through the 1990s, possibly moving beyond academic circles and into legislation. For a representative sample of both sides of this issue currently, see the many articles annotated in Bibliography, Section 9. We are more concerned with the aggregate revenue effects of the tax structure than with issues of distribution or efficiency (except to the extent that the latter impacts revenues). The author, though, is sympathetic to both sides of the argument and he feels that the tension between the two will drive the debate. In other words, the position taken by the author is this: (a) in support of the argument on incentives, the highest marginal income tax rates at the federal level should not exceed 35% (as it presently does), (b) because of the desirable redistribution effects of a progressive tax rate, the same rate should not be below 30%. More importantly, so long as there is a budget deficit, there should be no change to the tax code unless it is deficit neutral or it increases revenues.

[10]The crowding out theory, clearly favored by the author, is controversial and is certainly not accepted by all economists. For contrary opinions, see Dean Baker and

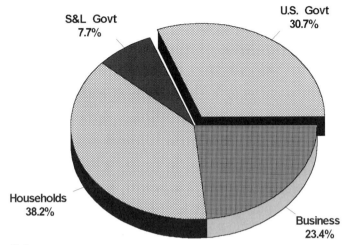

Figure 9.4
Total Funds Raised in Credit Markets, 1985 through 1994
Source: Federal Reserve Flow of Funds Data

to private borrowing and, hence, private capital formation by the government's competition for borrowed money. This theory begins with the reminder that the budget deficit is financed by borrowing money through the sale on the open market of marketable U.S. Treasury Securities, as was discussed in Chapter 1 and in Appendix A. This kind of activity puts the U.S. Treasury in competition with other borrowers for the limited funds available in domestic credit markets. Ultimately, it has the effect of putting upward pressure on interest rates.

We would expect to see the data confirm that federal borrowing is large even on a relative scale. The percentage of total funds raised in the decade between 1985 and 1994 that was borrowed by the U.S. Treasury is shown in Figure 9.4. Over that decade, federal borrowing claimed about 31% of total domestic borrowings.

There are many elements to the theory of crowding out. Implicit is an underlying theory of interest-rate determination that must be discussed

Todd Schafer (Bibliography, Section 3) and Robert Eisner (Bibl., Sec. 4). The author believes that the following articles add support, in some cases indirectly, to the general crowding out argument: Julia Darby and Jim Malley (Bibl., Sec. 3—the author regards this as an important advanced article for the professional, and a good starting point to work through the literature moving backwards), Richard J. Cebula and James V. Koch (both articles), and W. Robert Brazelton (Bibl., Sec. 3). There is no implication that these scholars would necessarily agree with the author's presentation.

briefly. Here are some of the major points to be reviewed in theories of the determination of interest rates:

(a) *Interest rates on all types of securities and deposits, from 13-week Treasury Bills to home mortgages, tend to rise and fall together, though not perfectly.*

Generally, over periods of time, though not necessarily in daily market activity, short-term and long-term interest rates tend to rise and fall together. For example, the normal spread between 13-week Treasury Bills and 30-year bonds is usually somewhere between 1.5 and 2.5%. If the 13-week T-bill rate is at 5½%, the long-bond rate, as the 30-year bond rate is called, would typically be around 7%. When the T-bill rate is at 7%, the long-bond rate might be at 9%, or even higher. While there is wide variance in this relationship, the rates generally move together.

(b) *The general level of interest rates is determined by market forces that reflect variations in the supply and demand for credit and the financial assets that represent that credit.*

The U.S. Treasury is simply one of several players in this game, albeit a large, important, and powerful one. The Treasury uses the finance markets to borrow money (through the sale of securities) in order to finance the budget deficit, and this has the same effect on interest rate levels as any other type of borrowing.

(c) *The Federal Reserve System actively intervenes in the credit markets by affecting the supply of credit, often with the intent of strongly influencing interest rates.*

Monetary policy, as executed by the Federal Reserve System, the nation's central banking authority, is very powerful when it comes to influencing interest rates. The Federal Reserve System often intervenes in the financial markets with the explicit purpose of raising or lowering interest rates.

(d) *Inflation or inflationary expectations, inevitably pushes interest rates up.*

This implies that if bad economic policy has the effect of introducing inflation to the economy, it will also raise interest rates, and it will be responsible for all attendant harm that arises from high interest rates. To complicate this further, the formation of *inflationary expectations*, which is the widespread belief that inflation will increase in the near future will *also* push interest rates up in anticipation of the inflation that is expected by everyone.

(e) *The level of interest rates, therefore, reflects the conflation of the many supply and demand forces that act upon them.*

These supply and demand forces include:

- the Treasury's demand for credit via the sale of its Bills, Notes and Bonds;
- Federal Reserve influence upon the supply of credit;
- domestic level of savings (which increases the supply of credit);
- consumer borrowing for mortgages, credit cards, auto loans, and so on;
- business borrowing for plant expansions, acquisitions, meeting short-run cash needs, and a host of other reasons;
- foreign interaction in domestic credit markets, influenced in turn by everything from currency exchange rates to overseas inflation rates;
- inflation and inflationary expectations.

All of these forces combine to push interest rates up or down, with some forces having a positive effect and others offsetting that. The actual movement of rates reflects the net effect of all of them working together.

Having reviewed these premises, let us now carefully explore the nuances of the crowding-out argument. To summarize the theory in words, when government borrowing rises due to budget deficits and becomes competitive with private borrowing, this has the tendency to push interest rate up, "crowding out" private borrowing. This then curtails the spending that otherwise would have resulted from private borrowing.

The Formal Crowding-out Argument

In order to pursue out line of reasoning here, it might be useful to present a visual image. Figure 9.5 presents a simplified version of the *loanable funds model* that is sometimes used in economics to present theories of interest rate determination. It is a general supply and demand model of the kind often seen in economics texts, except that it generically represents the credit market and it uses the interest rate as that special price—effectively the price of credit—that allocates credit over time. This proxy interest rate is meant to represent the general structure of interest rates. Remember, interest rates tend to rise and fall together, as we discussed earlier.

In this model the demand curve, labeled **D**, represents the *demand for credit*, which is borrowing activity. Any surge in borrowing activity coming from any source will cause the demand curve for credit to shift to the right. The borrowing activity embodied in this line represents the consumer demand for installment, business and consumer mortgage and other real estate loans, business borrowing for expansion and acquisition, foreign borrowing in the U.S. finance markets, and any other borrowing activity,

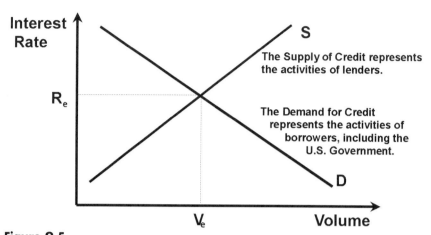

Figure 9.5
Interest Rate Determination: The Supply and Demand for Credit

including federal government borrowing to finance budget deficits. The demand curve slopes downward, as shown, because clearly the demand for credit—borrowing activity—will be higher at lower interest rates.

The supply curve, labeled **S**, represents all savings and lending activity in the United States. As will be seen later, this includes the ability of the Federal Reserve System to supply credit through its policy operations. The interest rate in this model, represented by value R_e on the vertical axis that might be a value of 7%, reflects the conflation of all variables represented in the model, including inflation and the formation of inflationary expectations. This means that in real markets, no single variable will necessarily dominate the direction of interest rates. This subtle point becomes very important in the discussion that follows.

Finally, the unit of measure along the horizontal axis is volume, since that is usually the quantity variable used in the discussion of the credit market. Therefore, the solution value for Volume, represented as V_e in the diagram, is equal to volume of credit, as measured in dollars, processed by the markets during the time period represented by the model, whether 1 day or 1 year. As the solution value for volume drifts right over time, that would represent *the actual, observable growth of credit* over time.

Now look at Figure 9.6 which shows the effect of budget deficits, considered in isolation, upon the demand for credit and the interest rate. The budget deficit requires Treasury financing, which increases the demand for credit in general, shown here as a shift in the credit demand curve from D_1 to D_2. This produces an increase in the level of interest rates,

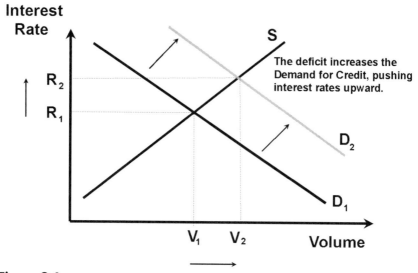

Figure 9.6
The Effect of Budget Deficits: Upward Pressure on Interest Rates

from R_1 to R_2, and a growth in the volume of credit from V_1 to V_2. Because of the higher interest rates shown, the private borrowing also represented in the demand curve is reduced, or to use the jargon of the model, "crowded out." To make the example more concrete, suppose that 30-year mortgage rates prior to this deficit shock were at 8%. The disturbance shown in Figure 9.6 might raise them to 8½ or 9%. That would likely discourage some of the borrowing in the private real estate sector of the economy.

A Serious Complication: Federal Reserve Intervention[11]

Does the result presented in Figure 9.6 guarantee that, in the real economy, if budget deficits rise then interest rates will also necessarily rise? The answer is no for two reasons. The first is drawn from the theory itself, which claims that actual, observable interest rates will reflect the impact of all things that act upon them. The deficit is only one element, albeit an

[11]Many earlier studies of crowding out and related matters ignored or downplayed the role played by the Federal Reserve System. A study by Robert W. Brazelton (Bibliography, Section 3) argues that when FRS policy is taken into account, budget deficits influence long-term interest rates.

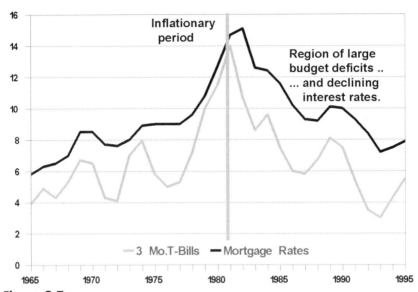

Figure 9.7
Interest Rates: Mortgage and 3-Month T-Bill, 1965–1995

important one. The line of reasoning shown in Figure 9.6 reflects only the *isolated* effect of budget deficits assuming no other changes in the economy. Of course, in a real economy everything is always in flux. That is why this theory merely argues that budget deficits have a *tendency* to push interest rates up or to put *upward pressure* on interest rates.

The second reason is empirical, as is made evident in Figure 9.7, which shows the performance of a short-term rate (for 3-month T-bills) and long-term rate (the 30-year mortgage rate) since 1965. This includes the modern periods of high deficits. Remembering that those deficits actually began in 1981, it is very clear from the graph that interest rates generally *fell*, and did not rise, at least in the earliest years of the deficit. This seems to contradict the theory, at least if the theory is considered superficially.

But again, the behavior of interest rates cannot be taken out of context. Rates were very high in 1981 because of the serious double-digit inflation that was experienced in the late 1970s. Stringent and effective Federal Reserve Policy under the guidance of Chairman Paul Volcker had wrung inflation out of the economy (and produced a serious recession to boot) by 1981, and the gradual decline in rates that began that year reflected in part the disappearance of the inflation premium in rates. Of equal important was a pronounced shift toward an easy-money policy

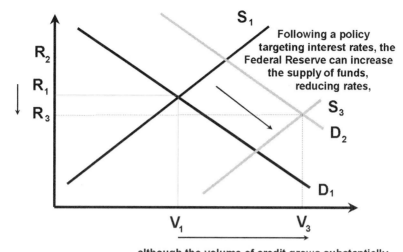

.. although the volume of credit grows substantially.

Figure 9.8
Offsetting Federal Reserve Policy: Interest Rate Accommodation

undertaken by the Federal Reserve System in the summer of 1982 that was pursued through the better part of the 1980s. To understand this, we will need to return to the model one more time.

In Figure 9.8 we see the potential combined effect of budget deficits that come from the federal budget and an easy money policy pursued by the Federal Reserve System. The Federal Reserve System has the means to increase the supply of money and credit to the economy through an expedient called *open market operations*. As represented in the model, this has the effect of shifting the supply curve substantially to the left, as shown, from S_1 to S_3. If the shift is substantial enough it can have the effect of *reducing* interest rates to levels even below the starting point, *despite* budget deficits. This is the scenario shown in Figure 9.8. R_1 represents the starting point, R_2 the interest rate that would be realized in the absence of interventionist Federal Reserve policy, and R_3 represents the actual interest rate realized because the interventionist policy was executed.

Clearly, in this last scenario rates are falling despite the deficit. The potentially dominant power of Federal Reserve policy is further reinforced when we realize that the Federal Reserve System often uses *interest rate targets* (this is certainly true in the present era). This implies that the policymakers at the Federal Reserve System might decide that level R_3 in Figure 9.8 is a desirable policy objective. If so, they could potentially increase the supply of money and credit until such time as the desired interest rate target is met. A larger budget deficit would simply require more of an increase in the supply of credit to accomplish the same goal.

If the Federal Reserve has this power, at least in theory, why worry about budget deficits? The theory argues that the harmful effects of budget deficits can be cashed out, producing yet another possibility of a policy that has few harmful effects. Spending can remain high, producing all of the employment benefits discussed earlier and keeping beneficiaries happy. Taxes, while not low, are lower than they would have to be with a balanced budget, and the deficit is finessed with counteractive Federal Reserve policy.

Unfortunately, the model gives us one more bit of information that undermines this policy panacea to the point of fatality. One last look at Figure 9.8 shows us that there is a spurious byproduct of the Federal Reserve's credit accommodation of the budget deficit. It has resulted in an *exceptionally high level of credit formation*. This is apparent when we realize that the Volume figure has grown from V_1 to V_3, representing a much higher level of credit and debt formation. Such an accommodative policy could never endure because it has the potential for two very undesirable side effects: inflation and the excessive growth of debt.

This complicated addition forces us to modify the theory's warnings into two components. According to the modified theory, rising budget deficits will tend to push interest rates up in the absence of interventionist Federal Reserve policy, or they will not push interest rates up if accommodative Federal Reserve Policy is used (or anything else happens to substantially increase the supply of credit in the economy). However, the second option has the undesirable effect of excessive credit formation, which in turn may have, in the right context, serious inflationary repercussions.

Monetizing the Deficit

It would be unfair to accuse the Federal Reserve System, which has a very complicated mandate, of intentionally accommodating the deficits of the present period. The last two chairmen of the Federal Reserve System, Paul Volcker and Alan Greenspan, have been openly critical of budget deficits and have consistently warned that the failure to bring the deficits down might result in the very scenario discussed in the theory above. The Federal Reserve's primary mandate is to guard against inflation, and the members of the Federal Open Market Committee (FOMC), the main policy group, have clearly warned that the appearance of inflation will prompt them to abandon any policy that appears to be validating interest rates at unnaturally low levels. Everyone believes them. Under such circumstances, the budget deficit would be on its own.

Nonetheless, there were no real inflationary threats through the mid-1980s, so the deficit was accommodated to some extent. The results are made apparent in Figures 9.9 and 9.10. Figure 9.9 shows that annual growth rates of the narrowest monetary aggregate, M1, and the broadest, the net debt growth rate, which is a good measure of the general rate of credit expansion. As we can see, they were actually higher than their equivalent values in the late 1970s, and they were often well into double-digit ranges. This is what would be expected if the deficit were being accommodated to some extent by a monetary policy intended to reduce interest rates and spur economic growth, even though sincerely on guard against inflation. This kind of accommodative policy is the modern form of *monetizing* the debt—offsetting the economic effects of high deficits and rapid federal debt formation by using an *easy* monetary policy designed to keep interest rates lower than would otherwise be the case. This has the final effect of allowing high levels of money, credit, and debt formation.

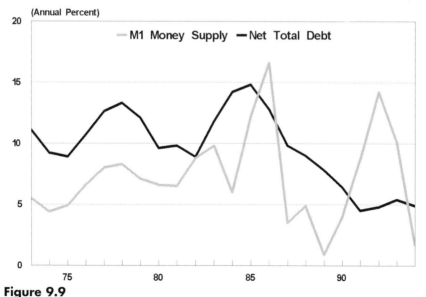

Figure 9.9
Money and Debt Growth Rates, 1973–1994
Source: Economic Report of the President, 1996

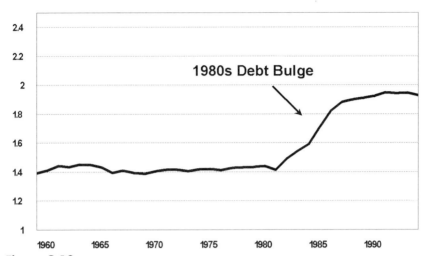

Figure 9.10
Debt/GDP Ratio, 1959–1994

Although inflation did not emerge during this period (the appearance of *inflationary expectations* or any early inflation indicators was always the signal to retreat from accommodative policy), these policies contributed to a permanent (or long-lasting) residual effect as shown in Figure 9.10. The U.S. economy became the ultimate debt economy. The *debt-to-GDP* ratio, which had remained stable for decades, rose substantially and probably permanently in a single long step. In effect, the 1980s became the decade where all sectors—government, business, and consumer—borrowed to meet economic goals.

Given that GDP is the rough proxy for the means to service debt at the national level, this implies that we may be a little more vulnerable to business cycles and economic distress. There is a reduced capacity for adjustment for debt-besieged consumers and businesses, not to mention for a government paying interest charges of $250 billion per year.

All of this suggests that there are some very sound economic reasons why deficit abuse should not continue. This is especially true when deficit equaling more than one-fifth of the budget and more than 5% of GDP. Continuing accommodation by the Federal Reserve becomes inherently dangerous (as Alan Greenspan has openly and pointedly warned), and for that reason accommodation will not continue in an emerging inflationary environment. Rising and volatile interest rates become more likely, which puts the economy in harm's way.

The Economic Impact of Deficit Reduction

While the argument may be made that large deficits should be reduced or the budget should be balanced, the economic impact of deficit reduction must be considered as well. Even if a reduction is worth the cost, understanding the consequences of the damage that can be done may lead to policies that are more gradualist and humane.

It is clear that when entitlements programs are cut certain benefits are lost by those parties that draw entitlements payments. A reduction in welfare, health, education, veterans, or retirement benefits will in each case impact a large group of voters who may regard balancing the budget as an abstract necessity but will be loath to lose specific benefits that they understand and enjoy. That is why even the most strident of elected budget cutters ultimately propose small, marginal cuts, such as trimming growth rates for the large programs that matter. Although private-sector economists and political commentators propose radical changes and deep cuts (they have nothing to lose by making such proposals) this zeal is never matched in Washington. Social Security retirement is regarded as almost entirely off-limits by liberals and conservatives, Republicans and Democrats alike. Eventually, Medicare may be trimmed somewhat (and even that remains to be seen), but no one who is elected talks seriously about deep program cuts. Even the most daring of plans calls for trimming the growth rate from 9.5% to 6.5%. And this trepidation is not due to the fact that our political representatives lack courage—it is due to the fact that they are elected. They understand that substantial cutbacks often do come at a great cost for the constituencies affected and these people are capable of registering their displeasure with their votes.

The degree of truth in this can be understood when we consider the economic pain caused by the one budgetary area that *has* been strongly impacted in the name of deficit reduction: defense. We saw in earlier chapters that defense has been cut sharply, and it was not just a trimming of growth rates. The amount spent on defense in 1997 will be nearly $40 billion less than the amount spent in 1989. The *regional multiplier* discussed earlier in the chapter becomes germane in applications like this. The impact of defense reductions was spotty, and it strongly affected local economies or entire regions that had previously benefitted from the payrolls of defense contractors or from local military bases.

It is perhaps the *employment* impact of defense cutbacks that most illustrates the damage done to individuals and to their careers. Generally, prior to the cutbacks, defense contractors in many regions provided excellent jobs at very good pay with the kind of job security that today seems part of a mythological past. Many stable lives were shattered by the sweep.

The truth of this was made very evident in a grim article prepared by Federal Reserve Bank of Boston Senior Economist Yolanda Kodrzycki gauging the impact of defense-related layoffs in New England between 1989 and 1994.[12] Nearly 114,000 jobs had been lost in the New England states and the survey, drawing from about 5,000 of that number, evaluated the results. The majority of those laid off had found work, but the median loss in hourly earnings was 18%, and one-fourth of those who had found jobs faced declines of 40% or more. Although most had received some job training after displacement, the income loss for older workers was even higher—workers above age 55 had suffered a decline in median hourly earnings of 31%. The result as presented in this study may imply that defense workers were overpaid (or, conversely, that their skills were very valuable, but only within the defense sector), but that does not take away from the fact that this transition, accomplished in the name of federal downsizing, was traumatic for very large numbers of people.

This is not sufficient reason to avoid program cuts if deficits are unacceptably large. A stagnant or crisis-prone economy that might be the byproduct of fiscal recklessness would likely do more harm—there is a lot of trauma in economic torpor. The example does suggest that cutbacks be gradual and sensitive to the problems of people who are caught up in them, and that they be tied to programs, such as retraining programs, educational benefits, or extended unemployment benefits that are designed to make the transition less painful.

What's Next?

Debates about the proper role and size of government, the allowable size of deficits, and appropriate corrective measures will likely rage eternal, given the range of opinion possible and the ideological variety found in a nation that values democracy and free speech. Most hard policy decisions, whether motivated by a liberal defense of large and inclusive government programs or by a conservative appeal for a government that is lean and inexpensive, will involve tradeoffs that complicate the decision by impacting different groups in different ways. Most policy decisions involve tradeoffs between the benefits of applied policy and the unavoidable costs of its implementation.

[12] Yolanda K. Kodrzycki, (Bibliography, Section 7).

On the positive side, the federal government provides a vast range of services to the beneficiaries of its programs. The federal government employs a very large number of people, providing them with well-paid careers and the prestige of a good job. Federal employment guidelines opened doors of opportunity to many people who might never have been given those chances in a world where unjust discrimination is still found. Additionally, the impact of federal spending on the economy—and especially on regional economies—can be substantial, generating income well above the initial stimulus.

On the negative side, it all has to be paid for. Large government demands high taxes or, worse, high taxes plus high levels of borrowing. Those who pay these taxes are not always convinced, sometimes with good reason, that the arrangement is equitable or fair. Taxes can be so high that they act as a disincentive to entrepreneurship, risk, and investment, which in turn has the potential to suffocate economic growth.

Deficits have to be financed by borrowing in competition with private borrowers in the finance markets. Large-scale federal borrowing can put upward pressure on interest rates. This can be offset by expansionary Federal Reserve Policy, but leads to excess credit formation and high growth rates in debt. In the face of inflation, such a policy would have to be abandoned.

Deficits should never be justified merely because federal spending creates jobs. Nonetheless, program cuts in the name of deficit reduction can take a heavy human toll, as was made evident by the large defense cuts already undertaken. This suggests that austerity policies should be gradual, designed in such a way that the transition is tolerable for those affected.

There is one more subject that deserves discussion: the tremendous intergenerational income transfers that are built into the present system. The economic cohort that people are calling Generation X is and will be paying very high taxes into programs that under current projections will not be there for them when their time comes to collect. This situation is intolerable and it demands a solution.

The final section of the book—the epilogue—discusses briefly the range of options for deficit reduction and budgetary integrity. It includes final observations by the author.

10

Epilogue

· · · · · · · · · · ·

· ·

A *consensus is emerging around* the world in support of government deficit reduction and fiscal moderation. The acceptable standards vary widely. The new European Union standard tries to restrict budget deficits to less than 3% of gross domestic product (GDP) and gross government debt to less than 60% of GDP. The present target in the United States is stricter. Both major political parties have at least nominal targets for balanced budgets by the year 2002. Although the balanced budget target may not be reached, by all appearances budget deficits will be small—probably less than 1% of GDP—when the U.S. economy and the rest of the world prepare to enter the third millennium.

This author does not believe that the balanced budget is an absolute necessity. Borrowing and debt can serve a useful purpose for government, as it does for consumers and businesses. The financial task of modern government should not be to eliminate the debt, which is impossible, nor should it be to mechanically reduce the deficit to zero, which might be harmful. The task of modern fiscal policy should be to keep the budget, the deficit, and the debt to a reasonable scale, given the strength and the capacity for growth of the American economy. If we allow them, deficits should be small. The European standard is too generous and the requirement for a balanced budget is probably too strict. Small deficits during recessions are advisable. A 1.5% standard, regarded as an acceptable upper limit rather than an average target, is more flexible. Having said this though, the author concludes that *it is far better to force the budget to balance than to allow the deficit to grow out of control if there are no realistic options between these two points or if a lack of political discipline makes moderation an impossibility.*

Considerable success has already been realized in the effort to reduce the deficit. The deficit was $290 billion in 1992 and it has been reduced considerably since then. Credit for this belongs to both political parties. The Clinton administration entered office resolving to maintain discretionary spending at flat levels set by the BEA, and this has contributed a great deal to the fiscal control seen in recent years. The Republicans, especially in the 104th Congress, have been zealous budget cutters in at least some programs, and more generally they have imposed an attitude of austerity upon Washington that was sorely needed. PAYGO provisions have generally been honored. On the other hand, much of the success in deficit reduction has been due to strong economic growth (for which the politcal parties can take little responsibility, despite their claims to the contrary) and the real test for Republicans and Democrats alike is still ahead. Eventually they must face the anticipated problems of the large entitlements programs: Medicare and Medicaid now, Social Security after that. Failure here would ultimately destroy all of the gains made elsewhere.

As this nation strives for deficit reduction, or at least for a more loosely defined fiscal responsibility, a number of issues will continue to dominate the direction and the scope of evolving fiscal policy. Here are some of the more important among them:

Gradualism and moderation. All parties seem to concede, as they should, that deficit reduction and, if that is the goal, a balanced budget, should be phased in slowly over a number of years. Hence the Republicans set the stakes by promoting a balanced budget by fiscal year 2002, and the Clinton administration later followed suit. This allows economic growth to have maximum impact on the revenue side, and it allows more moderate cuts, sometimes in growth rates only, on the outlay side. Generally a balanced budget will be reached using a plan like this if total outlays can be kept at a slower rate of growth than the nominal economic growth rate. Finally, because of their popular appeal and importance, most federal programs, especially the large ones, are going to be trimmed only slightly. Over time, some well-established programs that have truly outlived their purpose may be phased out altogether. This has happened in the past. The U.S. Postal Service, once heavily subsidized, is now on its own, and formerly subsidized power administrations are largely self-supporting.

Taxes. As was stated in the last chapter, we seem to be in rough tax limbo at the present time. Although European and Asian nations might try to meet the looming needs of government by raising taxes (and they might not—although the Japanese approach to their own social security underfunding is inauspicious), this will not be a political option in the United States, even as the long-range solution for Social Security. On the other hand, *cutting* taxes prior to actually achieving a balanced budget is unacceptable. To show how tax cuts could be included in a five year plan is equally unacceptable. A balance budget must be a *fact* rather than a plan; otherwise, budgetary discipline loses all credibility. It might be possible to shift the tax burden around some if certain inequities become clear, but general tax cuts must be postponed.

Discretionary spending. The present caps on discretionary spending seem to work quite well, and they certainly have done more for deficit reduction than any other factor aside from economic growth. However, as deficits shrink, some of these caps have to be lifted and allowed to rise, perhaps at least as high as the nominal economy is growing. Otherwise the conclusion reached by the Kerrey Commission (cited at the beginning of Chapter 6), that entitlements will eventually absorb 100% of the budget, will come true for the wrong reason. Defense, in particular, cannot be allowed to shrink indefinitely.

Medicare and Medicaid. This, especially Medicare, is the acid-test. If projected growth for medical costs cannot be brought under control, all bets are off. Because of the condition of the Medicare Hospitalization Trust Fund, the problem must be addressed immediately. As was shown in Table 8.8, *both* the Clinton and Republican 1996 balanced budget proposals require steep cuts in program growth rates in Medicare to accomplish their goals. The Clinton budget requires a reduction below current services projections of $41 billion in the year 2002 alone. The Republican proposal requires even larger cuts—more than $53 billion in fiscal year 2002 alone. This would require cutbacks of up to 20% in current program benefits (or their costs). This will affect the largest and most powerful voting constituency in the United States. There is no hope of accomplishing this without *requiring* Medicare recipients to move over to managed care, and even then the goal might prove elusive.

Medicaid, the need-based health-care program, could have its costs controlled by block grants, as discussed in the text. However, doing so merely puts the burden of cost containment on the states and removes from the federal government the responsibility for the consequences. More importantly, the issue of long-term nursing care for the elderly will continue to play a large role in this reform.

The reform to Medicare and Medicaid probably would be more successful under more inclusive health care reform, such as was attempted by the Clinton administration in the 103rd Congress. However, the contemporary political climate does not seem to be favorably disposed toward that kind of inclusive reform. This is probably because of the fear that an umbrella program could turn out to be another budgetary monster imposed on future generations. Regardless, health-care reform, whether all-inclusive or piecemeal, is an absolute prerequisite for budgetary control.

Social Security. This author does not favor trying to strengthen the Social Security Old-Age and Survivors Insurance Trust Fund through higher taxes while leaving projected benefits as they are. Higher taxes have always been the easy solution to Social Security problems (if in doubt, refer back to Table 7.7). Substantially reducing benefits for future retirees, such as raising the retirement age to 70, is not a very attractive option for the same reason. This forces the current generation to pay very high taxes into a program that promises to offer relatively little in return, especially compared to the payback rates experienced by earlier generations, such as the one that is now retiring. The most equitable solution would be one that allows high levels of tax-deferred savings. These savings might be mandatory or thet might be in lieu of FICA or other taxes. Again, there will be difficult tradeoffs in finding a more equitable and sounder program than the present one for a very simple reason. Programs that defer funds away from Social Security might allow the construction of a supplemental program that is stronger and fairer, but it will financially weaken the traditional program. Because the traditional program runs a surplus, this might contribute to large budget deficits.

Other entitlements and programs. The zeal for budgetary discipline does not mean that the budget axe must fall on every federal program in existence. Such programs presumably exist because they provide important or essential services to the public. As national needs change, so will program requirements. Politics is not likely to boil down to the practice of bean counting. A policy of fiscal moderation implies that reasonable standards are applied to program development, including financial integrity. So long as scrutiny is exercised and general budgetary guidelines are met, some programs can be increased in size as others are reduced in scope. In the future we may decide that it is wise to increase spending in some areas like defense, education, justice, or transportation. The primary rule to remember is this: never can the net effect of the realignment of priorities allow the deficit, the debt, and interest payments to grow again as they did after 1981.

To some extent, the public debate over the balanced budget leads us away from the more fundamental and important issues of federal fiscal policy. More important are the questions of the size of government, how the money is spent, and whether the arrangement is fair.

On the last point, we as a nation are obliged to address the question of whether the present arrangement is, indeed, fair to the social cohort that is generally referred to as Generation X. This includes young men and women in their 20s—or maybe a little older—and college students and their peers today. This group is destined to pay exceptionally high taxes. Just a few years after graduation, college students, most of who will still be unmarried and without home interest deductions, will find themselves in tax brackets where more than 30% of their income and 40% of their pay increases are taken away. This might not be so egregious if they lived in a cradle-to-grave European welfare state, but they do not. Aside from common goods provided by budgetary functions like defense, transportation, and justice, which we all enjoy, very little of the spending goes to this new class of taxpayers. None of the expensive medical or need-based programs benefit them, federal retirement is for someone else, as are agricultural subsidies. The Social Security system that they pay into is in its present configuration a sinking pit for their tax dollars that promises only substantially reduced benefits, higher taxes, or program bankruptcy.

Many critics identify the growth of entitlements as the biggest problem facing government. Perhaps that opinion should be refined. Entitlements that produce massive income transfers, including inter-generational income transfers, away from this economy's generation of the future to virtually everyone else is the biggest problem facing government. If this group ever discovers that they have the right to vote—so far apparent only to a minority—there may be yet another American political revolution.

In this book we have discussed the problems of heavy debt and high interest rates, and the undesirable economic effects of excessive deficits. As unacceptable as all of this is, it still does not constitute the primary reason for keeping our federal house in financial order. Large budget deficits and huge debt undermine the fiscal integrity of a government whose imputed purpose is to serve the people. Our federal government is the institutionalized form of our ideal of democracy and fair representation. It is the final expression of our social contract—a social contract that is admired and envied as an ideal around the world. A strong government—a government that serves the people—must be an example of both political integrity *and* economic integrity. If it slowly becomes a chimera, an illusion, a bag of tricks, deceitful and irresponsible, it ceases to serve the public well and it loses its claim to just representation of the people and its position of responsible leadership for the rest of the world.

Bibliography

· · · · · · · · · · · · · · · · ·

   This annotated list of sources and suggestions for additional reading is arranged by topic. As can be seen by the annotations, many of the subjects discussed in this book are very controversial, and research results can be made to support almost any position that one might take on certain topics. Not every conceivable explanation or policy option was presented in the main text but as was explained in the Preface, this book is neither a literature review nor a textbook on public policy. While we consistently try to be fair, the book generally reflects the point of view of the author. Opinions that are contrary to the author's are certainly abundant, and many of them can be found in the articles and books cited here.

   The author used original source material (actual budgetary documents, reports published by the CBO and OMB, numerous government publications, and legislative proposals and actual law) for much of what is contained in this book. C-SPAN, supplemented by a daily dose of *The Wall Street Journal* and the *Los Angeles Times* also provided background information. Consequently, the more formal and academic literature listed here tends to emphasize the economic perspective of this subject, and a considerable part of it addresses issues raised in Chapter 9 and in the Epilogue. Again, the author has his own take on all of this, and a lot of that can be contradicted or disputed by the references below.

   Citations are restricted mostly to articles that have appeared in the last 8 or so years, unless the material is cited somewhere in the text. Most older material has been supplemented, revised, or extended by the work cited below. Scholars searching for older material will find numerous references in these works.

The articles are arranged alphabetically by author according to the following sections:

Section 1: Balanced budget controversy, including constitutional amendments.

Section 2: Budget enforcement, budget enforcement acts, legislative procedures and related issues, including partisan issues.

Section 3: Crowding out and/or interest rate effects of the deficit and debt.

Section 4: Deficits and debt, general evaluation and discussion.

Section 5: Deficit and debt measurement, definitions, international comparisons.

Section 6: Economic impact of the deficit and/or the debt and fiscal policy, historical.

Section 7: Economic impact of the deficit and/or the debt and fiscal policy, modern era, including major theoretical controversies.

Section 8: Entitlements, Social Security, health programs, welfare, infrastructure, agricultural programs and related issues.

Section 9: Taxes, tax reform, supply-side economics, and related issues.

Most entries include a one-to-three line annotation. Each article is also ranked according to its degree of difficulty on the following scale:

G: **General** readership; should be understandable to everyone who has read this book.

U: **Undergraduate**; should be understandable to most advanced undergraduates majoring in economics, political science, or political economy, and to many general readers as well.

A: **Advanced** or very advanced; intended for graduate students or professionals. Not likely to be understandable to undergraduates nor the general audience.

Section 1: Balanced Budget Controversy, Including Constitutional Amendments

Alesina, Alberto, and Perotti, Roberto. "Fiscal Discipline and the Budget Process." *American Economics Review, Papers and Proceedings of the 108th Annual Meeting of the American Economic Associ-*

ation, May 1996, pp. 401–407. (Argues against balanced budget laws, offers reform suggestions—U.)

Corsette, Giancarlo and Roubini, Nouriel. "European versus American Perspectives on Balanced Budget Rules." *American Economics Review, Papers and Proceedings of the 108th Annual Meeting of the American Economic Association*, May 1996, pp. 408–413. (As the title states—U.)

Niskanen, William A. "The Case for a New Fiscal Constitution." *Journal of Economic Perspectives*, Spring 1992, pp. 13–24. (Proposes a constitutional amendment to require two-thirds vote to increase limit on public debt or increase taxes.—G.)

Reischauer, Robert D. "Balanced Budgets and Unreasonable Expectations." *Challenge*, September–October 1995, pp. 4–11. (Interview with former CBO director—difficult if not impossible to expect balanced budgets, lower taxes, and preservation of important programs such as defense and certain entitlements—G.)

Section 2: Budget Enforcement, Budget Enforcement Acts, Legislative Procedures and Related Issues, Including Partisan Issues

Collender, Stanley E. *The Guide to the Federal Budget—Fiscal 1996*, (and other years), Washington, D.C: Urban Institute, 1995. (As mentioned in the text, this is one of the two "living classics," along with Schick, on the material covered in Chapter 8, the budgetary process—U.)

Drew, Elizabeth. *Showdown: The Struggle Between the Gingrich Congress and the Clinton White House*, New York: Simon and Schuster, 1996. (An excellent overview of the troubled 104th Congress and the battles with the Clinton White House—G.)

Ferejohn, John, and Krehbiel, Keith. "The Budget Process and the Size of the Budget." *Annual Journal of Political Science*, January 1987, pp. 296–320. (U.)

Schick, Allen. *The Federal Budget: Politics, Policy, Process*. Washington, D.C: Brookings Institute, 1995. (Along with Collender, this is the other "living classic" on the budgetary process, the topic of Chapter 8—U.)

Wildavsky, Aaron, *The New Politics of the Budgetary Process*. Glenview, IL: Scott, Foresman, 1988. (Considered something of a classic, though now a little dated because of changes made in the law since publication—U.)

Section 3: Crowding Out and/or Interest Rate Effects of the Deficit and Debt

Baker, Dean, and Schafer, Todd. "The Clinton Budget Package: Putting Deficit Reduction First?" *Challenge,* May–June 1993, pp. 4–10. (Critical of crowding out theory, argues for moderate deficit reduction—interest burden of debt reduces ability of government to meet social needs and presents an obstacle to the effective use of countercyclical policy—G.)

Brazelton, W. Robert. "An Empirical Note on Deficits, Interest Rates, and International Flows." *Quarterly Review of Economics and Finance,* Spring 1994, pp. 113–116. (Federal budget deficits influence long-term interest rates, and measurements of the effects of this cannot ignore the purposeful policy decisions of the Federal Reserve System—A.)

Cebula, Richard J., and Koch, James V. "An Empirical Note on Deficits, Interest Rates, and International Capital Flows." *Quarterly Review of Economics and Business,* Autumn 1989, pp. 121–27. (Econometric—once capital flows from abroad have been factored into the study, federal budget deficits can be shown to have an influence over long-term interest rates—A.)

Cebula, Richard J. and Koch, James V. "Federal Budget Deficits, Interest Rates, and International Capital Flows: A Further Note." *Quarterly Review of Economics and Finance,* Spring 1994, pp. 117–120. (Econometric—budget deficits raise long-term interest rates, foreign capital inflows reduce them, and the evidence is inconclusive on the effects of FRS policy, except for the strong policy shift of October 1979–October 1982—A.)

Darby, Julia and Malley, Jim. "Fiscal Policy and Aggregate Consumption: New Evidence from the United States." *Scottish Journal of Political Economy,* May 1996, pp. 129–145. (Modern studies of the multiplier and of crowding out by federal spending are often represented as studies of the marginal rate of substitution between government spending and consumption. Although studies cited in this article show evidence of crowding out, this MRS estimator is unstable. The authors explore and affirm this instability, offer explanations, but do not acheive consistently robust results themselves—A.)

Evans, Paul. "Do Large Deficits Produce High Interest Rates?" *American Economic Review,* March 1985, pp. 68–87. (This older study concludes that budget deficits have no lasting impact upon interest rates—A.)

Section 4: Deficits and Debt—General Evaluation and Discussion (see also economic impact of the deficit)

Auerbach, Alan J. "The U.S. Fiscal Problem: Where We Are, How We Got Here, and Where We Are Going." in *NBER Macroeconomics Annual,* ed. S Fischer and J. Rotenberg. Cambridge, MA: MIT Press, 1994, pp. 141–175. (U.)

Bernheim, Douglas. "A Neoclassical Perspective on Budget Deficits." *Journal of Economic Perspectives,* Spring 1989, pp. 55–72. (Compares the neoclassical, Keynesian, and Ricardian paradigms. Dismisses the latter, claims the Keynesian only shows temporary effects, supports the neoclassical—A.)

Brown-Collier, Elba, K., and Collier, Bruce E. "What Keynes Really Said About Deficit Spending." *Journal of Post Keynesian Economics,* Spring 1995, pp. 341–355. (Keynes, who wrote little about budget deficits, believed that the best stabilization and growth policy arose from socializing investments, and the deficit might only be a consequence of that—U.)

Eisner, Robert. "Budget Deficits: Rhetoric and Reality." *Journal of Economic Perspectives,* Spring 1989, pp. 73–93. (The upper constraint on deficits should be the restriction that the growth of debt will not exceed the growth of output. No evidence that structural deficits contribute to inflation or have harmed stock market, and contemporary estimates tend to overstate the size and impact of the deficit and the debt—U.)

Eisner, Robert. "Clinton, Deficits, and the U.S. Economy." *Challenge,* May–June 1993, pp. 47–50. (Deficits can be too small as well as too large; a large part of budget deficits in early 1990s were due to slow growth—G.)

Eisner, Robert. "Deficits: Which, How Much, and So What?" *American Economics Review, Papers and Proceedings of the 104th Annual Meeting of the American Economic Association,* May 1992, pp. 295–298. (Argues that national savings should include public savings as well as private, that deficits are often justified and useful, and that no harm is done if debt grows no faster than national income or output—U.)

Federal Reserve Bank of Kansas City. *Budget Deficits and Debt: Issues and Options—A Symposium Sponsored by the Federal Reserve Bank of Kansas City,* 1995. Obtainable free from Public Affairs Department, Federal Reserve Bank of Kansas City, 925 Grand Boulevard, Kansas City, Missouri 64198-0001. (A good starting point on some of the deeper theoretical controversies over the budget deficit that includes articles by Greenspan, Masson, Mussa, Ball, Taylor, Martin, Auerbach, Giovannini, Peterson, Stark, Edwards, with discusion and moderation by Thiessen, Frenkel, Shigehara, Johnson, Meltzer, King, Schieber, Arellano, Flemming, Feldstein, Persson, and Wolfensohn—U.)

Federal Reserve Bank of Kansas City. *Debt, Financial Stability, and Public Policy: A Symposium Sponsored by the Federal Reserve Bank of Kansas City,* 1986. (Articles by Higgins, Kaufman, B. Friedman, Dornbush, Clausen, Eisenbeis, and Summers—U.)

Heilbroner, Robert and Bernstein, Peter. *The Debt and the Deficit: False Alarms and Real Possibilities,* New York: W.W. Norton, 1989. (This book generally disagrees with the theme of *Red Ink,* sees the current concern over the deficit as misplaced and alarmist, although does not justify deficits of any size; a good alternative read to *Red Ink*—G.)

Kotlikoff, Laurence. "The Deficit is Not a Meaningful Measure of Fiscal Policy," *Science,* August 12, 1988, pp. 791–795. (The title speaks for itself—G.)

Penny, Timothy J., and Garrett, Major. *Common Cents.* New York, NY: Avon, 1996. (Written by a retired 6-term Democratic Congressman, but very critical of his party, it provides a very readable overview on how we got to where we are—G.)

Poterba, James M. "Budget Institutions and Fiscal Policy in the United States." *American Economics Review, Paper and Proceedings of the 108th Annual Meeting of the American Economic Association,* May 1996, pp. 395–400. (Can anything be learned from state balanced budget rules?—U.)

Sawhill, Isabel V. "Distinguished Lecture on Economics in Government: The Economist vs. Madmen in Authority." *Journal of Economic Perspectives,* Summer 1995, pp. 3–13. (Generally supportive of government, and, to some extent, describes economists as over-critical, discusses some contemporary issues, such as welfare reform—G.)

Schultze, Charles L. "Is There a Bias Toward Excess in U.S. Government Budgets or Deficits?" *Journal of Economic Perspectives,* Spring 1992, pp. 25–43. (Most of the growth of government is explained by the growth of Social Security. Population above 65 in U.S. and internationally pull spending up; strong opposition to constitutional amendment to balance budget—U.)

Tobin, James. "Thinking Straight about Fiscal Stimulus and Deficit Reduction." *Challenge,* March–April 1994, pp. 15–18. (Emphasing deficit reduction over the economic impact of fiscal policy amounts to confusing the means with the end; certain fiscal measures that promote public sector investment are likely to be beneficial even if they do raise the deficit initially—G.)

Section 5: Deficit and Debt Measurement, Definitions, International Comparisons

Blejer, Mario, and Cheasty, Adrienne. "The Measurement of Fiscal Deficits: Analytical and Methodological Issues." *Journal of Economic Literature,* December 1991, pp. 1644–1678. (Various ways of measuring budget deficits, especially in international studies. Good explanation of *structural* or long-term deficit, accrual issues, etc.—A.)

Vickrey, William. "Meaningfully Defining Deficits and Debt." *American Economics Review, Papers and Proceedings of the 104th Annual Meeting of the American Economic Association,* May 1992, pp. 305–10. (Appeals for capital budgeting, argues against current efforts at deficit reduction—U.)

Section 6: Economic Impact of the Deficit and/or the Debt and Fiscal Policy: Historical

Higgs, Robert. "Wartime Prosperity? A Reassessment of the U.S. Economy in the 1940s." *Journal of Economic History,* March 1992, pp. 41–60. (Rejects the conventional argument that the Great Depression was solved by the fiscal effects of WWII. Instead attributes the recovery to the transformation into a "command economy" and improved expectations—U.)

May, Ann Mari. "President Eisenhower, Economic Policy, and the 1960 Presidential Election." *Journal of Economic History,* June 1990, pp. 417–427. (Good survey of Eisenhower years—Eisenhower was generally a balanced budget advocate, but he did reluctantly sign a small tax cut in 1954—U.)

Smiley, Gene and Keehn, Richard H. "Federal Personal Income Tax Policy in the 1920s." *Journal of Economic History*, June 1995, pp. 285–303. (As cited by supply-siders, the first of the big tax cuts were in 1921, 1924 and 1926. This explores the background and suggests that although the cuts might have stimulated the economy, there was considerable tax avoidance—U.)

Vernon, J.R. "World War II Fiscal Policies and the End of the Great Depression." *Journal of Economic History*, December 1994, pp. 850–868. (War related fiscal policy was by far the most important factor in the recovery from the Great Depression, accounting for 80% of the 1941 increase in GDP—U.)

Section 7: Economic Impact of the Deficit and/or the Debt and Fiscal Policy: Modern Era, Including Major Theoretical Controversies (see also historical, crowding out):

Abell, John D. "Twin Deficits During the 1980s: An Empirical Investigation." *Journal of Macroeconomics*, Winter 1990, pp. 81–96. (Econometric—suggests a strong connection between budget deficits and merchandise trade deficits; the best way to reduce the trade deficit might be to reduce the budget deficit—A.)

Bahmani-Oskooee, Mohsen, and Payesteh, Sayeed, "Do Budget Deficits Cause Capital Inflows? Evidence from the United States." *Quarterly Review of Economics and Finance*, Spring 1994, pp. 63–74. (Econometric—budget deficits do cause capital inflows into the United States, which are responding to interest rate effects of budget deficits—A.)

Bahmani-Oskooee, Mohsen. "On the Effect of U.S. Federal Deficits on its Trade Flows." *Journal of Post Keynesian Economics*, Fall 1991, pp. 72–82. (Econometric—The federal budget deficit has the effect of decreasing exports and increasing imports, contributing to the trade deficit—A.)

Barro, Robert J. "The Ricardian Approach to Budget Deficits." *Journal of Economic Perspectives*, Spring 1989, pp. 37–54. (Offers a good overview of the controversial "Ricardo Effect" or "Ricardian Equivalence"—budget deficits from tax cuts do not stimulate consumption because such cuts must be matched by increases in present value of future taxes, leaving budget constraints unchanged. Predicts no effect of budget deficits on interest rates—A.)

Beard, Thomas R., and McMillan, W. Douglas. "The Impact of Budget Deficits in the Interwar Period." *Journal of Macroeconomics,* Spring 1991, pp. 239–266. (In the period between 1922 and 1938, budget deficits seem to have no fiscal impact—A.)

Darrat, Ali F., and Suliman, M. Osman. "Real Deficits and Real Growth: Some Further Results." *Journal of Post Keynesian Economics,* Fall 1992, pp. 31–41. (Econometric—reevaluates the Eisner hypothesis using a VAR model; concludes that inflation-corrected deficits do exert a causal impact on real GDP—A.)

Davidson, Paul, ed., "Mini-symposium on 'Is Keynesian demand management policy still viable?'" *Journal of Post Keynesian Economics,* Winter 1994/95, pp. 185–307. (A series of articles re-exploring and largely defending Keynesian fiscal policy; articles by Cunningham and Vilasuso, Eisner, Fazzari, Galbraith, Kregel, Samuels, Wray, and Epstein—U.)

Eisner, Robert and Pieper, Paul J. "Real Deficits and Real Growth: a Further View." *Journal of Post Keynesian Economics,* Fall 1992, pp. 43–49. (Econometric—structural or cyclically adjusted deficits are related to changes in real economic activity—A.)

Fazzari, Steven M. "Why Doubt the Effectiveness of Keynesian Fiscal Policy" *Journal of Post-Keynesian Economics,* Winter 94/95, pp. 231–247. (A defense of traditional Keynesian policies, including the stimulating impact of deficit finance when there are slack resources in the economy—U.)

Friedman, Benjamin M. "Learning from the Reagan Deficits." *American Economics Review, Papers and Proceedings of the 104th Annual Meeting of the American Economic Association,* May 1992, pp. 299–304. (Six poignant observations for the experiments of the 1980s including the ERTA tax cuts that decreased revenues and growing deficits that did not cause interest rates to rise—G.)

Gale, William G. "Economic Effects of Federal Credit Programs." *American Economic Review,* March 1991, pp. 133–152. (Presents an advanced model of credit evaluation, experimentally uses it for subject in title, tentatively concludes that federal credit leads to real economic activity, but warns of numerous secondary effects—A.)

Gramlich, Edward M. "Budget Deficits and National Saving: Are Politicians Exogenous?" *Journal of Economic Perspectives*, Spring 1989, pp. 23–35. (Argues that deficits reduce national saving—U.)

Hooker, Mark A. "How Do Changes in Military Spending Affect the Economy? Evidence from some State-level Data." *New England Economic Review—Federal Reserve Bank of Boston*, March/April 1996, pp. 3–15. (Econometric—state-level evidence shows that military spending is a signficant determinant of regional economic activity—A.)

Kearney, Colm and Monadjemi, Mehdi. "Fiscal Policy and Current Account Performance: International Evidence on the Twin Deficits." *Journal of Macroeconomics*, Spring 1990, pp. 197–219. (Econometric—comparing data from eight countries, including U.S., concludes that any connection between budget deficits and current account balance is temporary; reducing budget deficits will not impact trade deficit—A.)

Kodrzycki, Yolanda K. "The Costs of Defense-related Layoffs in New England." *New England Economic Review—Federal Reserve Bank of Boston*, March/April 1995, pp. 3–23. (Cited in Chapter 9, shows that most impacted defense workers found new jobs, but at lower salaries—U.)

Raynold, Prosper. "The Impact of Government Deficits When Credit Markets are Imperfect: Evidence from the Interwar Period." *Journal of Macroeconomics*, Winter 1994, pp. 55–76. (Econometric article that challenges Ricardian Equivalence by considering imperfections in credit markets—A.)

Rock James M., ed. *The Debt and the Twin Deficits Debate*. Mountain View, CA: Bristlecone, 1991. (The second debate referred to here is the trade deficit, reflecting the theory that the two are linked. An excellent selection of readings on the subject that includes articles by Barro, Bernstein, Blinder, Eisner, B. Friedman, Gramlich, Heilbroner, Jameson, Rock, Smeeding, and Tullock—U.)

Rukstad, Michael. *Macroeconomic Decision Making In the World Economy, Text and Case*, 3rd. ed. New York: Dryden, 1992. (The Harvard case study approach. Includes discussion of cases in both monetary and fiscal policy, including Kennedy's 1964 tax cut, the Reagan and Bush administrations—U.)

Seater, John J. "Ricardian Equivalence." *Journal of Economic Literature*, March 1993, pp. 142–190. (The best graduate-level article on this subject. Ricardian Equivalence is an extension of the permanent income/life cycle hypothesis and concludes that no fiscal stimulus whatsoever comes from budget deficits; this theory is currently very popular—A.)

Section 8: Entitlements, Social Security, Health Programs, Welfare, Infrastructure, Agricultural Programs and Related Issues

Blank, Rebecca M. "Proposals for Time-limited Welfare." *Journal of Economic Perspectives,* Fall 1994, pp. 183–193. (Summary overview of AFDC, discusses costs of welfare and reform savings. Distinguishes between work goals and income goals, warns that reform will make poor women and children worse off—G.)

Cutler, David M. "A Guide to Health Care Reform." *Journal of Economic Perspectives,* Summer 1994, pp. 13–29. (Explains the 1993 Clinton plan, now dead, but also introduces general background on health care reform—G.)

Dunker, Kenneth F., and Rabbat, Basile G. "Why America's Bridges are Crumbling." *Scientific American,* March 1993, p. 66. (Referred to in Chapter 5, offers a grim view in infrastructural spending on bridges, estimates repair costs at $90 billion—G.)

Feldstein, Martin. "Richard T. Ely Lecture—The Missing Piece in Policy Analysis: Social Security Reform," *American Economics Review, Papers and Proceedings of the 108th Annual Meeting of the American Economic Association,* May 1996, pp. 1–13. (Critical of present system, urges privatization—U.)

Gottschalk, Peter, and Moffitt, Robert A. "Welfare Dependence: Concepts, Measures and Trends." *American Economics Review, Papers and Proceedings of the 106th Annual Meeting of the American Economics Association,* May 1995, pp. 38–42. (Introduces a new measure of welfare dependency that suggests that dependence upon welfare has not grown significantly except among younger women—A.)

Gramlich, Edward M. "Different Approaches to Dealing with Social Security." *American Economics Review, Papers and Proceedings of the 108th Annual Meeting of the American Economic Association,* May 1996, pp. 358–362. (U.)

Hamilton, David. "Welfare Reform in the Reagan Years: An Institutionalist's Perspective." *Journal of Economic Issues,* March 1990, pp. 49–56. (Welfare reform of 1996 was not the first. Here is a general overview of the welfare reform in the early 1980s—G.)

Hoffman, Elizabeth, and Libecap, Gary D. "Institutional Choice and the Development of U.S. Agricultural Policies in the 1920s." *Journal of Economic History,* June 1991, pp. 397–411. (Farm appeal to the federal government, especially for price support, and federal farm policy, had its origin in the 1920s with the Capper-Volstead Act, 1922, the Cooperative Marketing Act, 1926, and the Agricultural Marketing Act, 1929, which led to cooperatives—U.)

Kotlikoff, Laurence J. "Privatizing Social Security at Home and Abroad." *American Economics Review, Papers and Proceedings of the 108th Annual Meeting of the American Economic Association,* May 1996, pp. 368–372. (Interesting scheme to privatize Social Security—U.)

Kuhn, Betsy A.; Dunn, Pamela Allen; Smallwood, David; Hanson, Kenneth; Blaylock, Jim; and Vogel, Stephen. "Policy Watch: The Food Stamp Program and Welfare Reform." *The Journal of Economic Perspectives,* Spring 1996, pp. 189–198. (Detailed evaluation of proposed cutbacks in food stamp and welfare programs, measures impact. Written prior to 1996 welfare reform.—G.)

Meister, Barbara A. "Analysis of Federal Farm Policy Using the Social Fabric Matrix." *Journal of Economic Issues,* March 1990, pp. 189–224. (Detailed description of 1980s farm policies, evaluates program to boost exports and subsidies—U.)

Mitchell, Olivia S., and Zeldes, Stephen P. "Social Security Privatization: A Structure for Analysis." *American Economics Review, Papers and Proceedings of the 108th Annual Meeting of the American Economic Association,* May 1996, pp. 363–367. (U.)

Ohls, James C., and Beebout, Harold. *The Food Stamp Program: Design Tradeoffs, Policy, and Impacts.* Washington D.C: Urban Institute Press, 1993. (Sympathetic to and supportive of the Food Stamp Program with lots of background information—G.)

Porterba, James M. "A Skeptic's View of Global Budget Caps." *Journal of Economic Perspectives,* Summer 1994, pp. 67–73. (Caps on health care outlays, that is. Doubts that there will be cost savings from switching to managed care, and outright spending caps will fail—G.)

Rausser, Gordon C. "Predatory Versus Productive Government: The Case of U.S. Agricultural Policies." *Journal of Economic Perspectives,* Summer 1992, pp. 133–157. (Overview of federal policy toward agriculture that distinguishes between policies that enhance efficiency by correcting market failures or by providing public goods or transfering wealth to special interests—G.)

Sabelhaus, John. "Deficits and Other Intergenerational Transfers: Restoring the Missing Link." *Challenge,* January–February 1994, pp. 45–50. (Describes intergenerational transfers caused by programs like Medicare and Social Security, warns against excesses, proposes solutions—G.)

Sawhill, Isabel V., ed. *Welfare Reform: An Analysis of the Issues,* Washington, D.C.: Urban Institute, 1995. (A series of 15 articles exploring the issues introduced by the welfare reform movement of 1995. Includes a lot of background information on welfare. Highly critical of 1995 welfare proposals, which were very similar to those enacted in 1996—G.)

Scanlon, William J. "Possible Reforms for Financing Long-term Care." *Journal of Economic Perspectives,* Summer 1992, pp. 43–58. (Health care: provides background on issue, skeptical of comprehensive public program—G.)

Schielier, Sylvester J. and Shover, John B. "Social Security Reform: Around the World in 80 Ways." *American Economics Review, Papers and Proceedings of the 108th Annual Meeting of the American Economic Association,* May 1996, pp. 373–377. (Discusses lessons learned from reform in Chile, Australia, and Sweden—U.)

Sutch, Richard. "Has Social Spending Grown Out of Control?" *Challenge,* May–June, 1996, pp. 9–16. (Shows that although social spending has grown considerably as percent of GDP in last half-century, the growth rate has slowed down considerably since 1976, except for health care. Social Security difficulties might be eased by an echo generation of the grandchildren of the boomers—G.)

Suyderhoud, Jack P.; Loudat, Thomas A.; and Pollock, Richard. "Cumulative Tax Rates on the Working Poor: Evidence of a Continuing Poverty Wall." *Journal of Economic Issues,* March 1994. (Treats loss of welfare benefits when welfare recipients return to work as a tax, to be added to normal payroll and income taxes; discusses the disincentive effects—U.)

U.S. Department of Agriculture, Agricultural Research Service. "The Effects of Food Stamps on Food Consumption: A Review of the Literature." *Family Economic Review,* 1991. (As stated, a literature review and a good start on this subject, but not as current as other citations here—G.)

Wray, L. Randall. "Can the Social Security Trust Fund Contribute to Savings?" *Journal of Post Keynesian Economics,* Winter 1990–1991, with comments by Henry Aaron and Paul Davidson, pp. 155–174. (Deficits are an important source of effective demand; even if the Social Security Trust Fund goes into deficit, this will generate income growth—U.)

Section 9: Taxes, Tax Reform, Supply-Side Economics and Related Issues

Auerbach, Alan J. "Capital Gains Taxation in the United States: Realizations, Revenue, and Rhetoric." *Brookings Papers on Economic Activity,* 1988, 595–631. (U.)

Auerbach, Alan J. "Tax Projections and the Budget: Lessons from the 1980s." *American Economics Review, Papers and Proceedings of the 107th Annual Meeting of the American Economic Association,* May 1995, pp. 165–169. (Presents tentative model for evaluating effects of tax changes; offers tentative explanation for overly optimistic revenue forecasts of the 1980s—A.)

Ballentine, J. Gregory. "The Structure of the Tax System Versus the Level of Taxation: An Evaluation of the 1986 Act." *Journal of Economic Perspectives,* Winter 1992, pp. 59–68. (The TRA86 made it more difficult to increase taxes sufficiently to balance the budget, which should have had a higher priority—G.)

Bosworth, Barry, and Burtless, Gary. "Effects of Tax Reform on Labor Supply, Investment, and Saving." *Journal of Economic Perspectives,* Winter 1992, pp. 3–25. (Description of ERTA 1981 and TRA 1986. The tax reforms of the 1980s only marginally increased labor participation in the economy, if that, and did not contribute to investment—U.)

Calkins, Lindsay Noble. "Tax Effects, the Taxable/Tax-Exempt Yield Spread, and Tax Reform 1986." *Quarterly Review of Economics and Finance,* Winter 1992. (Econometric—evaluates the impact of changes in personal income tax rates upon the yield spread between corporate and municipal long-term bonds—A.)

Chimerine, Lawrence. "What Really Happened in the 1980s." *Challenge,* May–June 1996, pp. 29–34. (Highly critical of supply-side policies of the early 1980s; much damage was done by the tax policies of that decade—G.)

Dugger, William M. "The Wealth Tax: A Policy Proposal." *Journal of Economic Issues*, March 1990, pp. 133–144. (Proposes a tax on wealth to help pay down the deficit—G.)

Feenberg, Daniel R., and Porterba, James M. "Income Inequality and the Incomes of Very High Income Tax Payers: Evidence from Tax Returns." In *Tax Policy and the Economy*, Vol. 7, ed. James M. Porterba. Cambridge, MA: MIT Press, 1993, pp. 145–177. (The argument that reduction in high marginal tax rates stimulated strong growth in taxable revenues in the 1980s—A.)

Feldstein, Martin. "Behavioral Responses to Tax Rates: Evidence from the Tax Reform Act of 1986." *American Economics Review, Papers and Proceedings of the 107th Annual Meeting of the American Economic Association*, May 1995, pp. 170–174. (Evaluates reduction in highest marginal tax rates in 1986; suggests efficiency of tax system would be improved by reducing marginal tax rate of married women relative to that of their husbands—A.)

Gaffney, Mason. "Equity Premises and the Case for Taxing Rent." *American Economics Review, Papers and Proceedings of the 104th Annual Meeting of the American Economic Association*, May 1992, pp. 274–279. (Presents arguments for and against a land tax—U.)

Gravelle, Jane G. "Equity Effects of the Tax Reform Act of 1986." *Journal of Economic Perspectives*, Winter 1992, pp. 27–44. (TRA86 compressed and simplified the income tax rate structure. The redistributional effects are not clear; some tax burden shifted away from large families, little or no redistribution among generations. Some revenue was lost—G.)

Hailstones, Thomas J., ed. *Viewpoints on Supply-Side Economics*, Crockett, TX: Robert F. Dame, 1982. (Though a little dated and hard to find, this provides an excellent selection of articles on vintage early 1980s supply-side economics—U.)

Harmelink, Philip J. and Speyrer, Janet Furman. "An Evalutation of Alternative Methods of Taxing Social Security Benefits. *Journal of Post Keynesian Economics*, Fall 1992, pp. 3–30. (Develops a method of evaluating the effectiveness of various Social Security benefits taxes—A.)

Hildred, William M., and Pinto, James V. "Impact of the 1986 Federal Tax Reform on Passive Tax Expenditures of States." *Journal of Economic Issues*, March 1990, pp. 225–239. (Many states base their tax policies on federal policy. This evaluates the impact upon states of the Tax Reform Act of 1986—U.)

Hoover, Kevin D., and Sheffrin, Steven M. "Causation, Spending, and Taxes: Sand in the Sandbox or Tax Collector for the Welfare State?" *American Economic Review,* March 1992, pp. 225–248. (Does government spending cause taxes or do taxes cause government spending? This paper presents evidence that they are causally independent—A.)

Laffer, Arthur, "Supply-Side Economics." *Financial Analyst's Journal,* September/October 1981. (Referred to in Chapter 9, the "Laffer Curve" discussed here was prominent in the supply-side discussions of the early 1980s, although now largely ignored—U.)

Lindsey, Lawrence. "Individual Taxpayer Response to Tax Cuts: 1982–1984: With Implications for the Revenue Maximizing Tax Rate." *Journal of Public Economics,* July 1987, pp. 173–206. (A.)

Lindsey, Lawrence. *The Growth Experiment: How the New Tax Policy is Transforming the U.S. Economy.* New York: Basic Books, 1990.

Metcalf, Gilbert E. "Value-Added Taxation: A Tax Whose Time Has Come?" *Journal of Economic Perspectives,* Winter 1995, pp. 121–40. (A primer on VATs and an appeal for implementation in the U.S.—G.)

Minarik, Joseph J. "Federal Tax Policy for the 1990's: The Prospect from the Hill." *American Economics Review, Papers and Proceedings of the 104th Annual Meeting of the American Economic Association,* May 1992, pp. 268–273. (Written by a Congressman, discusses options for tax reform in 1990—G.)

Mott, Tracey and Slattery, Edward. "Tax Incidence and Macroeconomic Effects in a Kaleckian Model when Profits Finance Affects Investment and Prices May Respond to Taxes." *Journal of Post Keynesian Economics,* Spring 1994, pp. 391–409. (Using a model developed in the Kaleckian tradition, determine that taxing corporate profits or sales, rather than wages, as the source of government finance, produces the highest level of national output—A.)

Pechman, Joseph A. "The Future of the Income Tax." *The American Economic Review,* March 1990, pp. 1–20. (Landmark article; a staunch defense of the income tax; argues that it is more efficient than expenditure tax, like VAT, and that progressive tax structure makes income distribution more equal—G.)

Samuelson, Paul. "The American Economy: Before and After the Election." *Challenge,* March-April 1993, pp. 19–21. (Highly critical of Reaganomics and the tax cuts of the early 1980s—G.)

Sease, Douglas R. and Herman, Tom. *The Flat-Tax Primer: A Nonpartisan Guide to What it Means for the Economy, the Government—and You*, New York: Penguin, 1996. (This book explores in depth the Steve Forbes variant of the flat tax—G.)

Slemrod, Joel. "Did the Tax Reform Act of 1986 Simplify Tax Matters?" *Journal of Economic Perspectives*, pp. 45–57. (The outcome is mixed; TRA86 reduced itemization and leveled marginal rates, but simplicity remains elusive—G.)

Slemrod, Joel. "Do Taxes Matter? Lessons from the 1980s." *American Economics Review, Papers and Proceedings of the 104th Annual Meeting of the American Economic Association*, May 1992, pp. 250–256. (Excellent summary of new perspectives on the impact of taxes; appeals for elimination of aspects of tax code that reward taxpayers for misreporting income, changing the timing of transactions, and legal forms of business organization—U.)

Slemrod, Joel, ed. *Do Taxes Matter? The Impact of the Tax Reform Act of 1986*. Cambridge, MA: MIT Press, 1990. (Selection of readings; good summary overview of new supply-side theories, which evaluate behavioral changes due to taxes—U/A.)

Slemrod, Joel. "Income Creation or Income Shifting? Behavioral Responses to the Tax Reform Act of 1986." *American Economics Review, Papers and Proceedings of the 107th Annual Meeting of the American Economic Association*, May 1995, pp. 175–180. (Evaluates TRA86, suggests subtle effects of income shifting, urges caution in tax reduction policies—U/A.)

Swartz, Thomas R., Bonello, Frank J. and Kozak, Andrew F. *The Supply Side: Debating Current Economic Policies*. Guilford, CT: Dushkin, 1983. (Selection of reading on early 1980s version of supply-side economics—G.)

Financing the Deficit: The Market for U.S. Treasury Securities

· ·

As was discussed in Chapter 1, the annual budget deficit is financed through the sale of a mix of United States Treasury Securities. The total amount of these securities that is outstanding at any given time makes up the marketable debt component of the total interest-bearing debt of the U.S. Government (see Table 1.3 on p. 6 for the composition of the U.S. public debt). In general, if the federal government has a budget deficit of $100 billion in a given fiscal year, $100 billion of new marketable U.S. Treasury securities of the kind described below must be sold to finance that deficit, and marketable debt will grow by that amount. This appendix describes the debt instruments and the market for that debt.

Marketable debt of the U.S. Treasury stands at over $3.3 trillion, and consists entirely of U.S. Treasury Bills, Notes, and Bonds. These financial assets are the kind that most people who trade in the finance markets are familiar with.

Marketable U.S. Treasury Debt

Instrument	Maturity	Interest Category
U.S. Treasury Bills	13, 26, or 52 weeks	Discount
U.S. Treasury Notes	2–10 years	Coupon
U.S. Treasury Bonds	30 years	Coupon

By definition, these assets differ according to their maturity structure. A U.S. Treasury Bill will mature in 1 year or less (from its date of issue),[1] while a U.S. Treasury Note has a maturity of 2 to 10 years and a U.S. Treasury Bond has a maturity of more than 10 years, where thirty years is typical.[2] At maturity, the financial asset is redeemed, or "paid off" by the Treasury.

Bills also differ from notes and bonds in the manner in which the interest is paid. A U.S. Treasury Bill is called a discounted financial asset (as are most privately-issued bills) because no direct interest is paid to the owner of the bill. Instead, the bill is sold at less than its maturity value (sold at a discount), and it is redeemed at its maturity value, so the interest is implicit in its appreciation in price. For example, a $10,000 U.S. Treasury Bill, 52-week series, might be sold to an investor by the Treasury for $9,300. When it matures 1 year later the bill can be redeemed for $10,000, yielding a return of $700 (no interest would be paid otherwise). This return of $700 to an original investment of $9,300 amounts to an effective rate of return of about 7.5%.

In contrast, both U.S. Treasury Notes and U.S. Treasury Bonds pay **coupon** interest. Semiannual interest payments are made to the registered owners of these securities at the stipulated coupon rate. For example, an investor who purchases a 10-year $10,000 U.S. Treasury Bond yielding a coupon rate of 8% will receive two payments per year of $400 each.

U.S. Treasury Bills, Notes and Bonds are sold to whomever wants to buy them, which is why the sum of their value is classified as **marketable**

---

[1] A yield-bearing financial asset having a maturity of 1 year or less is typically called a bill. Such assets are also called "money market assets" and money market mutual funds are made up almost entirely of bills. As financial assets, they tend to be characterized by their relatively low yields but high safety or low risk (this is especially true of Treasury Bills).

[2] These bonds should not be confused with the popular and inexpensive **Series EE U.S. Savings Bonds,** which can be purchased for as little as $50. These are classified under Non-Marketable Debt and the amount outstanding in late 1995 was about $182 million.

debt. These financial assets can also be resold in a huge secondary market. For example, a 5-year U.S. Treasury Note might be sold to a private investor, who might then resell it 6 months later to a bank or mutual fund. Prices for these securities fluctuate in value on the secondary markets, just like stocks, and their prices are quoted daily in the nation's larger newspapers. Virtually anyone can buy these securities, including foreign governments and foreign citizens.

U.S. Treasury Bills, Notes, and Bonds are no longer sold in discreet denominations. That is, the Treasury does not sell large numbers of gilt-edged $10,000 bonds. Instead, the Treasury may announce an offering of 3-year notes on some future date for a total subscription of $100 million. Purchase requests (called tenders) may be for any part of this amount that is divisible by $1,000. The purchaser may, for example, buy notes worth $56,000, or any other amount divisible by $1,000. Minimum purchases vary with the type of asset; these are discussed below. The securities are sold through an auction process where potential buyers submit competitive bids on the *yield* (interest rate to be earned) of the securities being auctioned. The Treasury accepts the highest yield bids submitted, so the securities are released at competitive market rates.[3] Normally, the investor no longer receives a physical certificate. The transaction is carried as a bookkeeping entry on the Treasury's books, and the investor is merely given a receipt and receives periodic updates on the status of the account, somewhat like a modern bank account.

Here is some specific information about the Bills, Notes, and Bonds currently issued by the U.S. Treasury (this information, which was current as of January, 1997, does change periodically).

13-week and 26-week bills. The minimum investment is $10,000. These are auctioned every Monday and are sold at a discount (paying no direct interest).

52-week bills. The minimum investment is $10,000. These are auctioned every fourth Thursday and are sold at a discount.

2-year and 5-year notes. The minimum investment for 2-year notes is $5,000; for 5-year notes it is only $1,000. These are auctioned once a month, usually on the third Wednesday. These pay coupon interest semiannually.

3-year and 10-year notes. The minimum investment for 3-year notes is $5,000; for 10 year notes only $1,000. These are usually

---

[3]Small investors are allowed to submit *noncompetitive tenders,* which do not require a competitive bid on yield. These investors are issued securities with yields equal to the yield that are accepted on competitive bids.

auctioned during the first week of February, May, August, and November. These pay coupon interest semiannually.

30-year bonds. The minimum investment is $1,000. They are auctioned semiannually in the first week of August and February. These pay coupon interest semiannually.

A purchaser can buy these directly from a Federal Reserve District Bank or one of its branches. As stated earlier, the purchaser submits a **tender** for a competitive bid or a noncompetitive tender. The latter, used normally by small purchasers, accepts the yield determined by the competitive bidding.

Regardless of the size of the issue, the securities' prices are listed in the financial press at par-equals-100. Therefore secondary market prices will fluctuate around this amount. The security is said to be trading at a **premium** if the quoted price is *above* 100 and at a **discount** if the quoted price is *below* 100. The same securities can be purchased from brokers. If they are to be sold before maturity (usually the case for everything except for bills) they *must* be sold through brokers. A broker requires a commission, but no commission is charged by a Federal Reserve District Bank. These securities are often sold in huge blocks to primary investors and are then brokered to the public by breaking up the blocks.

There are also many mutual funds that specialize in U.S. Treasury securities. These offer the investor a diversified portfolio at low cost and for small transactions.

The Difference between U.S. Government Outlays and Government Purchases

· ·

As any good student of macroeconomics knows, the performance of the national economy is measured by the **National Income and Expenditure Accounts** compiled by the Department of Commerce, Bureau of Economic Analysis. It is from this important statistical series that we derive our estimates of gross domestic product, national income, personal consumption and related data that indicate income and spending trends.

The tables from the National Income and Expenditure Accounts that break down gross domestic product by expenditure categories always include an account called Government Purchases (sometimes Government Purchases of Goods and Services). This is sometimes broken down into two categories: Federal government purchases and state and local government purchases. A comparison between the spending category called federal government purchases in the national income accounts to total outlays of the federal government shows a huge difference. Compare the difference in Table B.1, which uses annualized data from the National Income Accounts for the third quarter of 1995 (the end of the federal fiscal year), and data for federal outlays from Chapter 1, p. 5. It is rather apparent that federal government outlays are nearly triple the magnitude of federal government purchases from the National Income Accounts! How

Table B.1

National Income and Expenditure Accounts and U.S. Government Outlays Third Quarter 1995 and FY 1995 (estimated) ($ million)

Consumption	$4960.0
Investment	1074.8
Net exports	–100.8
Federal government purchases	**507.1**
State and local government purchases	857.3
equals	
Gross domestic product	$7298.5
Memo:	
Federal government outlays	**$1519.1**

Sources and comments: GDP estimates are for the third quarter, 1995, annualized, and are estimated from data provided by the Federal Reserve Bank of St. Louis. Datum on outlays is taken from Chapter 1.

is this difference explained? As discussed in Chapter 1, federal government outlays (sometimes called expenditures) measures the actual amount of money spent by the federal government over some designated period, typically 1 year.

Federal government purchases, a smaller component of government outlays, is the measure of the amount spent to acquire actual goods and services for use by the federal government in the public name. Defense expenditures, the federal court and prison systems, expenditures for road construction, and spending for education are all good examples of federal government purchases. The same distinction can be made at the level of state and local government. The National Income Accounts, for example, include a large category labeled State and Local Government Purchases (find the entry in Table B.1) which shows a higher level of spending than at the federal level.

Why are these categories different (and why are purchases less than outlays)? This is because there is a very large category of government spending labeled **transfer payments.** These are direct payments to individuals by a government where no service or commodity is received in exchange. Payments by the Social Security System, Medicare, unemployment compensation, and welfare payments at the state and local level are good examples of transfer payments. Interest on the debt is also a transfer payment.

Entitlements are related to transfer payments. These are defined as benefits that must be paid to all who meet the eligibility requirements as mandated by law. Again, Social Security, disability payments, and Medicare payments are good examples of entitlements. All entitlements are classified as transfer payments, but transfer payments also include some categories of spending, like interest paid on the federal debt, that are not entitlements.[1]

The exact relationship between purchases, expenditures, and transfer payments is shown in this formula (using data from FY 1995 as an example):

Government Purchases	=	Government Outlays	–	Transfer Payments
($507.1 billion)	=	($1,519.1 billion)	–	($1,012.0 billion)

Look carefully at the numbers. Quite clearly, more than two-thirds of federal expenditures are for transfer payments; the majority of that is for entitlements.

Why the careful distinction between purchases and expenditures?

Purchases are meant to be a rough measure of *the claim upon national output by government.* In other words, if for the moment the U.S. economy can be thought of as an enormous factory of goods and services producing a given amount of output in 1 year, government purchases measure the dollar value of that amount for use by the government.

Transfer payments, in contrast, do not constitute claims upon national output by government. In the case of transfer payments, the government merely serves as a conduit of funds, where *payment merely passes from the hands of one private party, the taxpayer, to another private party, the recipient of the funds.* Ultimate purchasing power never leaves the private sector, but is redistributed by government from one private party to another. For example, in the case of the Social Security retirement plan (OASI), the payment passes from some young person paying the OASI employment tax required by law to a retired person drawing Social Security benefits. In this case, the ultimate claim upon national output stays in the private sector.

Federal government *outlays* cannot be used in the calculation of the National Income and Expenditure Accounts because to do so would constitute doublecounting. Social Security expenditures (from the OASI

---

[1]Entitlements are discussed extensively in Chapter 6. The reader might also consult the definition of "entitlements" in the Glossary.

program to beneficiaries) show up in the *consumption* category when the funds are spent by retirees.

When looking at the National Income and Expenditure Accounts, it can be seen that the two government accounts combined (total government purchases) constitute about 19% of GDP, with the federal government claiming about 7% of national output (a surprisingly low figure), and state and local governments claiming the remaining 12%.

Accrual, Cash, and Capital Accounting and Budgeting

. . . .

As was stated in Chapter 4, the *unified budget,* whether presented as a budget by budgetary function or by government agency, is largely a *cash* budget, reflecting receipts and outlays of actual cash (in the form of checks, for the largest part).

Businesses, in contrast, almost always use an *accrual* budget. Likewise, businesses treat their *capital* budgeting differently than their budgeting for *operations.* State and local governments typically also use the government equivalent of capital accounting. The federal government is singular in that it does not maintain a separate capital budget, and it generally does not use capital budget accounting. This has some subtle but important implications for the deficit issue.[1]

[1]Any standard accounting text will give the reader more background on these issues. The uninitiated might consult Joseph A. Cashin and Joel J. Lerner, *Schaum's Outline Series: Theories and Problems of Accounting 1, Third Edition,* McGraw-Hill, 1986. Capital (fixed asset) accounting is discussed in Chapter 13, and accrual accounting (receivables and payables) are discussed in Chapter 12.

Capital (Fixed Asset) Budgeting Issues

In a business budget, capital equipment and property that have high value and durability, such as land, buildings, machinery, vehicles, and office equipment are treated differently than payments for labor and non-durable commodities such as wages, utilities, and rent. When any of the latter are purchased (salaries and rent are paid, gasoline is purchased) the transaction is recorded as an expense at the time of purchase matched either by a *cash* outlay, if paid for directly, or typically by a *payable* account entry (a debt), which is later settled by cash.

When a building or a truck is purchased, on the other hand, the full purchase price is *not* recorded as an expense in the year of the transaction. Instead, the property is depreciated over a long period of time. This means that the expense is allocated gradually over the lifetime of the asset, usually a number of years. Far more important to our discussion, it is considered acceptable and even prudent to finance the purchase of such capital equipment (fixed assets) with *debt.*

Even consumers use this rough standard. Houses, which may have useful lives of more than a century, are almost always purchased with 30- or 15-year mortgages, and even automobiles, with projected lives of a dozen or so years, are purchased with loans of shorter duration.

Although they don't depreciate their buildings and other fixed assets, state and local governments usually *do* finance their major fixed assets with *debt.* This is typically in the form of dedicated bond issues, and not *cash.* This is the reason why the *municipal note and bond market* is so large. Large-scale infrastructure spending, such as freeways and school and hospital construction, is financed by note and bonds sales, often dedicated to the projects beings financed (school bonds or freeway bonds). Ideally, noncapital spending (police and fire protection, welfare outlays) is financed by receipts (mostly from taxes) in the year of the outlay, although this gray line is being crossed in some states like California.

This is why it is possible for heavily indebted states to maintain that they operate with a balanced budget. This means that their *cash* or *operating* budget is balanced. The capital budget that is financed by debt and is normally in the red by federal standards, is not part of the equation. If state and local governments used the same kind of accounting as is used by the federal government, most would be running budget deficits.

The federal government makes no distinction between cash and capital spending. Generally all are treated as cash outlays. In effect, the federal government pays cash for everything from weapons systems to Social

Security benefits. When it comes up a little short each year, it borrows the difference.

Certain types of federal spending could be treated much like capital spending. The most obvious candidate is military procurement, especially for major weapons systems (authorizations for such systems extend for years, as is discussed in Chapter 8, but they are not *funded* in any special way), but any spending for infrastructure, such as for roads and airports, government buildings in general, and land purchases, could qualify.

Because there *is* no capital budget under present federal budgeting conventions, requiring a balanced budget for *all* spending—including those categories that would normally fall into a capital budget—may be too restrictive. This is roughly akin to telling businesses that they can not borrow to finance their expansions, or states that they can not borrow to build freeways, or even consumers that they can not borrow to buy homes and cars. For capital spending, debt can be justified and the judicious use of debt is sometimes preferable to severe *cash-only* restrictions.

Accrual versus Cash Accounting

The second major distinction between normal business accounting and the practices used by the government is found in the fact that the federal government does not use *accrual accounting* practices. For the most part (with important exceptions explained below), the government uses *cash accounting*.

So what is the difference? Under accrual accounting, an expense would be recorded as such when the expense obligation is incurred, regardless of whether cash is paid at the time. So, for example, using an accrual method of accounting, if a business buys something using *debt* rather than a cash payment, the expenditure is recorded at the time of the transaction, rather than at the time the cash is paid. In contrast, using a *cash* budget, the expense is recorded at the time the cash is paid. The federal government uses the latter technique.[2]

Likewise, if a business using an accrual method sells a product on credit, the revenue is recorded at the time of the transaction rather than when the bill is paid. The federal government, though, does not record its revenues when our tax obligations arise. It records them when we actually

[2]For the reader with some accounting background, *accrual* accounting uses accounts such as *accounts receivable* and *accounts payable*. The federal budget does not use such conventions.

make our payments, both throughout the year with deductions and periodic contributions (such as through the quarterly IRS Form 1099s that is used by the self-employed) and when we file our taxes.

In some respects, the federal government uses a quasi-accrual method. For all federal programs, two levels of budget authority are required. One authorizes actual outlays (generally cash) for the year, the other authorizes what is called *budget authority*. This allows agencies like the Department of Defense to make contracts with private parties (for such things as weapons systems, for example) and it extends obligations into future years. Such budget authority at least makes note of implied future spending obligations (and contracts cannot be negotiated without it). These procedures are discussed in detail in Chapter 8.

A pure accrual budget would be impractical for the federal government, especially on the revenue side. Because taxes are not contracted on a transactions basis (no one sits down with a federal representative on October 1 and says "deliver a little defense protection and I'll pay you $900 in taxes"), calculating *taxes receivable* as receipts would be a dubious proposition at best. Efforts are always made to estimate tax receipts, but *accrual* accounting does not rely upon *estimates* of receipts; it relies upon concrete promises made in the name of debt.

There is a second and very important qualification to the statement that the federal government uses a *cash* accounting method. The federal government manages a large number of credit programs, either by offering loans directly to private parties or, more typically, by insuring loans made privately. Examples of this include loan guarantees for Federal Housing Administration and Veterans Administration loans, direct student loans and loan guarantees, Small Business Administration loans, Public Law 480 (agricultural export) loans and many others.[3] Federal accounting gets complicated with the treatment of the loans and loan guarantees. Although credit programs involve sizeable cash transfers between the government and private parties, the only major components that usually show up as outlays are any subsidies associated with loans or loan guarantees, and the present value of estimated future losses for loans that are made or guaranteed in the current fiscal year and the present value of future subsidies linked to any loans or loan guarantees made in the current fiscal year. In effect, this means that if a loan program, such as a student loan program, is undertaken and the money lent directly or private

[3]For a full discussion of these credit programs, see *Budget of The United States Government, Analytic Perspectives, FY1997*, Chapter 8. For a list of the federal credit programs, see Table 8.1, p. 120.

loans are guaranteed in fiscal year 1997 (both are possible with student loans), then an estimate must be made of future subsidy costs and future estimated losses for the loan package, and this must be reflected as outlays in fiscal year 1997, the year in which the loan is made. This would be added to administrative program costs. The loan itself would not be reflected as an outlay. Because estimates of future losses and subsidies clearly are *not* cash disbursements but *are* recorded as outlays, this is a clear (and sensible) departure from a strict *cash* accounting standard.

The Office of Management and Budget (OMB) has in recent years made efforts to estimate capital budgeting or fixed asset spending and other types of federal investment spending. The OMB is working on plans for improving the budgeting of fixed assets, although these efforts have not yet impacted primary budget procedures. For a discussion of capital budgeting see *Budget of the United States Government, FY1997, Analytic Perspectives,* Chapter 6. For FY 1997, the OMB estimated federal planned investment outlays, the rough equivalent of capital spending, at $225.2 billion.

Outlays by Function, Subfunction, and Major Program (1995 and 1996 Estimates, $ Million)

Note: All outlays above $100 millions are shown, except those labeled "other" or the equivalent. Because of omissions of the smallest totals and "other," program subtotals may not sum to program totals.

Func num	Sub func	Function or program	1995	1996e
050		NATIONAL DEFENSE	272,066	265,556
	051	Department of Defense—Military	259,442	254,258
		Military personnel	70,809	67,177
		Operation and maintenance	90,881	91,485
		Procurement	54,982	48,116
		Research, development, testing	34,594	34,434
		Military construction	6,823	6,524
		Family housing	3,571	4,028
	053	Atomic Energy Defense Activities	11,777	10,245
		Weapons activities	3,656	3,389
		Defense environmental restoration	5,621	5,237
		Nuclear waste disposal	132	86

Func num	Sub func	Function or program	1995	1996e
	054	Defense-related Activities	847	1,053
150		INTERNATIONAL AFFAIRS	16,434	14,830
	151	International Development & Hum Assistance	7,599	6,895
		Agency for International Development	4,055	3,763
		Multilateral development banks	1,424	1,850
		Food aid	1,496	1,191
		Refugee programs	705	837
		Voluntary contributions	496	308
		Peace Corps.	235	226
	152	International Security Assistance	5,252	5,292
		Foreign military financing grants and loans	2,981	3419
		Economic support fund	2,739	2596
		Repayment of foreign military financing loans. .	−674	−634
	153	Conduct of foreign affairs	4,192	4138
	154	Foreign information and exchange activities	1,417	1203
		U.S. Information Agency	1,163	1194
		Board for Internation Broadcasting.	230	0
	155	International financial programs	16,434	14,830
		Export/Import Bank.	151	453
		International Monetary Funds	−265	19
		Exchange stabilization fund	−2,467	−2,055
		Foreign military sales abroad fund	948	130
		Special defense acquisition fund	−85	−129
250		GENERAL SCIENCE, SPACE, AND TECHN	16,724	16,877
	251	General Science and Basic Research	4,131	3,978
		National Science Foundation programs	2,791	3,000
		Department of Energy general science programs	1,340	978
	252	Space flight, research, and supporting activities	12,593	12,899
		Science, Aeronautics, and Technology	2,200	4,538
		Human space flight	3,528	5,070
		Mission support.	1,763	2,038
		Space flight control and data communications. .	1,409	380
		Construction of facilities	305	86
		Research and development	3,286	748
270		ENERGY	4,936	3,217
	271	Energy supply	3,584	2,009
		Research and development	4,006	3,807
		Naval petroleum reserves	−209	−285
		Federal power marketing	−447	−498
		Tennessee Valley Authority	1,104	636
		Uranium enrichment	109	48
		United States Enrichment Corporation	−355	93
		Uranium enrichment decontamination and decomm.	349	287
		Decontamination transfer	−134	−350

Func num	Sub func	Function or program	1995	1996e
		Nuclear waste program	376	218
		Nuclear waste fund receipts	−597	−630
		Rural electrification and telephone loans	191	148
		Credit liquidating account (REA)	−828	−1,498
	272	**Energy Conservation**	671	681
	274	**Emergency Energy Preparedness**	223	171
	276	**Energy Information, Policy, and Regulation**	458	356
300		**NATURAL RESOURCES AND ENVIRONMENT**	**22,105**	**21,550**
	301	**Water Resources**	**4,791**	**4,729**
		Corps of Engineers.	3,870	3,777
		Bureau of Reclamation	824	946
	302	**Conservation and Land Management**	**5,318**	**4,876**
		Forest Service.	3,371	2,821
		Management of public lands.	1,010	942
		Mining reclamation and enforcement	313	233
		Conservation reserve program	1,732	1,841
		Other conservation of agricultural lands	806	926
	303	**Recreational Resources**	**2,828**	**2,568**
		Federal land acquisition	265	181
		Operation of recreational resources.	2,748	2,585
	304	**Air Pollution Control and Abatement**	**6,512**	**6,517**
		Regulatory, enforcement, and research programs	2,621	2,620
		Hazardous substance superfund	1,473	1,389
		Oil pollution funds.	151	159
		States and tribal assistance grants	2,455	2,500
		Superfund recoveries and other.	−261	−210
	306	**Other Natural Resources**	**2,656**	**2,860**
350		**AGRICULTURE**	**9,773**	**7,718**
	351	**Farn Income Stabilization**	**7,015**	**4,987**
		Commodity Credit Corporation	6,030	3,199
		Crop Insurance	387	2,006
		Agricultural credit insurance.	424	389
		Credit liquidating accounts.	−573	−1,302
	352	**Agricultural Research and Services**	**2,758**	**2,731**
		Research programs.	1,196	1,213
		Marketing programs	175	166
		Animal and plant inspection programs	495	421
		Economic intelligence.	136	134
		Offsetting receipts	−137	−138
370		**COMMERCE AND HOUSING CREDIT**	**−14,441**	**−10,744**
	371	**Mortgage Credit**	**−1,038**	**−3,999**
		Federal Housing Administration	−210	−2,402
		Government National Mortgage Assn.	−463	−472
		Rural housing programs.	1,061	725

Func num	Sub func	Function or program	1995	1996e
		Credit liquidating accounts................	−1,428	−321
	372	**Postal Service**	**−1,839**	**−189**
		Payments to postal service fund	130	122
	373	**Deposit Insurance**	**−17,827**	**−13,465**
		Resolution Trust Corporation fund..........	−10,668	−2,424
		Bank insurance fund	−6,916	−1,531
		FSLIC resolution fund	1,090	−3,463
		Savings Association Insurance Fund	−1,101	−5,886
		National Credit Union Administration	−274	−182
	376	**Other Advancement of Commerce**	**6,263**	**6,909**
		Small and minority business assistance	673	863
		Science and technology..................	468	616
		Economic and demographic statistics	339	318
		Payments to copyright owners	316	300
		Universal Service Fund...................	4,300	4,300
		Regulatory agencies	210	210
		International trade and business promotion....	335	386
		Credit liquidating accounts................	−378	−84
400		**TRANSPORTATION**	**39,350**	**39,769**
	401	**Ground Transportation**	**25,297**	**26,124**
		Highways	19,435	20,363
		Highway safety	353	389
		Mass transit..........................	4,473	4,471
		Railroads.............................	1,035	907
	402	**Air Transportation**	**10,020**	**9,865**
		Airports and safety (FAA)	9,207	8,551
		Aeronautical research and technology	784	1,290
	403	**Water Transportation....................**	**3,732**	**3,471**
		Marine safety and transportation	3,531	3,238
		Ocean shipping	312	298
	407	**Other Transportation....................**	**301**	**309**
450		**COMMUNITY AND REGIONAL DEVELOPMENT**	**10,641**	**12,878**
	451	**Community Development**	**4,744**	**5,519**
		Community development block grants	4,333	5,093
	452	**Area and Regional Development**	**2,615**	**2,689**
		Rural development......................	622	789
		Rural economic development assistance.......	354	459
		Indian programs.......................	1,408	1,366
		Appalachian regional commission............	193	182
		Tennessee Valley Authority	210	105
		Credit liquidating accounts................	186	163
		Offsetting receipts	−357	−375
	453	**Disaster Relief and Insurance**	**3,282**	**4,670**
		Small Business Administration disaster loans...	705	513

Func num	Sub func	Function or program	1995	1996e
		Disaster relief..........................	2,116	3,928
		Credit liquidating accounts.................	−285	−365
500		EDUCATION, TRAINING, EMPLOYMENT & SOC SERVICES	54,263	54,131
	501	Elementary, Secondary, and Vocational Education	14,694	16,002
		Education reform......................	61	538
		School improvement programs..............	1,391	1,587
		Education for disadvantaged..............	6,808	7,113
		Special education......................	3,177	3,511
		Impact aid...........................	808	830
		Vocational and adult education............	1,482	1,513
		Indian education programs...............	729	657
	502	**Higher Education**	**14,172**	**11,440**
		Student financial assistance...............	7,047	7,395
		Federal family education loan program.......	3,601	2,297
		Federal direct loan program..............	840	545
		Higher education......................	871	898
		Credit liquidating account...............	1,588	73
	503	**Research and General Education Aids**	**2,120**	**2,269**
	504	**Training and Employment**	**7,430**	**7,617**
		Training and employment services..........	4,690	4,846
		Trade adjustment assistance..............	103	95
		Older Americans employed...............	411	380
		Payments to states for AFDC work programs..	953	959
		Federal-state employment service..........	1,185	1,261
	505	**Other Labor Services**	**965**	**962**
	506	**Social Services**	**14,882**	**15,841**
		National service initiative................	426	572
		Family support and preservation...........	38	132
		Social services block grant..............	2,797	3,183
		Rehabilitation services..................	2,333	2,593
		Payments to states for foster care and adoption ser	3,243	3,740
		Children and families services program.......	4,726	4,898
		Aging services program.................	952	776
		Interim assistance to states for legalization....	358	3
550		**HEALTH**	**115,418**	**121,211**
	551	**Health Care Services**	**101,931**	**107,686**
		Medicaid grants.......................	89,070	94,892
		Federal employees and retired employees health benefits......................	3,694	3,594
		Coal miners retirees health benefits..........	336	328
		Indian health........................	2,012	1,932
		Substance abuse and mental health services....	2,444	2,105
		Other health care services................	4,375	4,898

Func num	Sub func	Function or program	1995	1996e
	552	Health Research and Training	11,569	11,533
		National Institutes of Health	10,883	10,924
		Breast cancer and other health research	114	67
		Clinical training	286	286
		Other research and training	286	256
	554	Consumer and Occupational Health and Safety	1,918	1,992
		Food and safety inspection	522	553
		Other consumer safery	900	915
		Occupational safety and health	496	524
570		MEDICARE	159,855	177,856
		Hospital insurance	114,883	126,531
		Supplementary medical insurance	65,213	70,897
		Medicare premiums and collections.	−20,241	−19,842
600		INCOME SECURITY	220,449	228,342
	601	General Retirement and Disability Insurance	5,106	4,973
		Railroad retirement	4,055	4,406
		Special benefits for disabled coal miners	1,288	1,222
		Pension Benefit Guaranty Corporation	−430	−858
	602	Federal Employee Retirement and Disability	65,834	67,936
		Civilian retirement and disability programs	38,860	40,169
		Military retirement.	27,797	28,511
		Federal employees workers compensation	71	249
		Federal employees life insurance fund	−894	−993
	603	Unemployment Compensation	23,638	25,986
	604	Housing Assistance	27,524	26,573
		Subsidized, public, homeless, and other		
		HUD housing.	27,009	26,059
		Rural housing assistance.	510	574
	605	Food and Nutrition Assistance	37,594	39,034
		Food stamps	25,554	26,346
		State child nutrition programs.	7,499	8,233
		Special supplemental for women, infants, children	3,404	3,687
		Other nutrition	1,137	1,064
	609	Other Income Security	60,753	63,840
		Supplemental security income (SSI)	26,488	26,621
		Family support payments	17,133	17,366
		Earned Income Tax Credit (EITC)	15,244	18,124
		Refugee assistance	393	399
		Low income home energy assistance	1,419	1,252
		Payments to states for day-care assistance	933	935
		SSI offsetting receipts	−927	−983
650		SOCIAL SECURITY	335,846	350,924
		Old-age and survivors insurance (OASI)	294,468	306,009
		Disability insurance (DI)	41,377	45,062
700		VETERANS BENEFITS AND SERVICES	37,938	37,748

Func num	Sub func	Function or program	1995	1996e
	701	**Income Security for Veterans**	**18,966**	**18,121**
		Compensation	14,815	14,077
		Pensions	3,024	2,757
		Burial benefits and miscelleaneous assistance	109	115
		National service life insurance trust fund	1,249	1,403
		All other insurance programs	43	52
		Insurance program receipts	−274	−283
	702	**Veterans Education, Training, and Rehabilitation**	**1,124**	**1,117**
		Readjustment benefits (GI Bill and related)	1,191	1,273
		All volunteer force educational assistance tr fu	−104	−194
	703	**Hospital and Medical Care for Veterans**	**16,428**	**17,081**
		Medical care and hospital services	16,262	16,987
		Construction	637	635
		Fees and other charges for medical services	−440	−466
	704	**Veterans Housing**	**329**	**284**
		Loan guaranty	105	117
		Guaranty and indemnity	508	25
		Credit liquidating accounts	−286	140
	705	**Other Veterans Benefits and Services**	**1,091**	**1,145**
		Cemetaries, administration of benefits, and other	986	1,052
		non−VA support programs	105	93
750		**ADMINISTRATION OF JUSTICE**	**16,223**	**18,764**
	751	**Federal Law Enforcement Activities**	**6,384**	**7,475**
		Criminal investigations (FBI,DEA,FinCEN,ICDE)	3,355	3,410
		Alcohol, tobacco, and firearms investigations	372	378
		Border enforcement activities (Customs, INS)	3,449	4,283
		Protection activities (Secret Service)	528	571
		Equal Employment Opportunity Commission	233	232
		Other enforcement	403	536
	752	**Federal Litigative and Judicial Activities**	**6,123**	**6,368**
		Civil and criminal prosecution and representation	2,757	2,769
		Federal judicial activities	2,924	3,313
		Representation of indigents in civil cases	429	280
	753	**Federal Correctional Activities**	**2,749**	**3,013**
	754	**Criminal Justice Assistance**	**967**	**1,908**
800		**GENERAL GOVERNMENT**	**13,835**	**13,590**
	801	**Legislative Functions**	**1,995**	**2,066**
	802	**Executive Direction and Management**	**248**	**295**
		Executive Office of the President	178	181
	803	**Central Fiscal Operations**	**7,936**	**7,576**
		Tax administration	7,716	7,433
	804	**General Property and Records Management**	**920**	**661**
		Real property activities	374	215

Func num	Sub func	Function or program	1995	1996e
		Records management	219	196
	805	Central Personnel Management	126	150
	806	General Purpose Fiscal Assistance	2,057	2,096
		Payments and loans to District of Columbia . . .	709	700
		Payments to states and counties from		
		Federal Services	320	295
		Payments to states from receipts under		
		Mineral Leases	474	508
		Payments in lieu of taxes	101	100
		Payments to territories and to Puerto Rico	136	149
		Tax revenues for Puerto Rico	206	232
	808	Other General Government	1,630	1,600
		Treasury claims	1,104	1,000
	809	Deductions for Offsetting Receipts	–1,077	–854
900		NET INTEREST	232,173	241,059
	901	Interest on the Public Debt	332,414	344,628
	902	Interest Received by On-budget Trust Funds	–59,867	–61,158
		Contributions to civil & foreign service		
		retirement fund.	–28,056	–29,242
		Military retirement.	–10,915	–10,900
		Medicare	–12,806	–12,299
	903	Interest received by Off-budget Trust Funds	–33,305	–36,440
	908	Other Interest	–7,069	–5,971
		Interest on loans to Federal Financing Bank . . .	–7,422	–6,116
		Interest on refunds of tax collections.	2,655	2,890
		Payment to Resolution Funding Corporation. . .	2,328	2,328
		Interest paid to loan guarantee financing		
		accounts.	2,541	778
		Interest received from direct loan financing		
		accounts.	–2,726	–1,754
		Interest on deposits in tax and loan accounts. . .	–946	–933
950		UNDISTRIBUTED OFFSETTING RECEIPTS	–44,455	–42,268
	951	Employer Share, Employee Retirement		
		(On-budget)	–27,961	–27,138
		Contributions to military retirement fund	–12,238	–11,250
		Postal Service contributions to		
		retirement/disability fund	–5,431	–5,637
		Other contributions to retirement/disablity fund	–7,843	–7,885
	952	Employer Share, Employee Retirement		
		(Off-budget)	–6,432	–6,291
	953	Rents and Royalties on Outer Continental Shelf	–2,418	–2,689
		TOTAL OUTLAYS	1,519,133	1,572,411

The Republican Contract with America

. . . .

As Republican Members of the House of Representatives and as citizens seeking to join that body we propose not just to change its policies, but even more important, to restore the bonds of trust between the people and their elected representatives.

That is why, in this era of official evasion and posturing, we offer instead a detailed agenda for national renewal, a written commitment with no fine print.

This year's election offers the chance, after four decades of one-party control, to bring to the House a new majority that will transform the way Congress works. That historic change would be the end of government that is too big, too intrusive, and too easy with the public's money. It can be the beginning of a Congress that respects the values and shares the faith of the American family.

Like Lincoln, our first Republican president, we intend to act "with firmness in the right, as God gives us to see the right." To restore accountability to Congress. To end its cycle of scandal and disgrace. To make us all proud again of the way free people govern themselves.

On the first day of the 104th Congress, the new Republican majority will immediately pass the following major reforms, aiming at restoring the faith and trust of the American people and their government.

- **First,** require all laws that apply to the rest of the country also apply equally to the Congress;
- **Second,** select a major, independent auditing firm to conduct a comprehensive audit of Congress for waste, fraud, or abuse;
- **Third,** cut the number of House committees, and cut the committee staff by one-third;
- **Fourth,** limit the terms of all committee chairs;
- **Fifth,** ban the casting of proxy votes in committee;
- **Sixth,** require committee meetings be open to the public;
- **Seventh,** require a three-fifths majority vote to pass a tax increase;
- **Eighth,** guarantee an honest accounting of our Federal Budget by implementing zero base-line budgeting.

Therefore, within the first 100 days of the 104th Congress, we shall bring to the House Floor the following bills, each to be given full and open debate, each to be given a clear and fair vote and to be immediately available this day for public inspection and scrutiny.

1. The Fiscal Responsibility Act: A balanced budget/tax limitation amendment and a legislative line-item veto to restore fiscal responsibility to an out-of-control Congress, requiring them to live under the same budget constraints as families and businesses.

2. The Taking Back our Streets Act: An anti-crime package including stronger truth-in-sentencing, "good faith" exclusionary rule exemptions, effective death penalty provisions, and cuts in social spending from this summer's "crime" bill to fund prison construction and additional law enforcement to keep people secure in their neighborhoods and kids safe in their schools.

3. The Personal Responsibility Act: Discourage illegitimacy and teen pregnancy by prohibiting welfare to minor mothers and denying increased AFDC for additional children while on welfare, cut spending for welfare programs, and enact a tough two-years-and-out provision with work requirements to promote individual welfare programs, and enact a tough two-years-and-out provision with work requirements to promote individual responsibility.

4. The Family Reinforcement Act: Child support enforcement, tax incentives for adoption, strengthening rights of parents in their children's education, stronger child pornography laws, and an elderly dependent care tax credit to reinforce the central role of families in American society.

5. The American Dream Restoration Act: A $500 per child tax credit, begin repeal of the marriage tax penalty, and creation of American Dream Savings Accounts to provide middle class tax relief.

6. The National Security Restoration Act: No U.S. troops under U.N. command and restoration of the essential parts of our national security funding to strengthen our national defense and maintain our credibility around the world.

7. The Senior Citizens Fairness Act: Raise the Social Security earnings limit which currently forces seniors out of the work force, repeal the 1993 tax hikes on Social Security benefits and provide tax incentives for private long-term care insurance to let Older Americans keep more of what they have earned over the years.

8. The Job Creation and Wage Enhancement Act: Small business incentives, capital gains cut and indexation, neutral cost recovery, risk assessment/cost-benefit analysis, strengthening the Regulatory Flexibility Act and unfunded mandate reform to create jobs and raise worker wages.

9. The Common Sense Legal Reform Act: "Loser pays" laws, reasonable limits on punitive damages and reform of product liability laws to stem the endless tide of litigation.

10. The Citizen Legislature Act: A first-ever vote on term limits to replace career politicians with citizen legislators.

Further, we will instruct the House Budget Committee to report to the floor and we will work to enact additional budget savings, beyond the budget cuts specifically included in the legislation described above, to ensure that the Federal budget deficit will be less than it would have been without the enactment of these bills.

Regarding the judgment of our fellow citizens as we seek their mandate for reform, we hereby pledge our names to the Contract with America.

[Author's note: Legislation linked to the Republican Contract with America was introduced at the beginning of the 104th Congress in January, 1995. Each of the 10 acts named above were accompanied by proposed bills. Very little was enacted into legislation by the 104th Congress].

APPENDIX

The Balanced Budget Amendment to the United States Constitution

104th Congress House Joint Resolution 1

Joint Resolution

Proposing a **balanced budget** amendment to the Constitution of the United States.

Resolved by the Senate and House of Representatives of America in Congress assembled (two-thirds of each House concurring therein), That the following article is proposed as an amendment to the Constitution of the United States, which shall be valid to all intents and purposes as part of the Constitution when ratified by the legislature of three-fourths of the several States within seven years after the date of its submission to the States for ratification:

"Article. 1A—

'Section 1. Total outlays for any fiscal year shall not exceed total receipts for that fiscal year, unless three-fifths of the whole number of each House of Congress shall provide by law for a specific excess of outlays over receipts by a rollcall vote.

'Section 2. The limit on the debt of the United States held by the public shall not be increased, unless three-fifths of the whole number of each House shall provide by law for such an increase by a rollcall vote.

'Section 3. Prior to each fiscal year, the President shall transmit to the Congress a proposed **budget** for the United States Government for that fiscal year in which total outlays do not exceed total receipts.

'Section 4. No bill to increase revenue shall become law unless approved by a majority of the whole number of each House by a rollcall vote.

'Section 5. The Congress may waive the provisions of this article for any fiscal year in which a declaration of war is in effect. The provisions of this article may be waived for any fiscal year in which the United States is engaged in military conflict, which causes an imminent and serious military threat to national security and is so declared by a joint resolution, adopted by a majority if the whole number of each House, which becomes law.

'Section 6. The Congress shall enforce and implement this article by appropriate legislation, which may rely on estimates of outlays and receipts.

'Section 7. Total receipts shall include all receipts of the United States Government except those derived from borrowing. Total outlays shall include all outlays of the United States Government except for those for repayment of debt principal.

'Section 8. This article shall take effect beginning with fiscal year 2002 or the second fiscal year beginning after its ratification, whichever is later.' "

Author's note: This version of the amendment passed the House of Representatives on January 26, 1995. It later failed in the Senate by one vote, then failed again in the Senate a year later.

This version of the amendment has four serious flaws:

1. It has no enforcement provision. What is to happen if the conditions are not met? It has the potential to provoke a constitutional crisis—is the Supreme Court to decide how the budget will be balanced?
2. **Section 2** stipulates that "the limit on the debt of the United States held by the public shall not be increased." This is vague. There is no limit on the debt held by the public currently. The statutory

limit on the public debt applies to gross debt, not debt held by the public. (See p. 17 in Chapter 1).

3. The U.S. government is going to run a budget deficit in any recession year—because of the impact on taxes that is nearly unavoidable. This amendment makes no provision for that. Are outlays to be cut back automatically in the middle of a recession?

4. Economic policy of this kind does not usually make its way into the same document that contains our Bill of Rights. It may not be a wise precedent to start putting economic policy into the Constitution of the United States Government.

This issue again came to a vote in the Senate in March, 1997, when it failed again.

The Welfare Reform Act of 1996

· ·

As discussed in Chapter 6, the 104th Congress made some substantial changes to federal welfare programs. In this appendix we describe the salient features and we discuss in greater detail HR 3734, the Welfare Reform Act of 1996, now Public Law 104-193, signed into law on August 22, 1996.[1]

Major Provisions of Public Law 104-193

1. **Changes AFDC from entitlements status to block grants.** Specifically, the law eliminates the old Aid to Families with Dependent Children (AFDC) program, operated as an entitlements program, with the new Temporary Assistance for Needy Families (TANF) program, funded as a block-grant program. This was the most far-reaching change in the law. The block grants come with numerous and substantial provisions and

[1] The text of Public Law 104-193 and Titles 8, 9, and 42 of the United States Code superseded by this law provides the source material for this summary. When this appendix was written the law was new and subject to interpretation, so some elements included here may no longer be accurate.

restrictions, many of which are described elsewhere in this appendix. The Food Stamp Program, Medicaid, nutritional programs such as the School Lunch program and nutritional aid to women, infants, and children (WIC), and most housing programs remain as entitlements and were not converted to block grants.

Qualifications, exemptions, and exceptions. As stated, the new law changed the AFDC program from an entitlements program to a block-grant program. There are some subtle qualifications to this feature. First, rather than replace altogether the entitlements status of the program, the law effectively removed it at the federal level and placed it at the state level. To receive a block grant, each state must submit a comprehensive child-based welfare plan that will entitle qualified families to benefits. Such plans will differ from one state to another, but that was also true under AFDC. Second, the old AFDC was a state grant program just like the new one. The old AFDC differed from the new TANF in that the latter caps the size of the federal contribution by a formula based upon prior payouts to individual states between 1992 and 1995 and is subject to annual appropriations. The amount of TANF funding is expected to be around $16 billion annually, compared to $17.1 for fiscal year 1995 AFDC funding. AFDC outlays were not capped, nor were they subject to annual appropriations. They were determined by the level of federal entitlements, which in turn was determined in part by the size of the caseload. This difference is what makes the TANF arrangement a "block" grant instead of just a grant. States with large welfare populations that fall short on this funding, now capped, will have to make up the difference. If states are able to successfully remove people from welfare because of changes in entitlements at the state level or because of the new time limits and work requirements described below, this will not happen.

2. Places time limits on some welfare benefits. The law limits family assistance from the new TANF program (the old AFDC program) and food stamps to 5 years (60 months) total cash assistance over a lifetime. TANF requires that the family receiving assistance include a minor child or pregnant woman.

Qualifications, exemptions, exceptions. The 60-month lifetime limit means a limitation of 60 months of benefits to the head of the family in question that may be paid intermittently. It is not a limit of 5 calendar years from the date of the first benefit paid. This limit does not include child nutrition programs, or Medicaid. Time spent on welfare prior to the law going into effect will not be counted, so no family will reach this limit until the year 2002. Under prior law, it appeared that about one-third of all families exceed 60 months of benefits.

3. Imposes work and/or training requirements. The new law generally imposes stiff work requirements for welfare recipients who receive benefits from the new Temporary Assistance for Needy Families (TANF) and food stamp programs. The law imposes requirements on aid recipients *and* the states that administer the aid. Generally, the law requires parent or caretaker (hereafter caretaker) adult recipients of TANF aid to engage in work or to receive specified job search or training activity after 24 months of receiving aid (whether or not consecutive), or even sooner if the state determines that the caretaker is ready to engage in work. To be engaged in work or in suitable training, the caretaker must work at least part-time for a minimum number of hours per week specified by the law on a sliding scale: in fiscal year 1997 the minimum work week is 20 hours, but by fiscal year 2000 and thereafter the minimum is set at 30 hours per week. For two-parent families, one parent must work at least 35 hours per week. The other parent must also work 20 hours per week if the family receives federally-funded child care assistance.

The individual *states* also must meet requirements in forcing recipients to work. On an escalating scale, states are required to have 50% of all families and 90% of two-parent families engaged in work by these criteria by fiscal year 2002 (because of new entrants into TANF programs and the 24-month exemption, these participation rates will never reach 100%). States that fail to meet these targets can be penalized with reduction in federal TANF grants according to formulas specified by the new law.

Qualifications, exemptions, exceptions. The TANF work requirement defines work to be private or public work, subsidized or unsubsidized. Acceptable job search and training activities, none of which can permanently replace actual work, include (a) direct job search (6 weeks only); (b) on-the-job training, job preparation training, or job-skill training but only if directly related to employment; (c) enrollment in high school program if it leads to a Certificate of General Equivalency (High School Degree); (d) teenage head of household still enrolled in a high school and making ordinary progress; or (e) community service programs. Notably, the law does *not allow* attendance at a college to substitute for work activity. The law also has a displacement provision—no established employee may be laid off for the purpose of creating a vacancy for a TANF beneficiary. The TANF assigns higher work-requirement priority to two-parent families.

The viability and effect of the new work requirements are further discussed at the end of this document.

The Food Stamp program also has similar job training, job search and work requirements.

4. Elimination of immigrant welfare benefits. Disallows any federal funding for most types of public assistance for illegal aliens. Legal aliens are denied benefits outright for Supplemental Security Income (SSI, a need-based entitlements program mostly for the elderly, blind, and disabled) and food stamps. The federal law does not deny TANF benefits to legal aliens, but it does not grant them either. It leaves the determination of eligibility to the individual states after a 5-year waiting period has passed. For legal aliens, there are no benefit restrictions for National School Lunch and Child Nutrition Programs, education programs in general, and the medical costs of immunization, communicable diseases, and emergency medical care.

Qualifications, exemptions, exceptions. The old law prevented immigrant agricultural workers and immigrants with temporary visas from collecting most federal benefits for a period of 5 years [see 8 USC 1160 (f) and 8 USC 1255a (h)]. After passage of the law, it appeared that Medicaid benefits would be unaffected by the law and the final outcome of medical care for the poor would depend upon direct reform to Medicaid, if that happens.

Minor Provisions of Public Law 104-193

1. The law includes language that makes it appear that the intent is to improve the establishment of paternity of children born to unwed mothers and the enforcement of child care payments from fathers not with the family. The new law, however, is not much different from the old superseded AFDC law [42 USC Sec 602 (26)], which required the same thing.

2. The law provides substantial funding for child care assistance, certainly necessary if the back-to-work provisions of the new law have any chance of succeeding. Under two separate programs, the child-care federal funding grants to states range from about $3 billion in fiscal year 1997 to $3.7 billion in fiscal year 2002.

3. Again reflecting the Congress's flair for strange new savings accounts, the law also authorizes the creation of personal *Individual Devel-*

opment Accounts by the recipients of TANF relief. These are savings accounts that may be used for college education, first home purchase, or business capitalization. The welfare recipient must make a deposit in this account, and states and charities have the option of providing matching funds. Because people on welfare do not have the means to save much, it is hard to imagine that this provision of the law will play much of a role in welfare reform.

Author's Assessment of Public Law 104-193

Some of the features of Public Law 104-193 are likely to become permanent, but this will not be the last word on welfare reform. The law does a great deal of restricting and limiting without having much of a plan, not to mention adequate funding, for helping people move into real jobs through training and job placement activities. Although the unemployment rate is fairly low in the mid-1990s, the capacity of the economy to create millions of new low-end jobs for welfare recipients is doubtful. Under a literal interpretation of the law, around 5 million people, and possibly many more, will have to moved into jobs over the next few years. Even when the economy is operating at full capacity and growing quickly, it only creates about 3 million new jobs annually (and far fewer in slow years or during recessions). Only a fraction of these new jobs are suitable for people on welfare. It must be remembered that the law explicitly states that no one presently employed can be pushed out of a job in an effort to place welfare recipients in the job market, so the new jobs must be net new additions. The problem will be especially acute in cities with huge pockets of welfare, such as Washington, D.C. and Los Angeles. It is estimated by many critics that the law likely will push a large number of people, including children, deeper into poverty.[2]

In addition, the capacity for caseworkers to adjust to the new, complicated procedures for review and compliance will be difficult, especially with insufficient funding for training. This law imposes a tremendous burden at the operational level, at least in the early years of the program, while it imposes most of the cost and management of the transition on the individual states and their budgets.

---

[2]One of the most damning criticisms of the new law and of the treatment of poverty in general was published in *Scientific American*. See "Single Mothers and Welfare," by Ellen L. Bassuk, Angela Browne, and John C. Buckner, *Scientific American*, October 1996, pp. 60–67.

The final budgetary effects of the law are open to question as well. TANF block-grant outlays are expected to be set at just a little above $16 billion annually, without rising. This compares to $17.1 billion for the old AFDC program in fiscal year 1995. Food stamp outlays are trimmed slightly as well, and additional savings are realized by restricting benefits extended to aliens. The law is supposed to reduce federal outlays altogether by $50 billion to $60 billion between passage of the law and fiscal year 2002, which is a rather modest amount given the scope of the law (this is only about $10 billion per year). This gain will be diminished, however, by the impact of law at the state and local level. Some states will be reluctant to develop absolute "turn-away" policies for certain classes of welfare recipients (especially for aliens in states where the alien labor force is very important) simply because federal funding is cut off or restricted. Loophole provisions in medical care (allowing treatment for emergencies only, which means that everything becomes an emergency) may actually raise rather than lower medical costs. For these reasons and others, this is not the final chapter in welfare reform.

Glossary

· · · · · · · · · · · · ·

appropriations (and appropriations bills or acts) There are
two categories of federal spending, **mandatory** spending and **discretionary** spending. Discretionary spending requires annual
appropriations provided for in appropriations acts, which set
upper limits on **budget authority** and **outlays** for federal agencies
and programs, typically for a single fiscal year. Thirteen appropriations acts are passed annually by the appropriations subcommittees of both houses of the Congress. Some mandatory
entitlements programs, such as the Food Stamp Program, require
annual appropriations as well. Because most mandatory spending (including most entitlements) does not require appropriations, less than half of annual federal spending is regulated by the
appropriations process. Appropriations acts typically include
funding targets for mandatory spending programs not covered by
appropriations, although these targets are not enforceable. See
p. 160 for more information.

authority (budget) Budget authority specifically authorizes an agency
or program to undertake financial commitments, including contracts, that will result in immediate or future outlays. Budget

273

authority can be granted in originating legislation for a program, in authorization acts, or in appropriations acts. Budget authority can be *current,* which requires that it be renewed each year, or *permanent,* if review is not required each year (most entitlements programs have permanent budget authority), though in many cases occasional review (every few years) is mandated. Budget authority is also classified as *definite,* where a specific upper limit on dollar spending is set, or *indefinite,* where spending is determined by circumstances, such as the number of people who qualify for an entitlements program. See also **appropriations** and **authorization** and p. 160 for more information.

authorization (and authorization bills or acts) The origin of all federal spending, authorizing legislation allows an agency to undertake some program or task to fulfill a mandate of government. Authorizing legislation typically evaluates the financial requirements of a new or continuing program and it can impose financial constraints or provisions. Authorization is required before either budget authority or outlays can begin. Defense, the Environmental Protection Agency and NASA require authorization acts *(and appropriations acts)* every year. For example, each year a defense *authorization bill* and a defense *appropriations bill* must be passed separately. Many other types of spending, like agricultural programs, require a renewal of authorization periodically, such as every 2, 3, or 5 years. See p. 160 for more information.

baseline An economic projection of receipts and outlays for mandatory programs based upon current law (especially on entitlements), demographic estimates, and the economic assumptions of the OMB forecast. The baseline sets an *upper* limit on **mandatory spending** and a *lower* limit on **receipts.** The mandatory spending limits in the budget are desegregated by entitlement *category* (for example, social security benefits, unemployment benefits). The limits have a small **allowance** for error built in. If either the spending or revenue limit is breached without an offsetting **PAYGO** provision, and automatic **sequester** is generated. Programs controlled by baselines (in other words, entitlements) do not need to be reviewed by Congress annually, not do they need to go through appropriations, which implies that once in place, such programs can endure relatively unaltered. Again, this explains why the budget over the years is so strongly affected by demographics. (In some discussions of the budget, this term is sometimes used in reference to discretionary spending in addition to mandatory spending, although as a legal term it applies only to mandatory spending.) See also **current services budget** and p. 170 for more information.

balanced budget (and Balanced Budget Amendment)   A situation in which government revenues equal government outlays, where there is no budget deficit. (Under balanced budget proposals, budget surpluses are allowable, but not deficits.) The *Balanced Budget Amendment* refers to the occasional political campaign to pass an amendment to the U.S. Constitution that requires the U.S. government to match all outlays with revenues, except under stipulated situations. See Appendix F for more information.

borrowing authority   See budget authority.

budget authority   The authority given to any agency of government to incur financial obligations that will directly or eventually result in outlays. Budget authority is essentially *spending authority,* because that is what is being granted. Budget authority and outlays are very closely connected. Discretionary spending limits (**caps**), for example, are set for both outlays and budget authority. For **discretionary spending,** budget authority is set in **appropriations.** For **mandatory spending** like entitlements programs, authorizing legislation usually creates **permanent budget authority,** which is not normally reviewed annually through appropriations, although it is subject to periodic review as entitlements programs are reconsidered. Most **trust funds** are extended automatic budget authority under the existing law that created the trust fund. Budget authority for the Medicare, Unemployment insurance, and railroad retirement trust funds equal estimated obligations of the funds. Budget authority for the other large entitlements programs and most other trust funds are restricted by their **receipts.** Therefore, if the funds run a surplus in any given year, as is the case with the Social Security OASI Trust Fund, the surplus balance remains available indefinitely to fund future entitlements associated with the trust fund. In addition to authorizing outlays, budget authority includes **borrowing authority,** which is the right to meet obligations by borrowing funds (typically from the general fund of the U.S. Treasury), and **contract**

authority, which permits contract obligations in advance of actual appropriations or in anticipation of receipts, as are often incurred in defense contracting.

caps (discretionary spending limits)   Mandated by the BEA, sets upper limits on appropriations for **discretionary spending.** Such caps are imposed upon both budget authority and outlays in the aggregate and agency by agency. Current caps extend until FY 1998 and the Clinton administration has proposed extending them past FY 2000. The caps can be changed if economic assumptions change (inflation in particular), if "concepts and definitions" change, and they can be exceeded in the event of war or recession. Otherwise, exceeding a cap in either authority or outlays by more than a small **allowance** buffer will automatically trigger a **sequester.** See p. 167 for more information.

conference committee   When the House and the Senate first vote on bills addressing some specific topic (such as welfare reform), the House and Senate versions of the bills, when passed by the respective houses (**engrossed**), will differ, sometimes substantially. The respective bills are then sent to a joint House-Senate Conference Committee where a common single compromise bill is developed to be presented to both houses of Congress.

Congressional Budget Office (CBO)   The congressional counterpart of the **Office of Management and Budget (OMB),** the Congressional Budget Office is the agency primarily responsible for assisting the Congress in budgetary affairs, including aiding in the development of the **Congressional Budget Resolution** (the congressional version of the budget), developing options for reducing the budget, and preparing economic forecasts and budget assumptions for comparison to those made by the OMB.

Congressional Budget Resolution (also called the First Concurrent Budget Resolution)   This is the Congress's version of the budget, which, among other things, sets 5-year budget authority and spending limits for federal programs. The Congressional Budget Resolution, released after the President's February budget proposal (the deadline for the first concurrent budget resolution is April 15) is effectively the Congress's "answer" to the President, and as such it may differ significantly from proposals made in the President's budget. Each house passes its own separate version of the resolution, and a House and Senate **Conference Committee** then works out a joint compromise. This document is passed as the **First Concurrent Budget Resolution** (and is typically called the "Congressional budget" by the press). The document includes little more than bottom-line figures for agencies and programs, but does not mandate how major changes in the budget, if proposed, are to be made. If the Congressional Budget Resolution mandates major changes in programs, compliance by appropriate committees is accomplished (or attempted) through a procedure called **reconciliation.** A Congressional Budget Resolution is not submitted to the President for signature. Only the **on-budget** portion of the unified budget is included in the Congressional Budget Resolution. See also **reconciliation, off-budget** and p. 175 for more information.

consols   Bonds first issued by the British Government in 1751 when government debt was consolidated. These bonds are **perpetuities—** they never mature and they pay interest to the owner forever.

contract authority   See budget authority.

continuing resolution   In the context of the budget, a continuing resolution, when passed by both houses of Congress and signed into law by the President, provides temporary authority for government agencies to continue operating even though their funding has not been authorized for the current fiscal year. A continuing resolution is necessary, for example, if the required authorizations bills and appropriations bills have not been passed by the beginning of a new fiscal year (October 1). Failure to pass a continuing resolution under such circumstances will result in a shutdown of some government agencies. A continuing resolution typically has a deadline, sometimes of only a few weeks.

coupon (interest)   As opposed to **discounted** financial assets such as U.S. Treasury Bills, all yield-bearing U.S. Treasury financial assets having maturities of more than 1 year, including all traditional notes and bonds, pay semiannual interest payments to the registered owners of these assets. These are said to be **coupon** payments, and the rate paid is said to be the **coupon** rate. This is what people normally think of as a traditional interest payment; see also **discount.** U.S. Treasury Bills having maturities of 52 weeks or less do not pay coupon interest—they are discounted. See Appendix A for more information.

credit financing account   See loans.

credit liquidating account   Prior to 1992, federal direct loan obligations and loan guarantee commitments were recorded in the budget on a cash-flow basis, whereas since 1992 they have been recorded on a present-value basis, taking into account the present value of estimated future subsidies, loan defaults, and other loan costs (see **loans**). Transactions made prior to 1992 continue to be recorded the old way, on a cash-flow basis, and are recorded as credit liquidating accounts.

credit program account   See loans.

crowding out   An economic theory that claims that large budget deficits can put upward pressure on interest rates, curbing private borrowing such as business loans or mortgages. This crowding out of private borrowing can be offset by easy monetary policy, which can have the effect of indirectly monetizing the deficit. For a more detailed explanation, see p. 200.

current services budget   Current law requires the **Office of Management and Budget (OMB)** to prepare a current services budget, which is included in the budgetary documents released by the President every February. The current services budget makes a 5-year budget projection for budget authority, outlays, receipts, and the deficit based upon **economic assumptions** made by the OMB that reflect existing legislation and the obligations implied by that legislation, including entitlements obligations. In effect, the current services budget is the best-guess estimate of the future budgetary picture given the current legislative environment. The budget includes an estimate of the current services **baseline**, which is a projection of **receipts** and **mandatory spending** (mostly entitlements) under current law. This in turn relies upon estimates of entitlements benefits and the number of beneficiaries entitled to receive those benefits. The baseline provides a benchmark against which proposed changes in laws affecting spending or taxes can be compared. See p. 170 for more information.

deficit (budget)   A budget deficit is equal to total government outlays minus total government revenues when outlays are greater than revenues. For examples, see Chapters 1 and 2.

direct spending   Another name for **mandatory spending**.

discount This is a financial term that refers to how U.S. Treasury Bills and other money market yield-bearing assets (having maturities of less than one year) implicitly pay interest. Bills are sold at less than their maturity value (sold at a **discount**) and are redeemed at maturity value, so interest earned is implicit in the appreciation of price. See Chapter 1 for examples. Thirteen-week, 26-week and 52-week U.S. Treasury Bills are discounted. See also **coupon** and Appendix A for more information.

discretionary spending Generally, the more traditional non-entitlements component of the budget, like defense, where funds (called budgetary resources in the text of the legislation) are provided annually through appropriations acts. Discretionary spending is limited by **caps** (discretionary spending limits). Also called controllable spending. See p. 164 for more information. See also **mandatory spending.**

economic assumptions The assumptions made by the OMB are reflected in the President's budget and have a strong impact upon **baselines** and the **current services budget,** and they may have a strong impact upon discretionary spending **caps.** The CBO also makes economic assumptions and budget projections. See p. 172 for more information.

Economic Recovery Tax Act (of 1981) A radical change in tax laws passed in the first year of the Reagan administration. This law cut personal income tax brackets by about 23%, reduced the top marginal tax bracket from 70% to 50%, indexed personal tax brackets to inflation, and reduced certain business taxes. The net effect of this legislation increased budget deficits considerably. See p. 36 for more information.

engrossed After a bill has been passed by a house of Congress, but before it has been passed by both houses, it is said to be engrossed. After a version of a bill on the same topic has been passed by each house (hence, both are engrossed), the respective bills are sent to a joint House-Senate **Conference Committee.** Here differences are resolved and a single bill is then presented to both houses of Congress for action. See also **enrolled.**

enrolled After a bill has been passed by both houses of Congress, signed by the presiding officers, and sent to the President for action, the bill is said to be enrolled. See also **engrossed.**

entitlements   Spending, typically in the form of a benefit payment, that is mandated by federal law and extends benefits to those who qualify under the provisions of law. Almost all entitlements spending is classified as **mandatory spending** and is therefore not subject to **appropriations**. Most entitlements payments go to private citizens, but some also go to corporations or to state and local governments. Entitlements programs include Social Security, Medicare, Medicaid, federal pensions, need-based public assistance of all forms, and agricultural subsidies. Entitlements payments are legal obligations of the U.S. government. The only way an entitlement can be changed or the fiscal requirements altered is by amending the authorizing legislation that extends the benefit. Entitlements are discussed extensively in Chapters 6 and 7.

expenditures (government)   As opposed to **purchases**, U.S. government expenditures measures the actual amount of money spent by the government for all purposes over some designated period, such as one year. Federal monies spent within federal budget documents are usually called **outlays**. See also **outlays, purchases, receipts,** and **transfer payments.**

European Monetary Union and European Union   See **Maastricht Treaty.**

federal debt   The entire debt of the U.S. government, consisting of U.S. Treasury securities and various categories of nonmarketable debt (mostly debt to other government agencies). Budget **deficits** each year add to the federal debt. See p. 6 for more information.

federal funds   Outlays by programs and agencies are classified as either spending by **trust funds** or by **federal funds.** Federal funds are all outlays, including interagency or interprogram outlays, that are not classified as outlays by a trust fund.

Federal Reserve System (FRS)   The nation's central banking authority. Although a quasi-governmental agency, the FRS is technically not a branch of the U.S. government nor of the U.S. Treasury. The FRS is responsible for executing the nation's monetary policy, which has considerable impact upon interest rates and the rate of money and credit formation. The FRS acts as banker for the U.S. Treasury.

fiscal year   The fiscal year of the United States government begins on October 1, and ends on September 30. For example, FY1998 begins on October 1, 1997.

flat tax   Income taxes in the United States are graduated; income earners with higher taxable income pay a higher tax rate than those with lower taxable income. Proposals for a flat tax generally advocate eliminating graduated tax brackets and replacing them with a single tax rate paid by all. Most flat tax proposals have qualifications or provisions, such as exclusion for very low income, or different rules for capital gains, that complicate this simple rule.

interest on the federal debt (net)   The interest paid annually on the net federal debt to parties outside of the government. Net interest does not include interest paid internally to federal agencies for their ownership of nonmarketable U.S. Treasury securities. Net interest on the debt is also one of the three primary categories of outlays. Total outlays equal discretionary spending plus mandatory spending plus net interest. (It is called net interest because it excludes interest paid internally to other government agencies, such as the Social Security Trust Fund.) There is no **cap** nor limit of any kind on net interest. This value depends upon the size of the debt and the interest rates paid on the marketable component.

limit on the public debt   See statutory limit on the public debt.

line-item veto   Many bills are sent by the Congress to the President for signature into law with sections attached that are unrelated to the primary subject of the bill. Such riders sometimes consist of new laws that the President would not otherwise support. When the bill is signed, all provisions become law. A true line-item veto would give the President the right to veto certain sections of a bill while retaining the others and allowing them to become law. A weak version of the line-item veto was passed in 1996 and became effective January 1, 1997. The line-item veto in this case is restricted only to riders that involve appropriations; the full package will then be sent back to the Congress for reconsideration. In practice, this is not much different than the ages-old procedure for reconsidering vetoed legislation.

loans and loan guarantees The federal government provides both **direct loans** to qualified borrowers and **loan guarantees** for designated programs, which typically insures payment to a private lender for all or part of principal and interest on a guaranteed loan. Such loans and loan guarantees are made to international agencies, farmers, students, the housing sector, and so on. In the federal budget, all such lending programs have two accounts associated with the program:

1. A **credit program account** which includes the budget **outlay** as an estimate of the true cost of the program, calculated (typically) as the present value of expected future subsidy costs and default payouts for loans made currently, and paid to the **credit financing account.** It is through this noncash outlay that the budget and hence the deficit is impacted by loan programs.

2. A non-budgetary **credit financing account** which records all cash payments to and from the government arising from direct loans and loan guarantees. This account receives the outlay for the estimated loan costs discussed above. Cash flows from **credit financing accounts** do not impact net outlays, receipts, nor the deficit.

For more detailed information on the budgetary treatment of loans and loan guarantees, or any of the accounts discussed here, see *Budget of the United States Government, Analytic Perspectives, FY 1966,* pp. 321–322.

mandatory spending This category includes all large entitlements programs, such as Social Security, but also a host of smaller sundry programs. Mandatory outlays *and* revenues are constrained by the **baseline.** Mandatory spending authority is not provided by appropriations. It is usually provided by authorizations (the impact of which usually spans many years) or entitlement authority. Increases in mandatory spending *or* decreases in revenues must satisfy **PAYGO** criteria. Also called (believe it or not) uncontrollable spending. See p. 169 for more information. See also **discretionary spending.**

marketable debt Federal debt is divided into two components, marketable and nonmarketable debt. Marketable debt consists of financial assets, U.S. Treasury Bills, Notes and Bonds, that can be resold on a secondary market. See p. 7 and Appendix A for more information.

Maastricht Treaty   Signed on February 7, 1992, by the representatives of 12 European governments, this treaty created the **European Union** and it governs the transformation from the old European Economic Community—originally the Common Market—to a new union of European economic, social, legal, security and cultural cooperation. The Treaty requires some important economic conditions of member nations (of which there were 15 as of 1996), including the requirements that general government deficits be no higher than 3% of GDP, and general government debt be no higher than 60% of GDP. Failure to meet these criteria might result in exclusion from the new **European Monetary Union,** which on January 1, 1999, will allow the use by members of a common European currency, to be called the **Euro.** See p. 46 for more information.

maximum budget deficit   Required by BEA, an upper limit on budget deficits projected out 5 years. Exceeding the limit can trigger a **sequester.** Under the Clinton administration, the MBD seems to be deemphasized in the budget, or at least subordinated to **baselines** and **caps,** both of which have been strongly emphasized in the Clinton budgets.

national debt   See federal debt.

multiplier effect   An initial stimulus to spending in an economy will usually increase final spending and income by a multiple (such as 2.5) of the original stimulus. For example, a new payroll in a community of $1 million annually might raise income in that community by $2.5 million because of respending. This is said to represent the multiplier effect. The multiplier effect is important in discussions about the economic impact of government spending. See p. 191 for more information.

nonmarketable debt   That portion of the **federal debt** that cannot be sold on a secondary market. Most of this debt is held by U.S. government agencies such as the Social Security Trust Fund. See p. 8 for more information. See also **marketable debt.**

off-budget or **off-line**   A small portion of outlays and budget authority in the unified budget is classified as **off-budget** or **off-line** (the terms mean the same thing). The off-budget portion of the unified budget consists of the two Social Security Trust Funds (OASI and DI) and the Postal Service Trust Fund. Though the off-budget concept is obsolescent, this status technically exempts these trust funds from deficit calculations and general BEA regulations as discussed in Chapter 8. All categories of outlays and budget authority that are not classified as off-budget are, by default, classified as **on-budget** or **on-line.** The **Congressional Budget Resolution,** which must be passed each year, includes only the **on-budget** portion of the unified budget.

Office of Management and Budget (OMB)   The administrative agency of the executive branch of government (answerable to the President) responsible for formulating the President's budget and for providing general policy guidance on budgetary affairs. The OMB is also responsible for **sequester** previews. See also **Congressional Budget Office (CBO),** the congressional counterpart of the OMB.

on-budget or **on-line**   See off-budget.

outlays   Outlays record the payment of financial obligations of the U.S. Government, usually, but not always, in the form of cash (checks, currency or electronic funds transfers). When considering the Unified Budget, **net outlays** are synonymous with **expenditures.** Within agency budgets, outlays may take the following forms:

1. cash disbursements,
2. bookkeeping entries transferring funds from one federal agency or account to another,
3. present value estimates of future subsidy and default costs for loans and loan guarantees made by agencies of the U.S. Government.

For a more detailed discussion of outlays, see *Budget of the United States Government, Analytical Perspectives, FY 1996,* p. 320, or *Budget Systems and Concepts of the U.S. Government,* February 1994, p. 15.

PAYGO (pay-as-you-go)   A complicated provision of the BEA and of subsequent legislation that strongly affects mandatory spending and receipts. Generally, given **baseline** projections, if a new entitlement program is initiated or if an existing program has a change in legislation that requires more spending, or if legislation is enacted that reduces revenues, PAYGO requires that Congress and the President enact an **offset** that either reduces spending in another mandatory program or raises revenues. On August 20 and 15 days after the end of the congressional session, the **OMB** issues a **PAYGO scorecard,** which evaluates the fiscal impact of any new legislation affecting revenues or mandatory spending. Under **PAYGO** provisions, such programs cannot violate the **baseline.** If they do, an automatic **sequester** is triggered. See p. 169 for more information.

permanent budget authority   See budget authority.

perpetuities   Bonds that never mature. They pay interest to their owners forever. See also **consols.**

premium   All marketable U.S. Treasury Notes and Bonds are listed at the par price of 100. When these securities are resold on the secondary market they are typically sold at a price higher than par (sold at a premium) or at a price lower than par (sold at a discount). For example, a 30-year bond might be listed in the financial press at 115. This means that a denomination of this security that originally sold for $10,000 is now worth $11,500.

public debt   See federal debt.

public debt limit   See statutory limit on the public debt.

purchases (government)   A spending category from the National Income Accounts, where gross domestic product is desegregated into various spending categories, of which government purchases is one. This measures the amount spent by the U.S. government to acquire goods and services for use by the government. It represents the claim upon national output by government (the term also applies to state and local governments). Government purchases are always less than government **outlays,** because the latter includes **entitlements** and other **transfer payments** that merely pass purchasing power, via the government, from one area in the private sector to another. Government purchases are equal to government **expenditures** minus **transfer payments.** See Appendix B for more information.

receipts   Payments received by the government, typically in cash (checks, currency, and electronic funds), mostly for the payment of taxes, but also for other duties, fees, and charges. Net government receipts in the unified budget constitute the **revenues** used to calculate the size of the budget deficit. Funds transfers between government agencies and funds (called intrabudgetary transactions) often involve a special category of receipts called **offsetting receipts.**

reconciliation (and reconciliation bills) This is the procedure whereby the House and Senate Budget Committees attempt to enforce compliance with any new budgetary proposals or changes made in the **Congressional Budget Resolution** (also called the First Concurrent Budget Resolution) earlier in the year. The Congressional Budget Resolution in effect instructs the responsible committees on spending targets for programs under their jurisdiction, while allowing those committees considerable latitude in changing programs in ways that meet those targets if substantial changes are called for. Reconciliation refers loosely to the passage of the 13 annual appropriations bills and the corpus of legislation that affects mandatory spending not covered by appropriations, all of which are supposed to collectively ensure compliance with the Congressional Budget Resolution. In recent years, bills affecting reconciliation from many programs have been clustered together in inclusive **reconciliation bills** (under that label), forcing the President to veto or accept entire budget packages. See also Congressional Budget Resolution for more information.

rescission The outright cancellation of previously approved budget authority. In effect, this will cancel outlays that have already been approved. Rescission is a practice that can effectively kill a program.

revenues See receipts.

scorecard (PAYGO) The on-going review by the **Office of Management and Budget** (OMB) of mandatory spending and revenue measures and how they affect **PAYGO** requirements. See **PAYGO.**

scoring (tax scoring) This refers to a practice in budget estimating that assumes that because certain tax rates are cut, the tax base will grow substantially through the resulting economic stimulation, possibly enough to be deficit-neutral or even to cause revenues to rise.

sequester A cancellation of funds (budget resources) required by the BEA if there is a violation of spending **caps** for **discretionary spending** or for **PAYGO limits** for **mandatory spending** and **revenues.** First authorized by GRH (where it failed) and now the key enforcement provision of the BEA. Sequestration, which can be invoked technically by the OMB, can come at various times within a congressional session or after the session has ended. See p. 179 for more information.

statutory limit on the public debt The sum total of most gross federal debt, which consists almost entirely of marketable and non-marketable interest-bearing securities, is subject to an upper limit by law. When that limit is reached, the U.S. Treasury can no longer engage in borrowing activities until the limit is again raised by an act of Congress. See Table 1.7 for the current debt limit. The debt limit was first established in 1917 and it has been raised more than 60 times since 1940. It is a completely ineffective means of controlling the deficit or the debt. See p. 17 for more information.

structural deficit As opposed to an actual budget deficit in any fiscal year, a structural deficit is an estimate of what the deficit would be or would have been (when estimating prior years) assuming an economy that is at full employment or is operating at an optimal sustainable level of output (ordinarily the same thing). Because economies seldom operate at full employment, the structural deficit is usually below the actual deficit. See also **systemic deficit**.

supply-side economics Supply-side economics is a corpus of economic theory popular in the early 1980s used as a partial justification for the tax cuts of that era. Essentially, theorists argued that when tax rates are too high they act as a disincentive to economic growth by discouraging innovation, risk, and investment. If true, this would mean that national income, or the nation's tax base, would be retarded or would be growing far below potential. Tax revenues collected are equal to the product of tax rates times the tax base. Therefore, a *reduction* in the tax rate might actually *raise* tax revenues if the resulting economic stimulus caused the tax *base* to grow proportionately more than the reduction in tax rates. Although in certain contexts the theory has merit, a policy based upon such theory is always a gamble. If insufficient economic growth follows the tax cut, a budget deficit will emerge. The supply-side arguments of the 1990s tend to emphasize the reduction of the highest marginal tax brackets only, rather than all tax brackets, unless this can be shown to be deficit-neutral. Flat-tax proposals can be construed to be a special application of modern supply-side economics, though not all contemporary supply-siders support the flat tax (the 1990s school of thought is not well defined).

surplus (budget)   A budget surplus is equal to **total government revenues minus total government outlays** when revenues are greater than outlays. See also budget **deficit.**

systemic deficit (a term created by the author)   As opposed to a budget deficit caused by temporary problems, such as a recession or war-related expenditures, a systemic deficit will endure for years regardless of economic conditions. It is due to some systemic, lasting, and fundamental budgetary problem, such as taxes that are far too low or high expenditures linked to popular political programs, where a remedy is very difficult, given the prevailing political system and the way it works. See also **structural deficit.**

tax base   In an income-based tax system, such as that used primarily by the U.S. government, the income that is taxed is referred to as the tax base. For income taxes, tax receipts will equal the tax rate(s) times the tax base.

tender   Purchase requests for U.S. government Treasury Bills, Notes, and Bonds are submitted, normally though Federal Reserve District Banks or their branches, on documents called tenders. See Appendix A for more information.

transfer payments   These are direct payments by the U.S. government (and state and local governments) to individuals or corporations in the private sector where no service or commodity is received in exchange. All **entitlements** are transfer payments, as is **interest** on the federal debt. Examples include Social Security, Medicare, and unemployment payments. See Appendix B for more information.

trust fund   In the context of the federal budget, a trust fund is a government account that accumulates funds as bookkeeping entries. Trust funds acquire their funds by having them transferred from other areas of the budget or by running independent surpluses. For example, taxpayers pay more into the Old Age & Survivors Insurance (OASI) Fund than disbursements from that fund, so the difference accumulates as a trust fund. Usually, the U.S. Treasury issues **non-marketable debt** to the trust fund agency. Many **entitlements** are funded by trust funds. Trust funds are discussed in detail in Chapter 7. See also **federal funds.**

undistributed offsetting receipts This accounting category is classified as budgetary function number 950 and is always found in the Unified Budget as a negative number (see Table 4.2a, The Unified Budget of the United States Government, the last outlay entry). Most of this consists of receipts by federal employee retirement trust funds, including military, from various agencies of the government. These receipts are bookkeeping transfers represented as outlays for the individual agencies that are required to contribute to these retirement trust funds. Because the outlays are included in the calculation of net outlays for other budgetary functions (such as defense and transportation) but the funds never leave the federal government nor are they spent, they are shown as a negative entry to eliminate double counting. To learn what other categories are included in Undistributed Offsetting Receipts, see *Budget of the United States Government, Analytic Perspectives, FY 1997*, Table 4.3.

unfunded mandates If a federal law is passed that imposes some new requirement on a state or local government that has a cost for which the law provides no funding from the federal level, the law is said to include an unfunded mandate. An example would be if a federal law requiring state governments to provide a new type of welfare benefit or an educational program without funding the benefits or the program. On March 22, 1995, a law was passed with the stated purpose of curbing unfunded mandates, but it mostly set up a new review and oversight procedure, and the true effectiveness of the law remains to be seen.

value-added tax (VAT) A value-added tax (VAT) is essentially a national sales tax, much like state sales taxes, but imposed nationally by the federal government. Some items, such as food, might be classified as exempt. Great Britain uses a VAT of 17.5% as a major source of tax revenues. Like a state sales tax, the VAT is included in the final retail price of an article.

Index

. . . .

Entries followed by n or t denote notes and tables, respectively.

*This is dedicated to
Sonia, Leslie, and Jennifer Evans
and to the memory of
Tom Burrows*